Sociology and Hip Hop

An Anthology

First Edition

EDITED BY

Earl Wright II
Rhodes College

Kierra N. Toney
University of Cincinnati

Keri Eason
University of Cincinnati

Anthony J. Stone, Jr.
University of Cincinnati

 cognella®
SAN DIEGO

Bassim Hamadeh, CEO and Publisher
Jennifer Codner, Senior Field Acquisitions Editor
Michelle Piehl, Senior Project Editor
Susana Christie, Senior Developmental Editor
Alia Bales, Production Editor
Jess Estrella, Senior Graphic Designer
Trey Soto, Licensing Specialist
Ursina Kilburn, Interior Designer
Natalie Piccotti, Director of Marketing
Kassie Graves, Senior Vice President of Editorial
Jamie Giganti, Director of Academic Publishing

3970 Sorrento Valley Blvd., Ste. 500, San Diego, CA 92121

Contents

Part 3   Performing Hip Hop Identity Against
            Inequality   130

By Anthony J. Stone Jr.

Part 4   Hip Hop as Resistance   199

By Kierra Toney

INTRODUCTION TO SOCIOLOGY OF HIP HOP

By Earl Wright II

Sociology is a science that seeks to understand human behavior through rigorous methods of research. Historically, the lens through which sociologists have examined the world has been nearly exclusively white, male, heterosexual, and Christian. Because of the limited frame that has defined the discipline, the scope and impact of the science has been somewhat limited. Fortunately, over the past few decades, the discipline has become more diverse and that has led to its broader relevance as new ways of looking at the science and different questions raised within the discipline have curated a generation of scholars whose lived experiences provide unique insights into different ways of understanding and presenting it to outsiders. No view is more unique or different from that of traditional sociologists than that of those whose research and pedagogy are influenced by hip hop music and culture.

Once viewed as a fad that would quickly disappear, hip hop is the most popular and influential form of popular culture in the United States and the entire world. Since its establishment in 1971, hip hop has been a consistent leader in and influencer on pop culture through music, fashion, dance, art, and nearly every other industry you can name. Until recently, however, there was one area that hip hop had failed to integrate with any degree of seriousness—academia. Sociologists are only now beginning to understand the usefulness of hip hop in expanding understandings of what the discipline is to outsiders and how it can be used to positively impact the world. While a good number of people are only now understanding the usefulness of hip hop to the discipline, many of us have been employing aspects of the art in our classes for many years and have been effective in broadening conceptions of sociology to those who, heretofore, were indifferent or did not "see" themselves in it. What we are attempting in this book is to demonstrate how sociologists can better explain their work by using hip hop. This is the impetus for this effort. Although we acknowledge this is a small step toward a larger goal, the readings included in this book provide a template for others interested in using hip hop in their particular area of expertise (e.g., business, health, education, medicine, etc.) to broaden their impact and relevance. Ultimately, the primary objective of this book is to serve as a bridge for those interested in understanding our society through a scholarly lens crafted by hip hop–influenced scholars.

PART 1

Hip Hop Beyond the Stereotype

By Earl Wright II

Hip hop was born on August 11, 1973, when DJ Kool Herc threw a back-to-school party in his Bronx, New York, neighborhood that his sister, Cindy Campbell, heavily promoted. Beyond promoting hip hop's first event, Campbell was influential in crafting the art's early dance and fashion stylings. Herc and Campbell did not know they were starting a cultural phenomenon that would spread across the United States and eventually the world to become the most impactful form of popular culture on the planet. I was two years old when hip hop was born and remember hearing the first rap songs ever played on the FM stations in my hometown of Memphis, Tennessee. The sounds emanating from hip hop artists, including the music and lyrics, were different from anything I had been exposed to as someone raised in the Deep South and constantly surrounded by music of artists from the blues, R&B and country worlds. "Rapper's Delight" by the Sugarhill Gang introduced my friends and me to the term *hip hop*. "The Message" by Grandmaster Flash and the Furious Five showed me how this new art form could be used to expose inequities within a society while simultaneously using one's influence to push for policy changes. Both songs caught my attention because they were unlike anything I'd heard before. While I could not sing, I definitely knew I could rap a poem I'd written over any instrumental or human beatbox available. I did not become a huge hip hop fan until 1985. During that year, the song "Rappin' Duke" caught my attention. Shawn Brown's song was a fun parody of the late actor John Wayne and cowboy culture. However, it was Run-DMC's *King of Rock* album that knocked me off my feet and made me a lifelong hip hop fan. Moreover, it was around this time that I began to believe hip hop, like other forms of music, could be used to help people better understand the society in which we live.

Before I became immersed into hip hop, the sounds of Motown music filled my home—more specifically, the music of Marvin Gaye. I learned early in life about the liberating potential of music. When Gaye sang "What's Going On?" it was a clarion call to this nation that the war in Vietnam should be discontinued for many legitimate reasons. The least of which was the drafting of mostly poor and disproportionately Black soldiers to fight a war many believed was unnecessary. Just as Gaye's "What's Going On?" informed me of the brutality of war and death, "The Message" by Grandmaster Flash and the Furious Five stirred into me the idea that artists could change the world, even classrooms. Music and the arts are integral components of any society because they serve a number of functions. The least of which is that they make us sad and happy, provide avenues for us to express ourselves, and, possibly, serve as supplemental tools in educational settings. Because of its global popularity, rap music is the vehicle to accomplish all of the above while spreading its messages far and wide to audiences, including persons who may be the complete opposite of yourself. In its truest form, hip hop allows us to analyze and make sense of our world. Over my teaching career, I've used hip hop in the classroom at various times to accomplish all of the wonderful things discussed here.

Throughout most of my years of schooling, I was an average student. I did not study regularly, complete homework assignments, or perform to the best of my abilities throughout high school and the first few years of college. In fact, probably the only reason I graduated from high school was because student-athletes needed to maintain a 2.0 GPA to be eligible for participation. That was my motivation. I played sports year-round with football and track and field being my primary passions. I was as surprised as anyone else when I received a scholarship to play Division 2 football in Kentucky. Unfortunately, and consistent with my high school career, I did not fully strive for perfection in the classroom as I had on the gridiron. My lack of attention to schooling resulted in my being forced to leave college and return home with a sub 1.0 GPA. This wake-up call finally convinced me to pay serious attention to school. After being admitted into my hometown college—on academic probation—I finally began to take school seriously. By the time I entered graduate school, I was a focused student looking for ways to catch the attention of young persons like myself who did not take school seriously and convince them to change their ways. Little did I know one vehicle for doing just that would be hip hop.

While I was a dedicated graduate student, I wasn't very successful. At least, initially. My undergraduate degree was in history, and I was now in a sociology program being introduced to new and foreign concepts and theories. It was in this setting that I learned how to fuse hip hop into schooling. The inspiration sprung from a class I was taking titled Deviance. In this course, we learned how the criminal justice system failed poor and minority people. The most substantive part of the course was the instructor's insistence that we be able to identify, define, and explain the leading deviance theories in the field. In each class, the instructor would present to us many theories to answer questions about how and why people commit crimes, why law enforcement was tougher on the poor versus the affluent, and other similar topics. I didn't understand what the instructor was asking of us, but I continued to attend the class and complete the assigned readings. Toward the end of the semester, I had become discouraged and questioned whether I had made a good decision choosing to attend graduate school.

One day I left class and, as usual, immediately began blasting the latest Tupac Shakur album, *Me Against the World*, in my car. The music was initially background noise that I paid little attention to as my mind was focused on trying to remember the theories I had been exposed to a few minutes earlier. While driving home, my mind meandered between the deviance theories and Shakur's lyrics. I became entranced in his wordplay. This was, probably, the first time I'd seriously listened to rap lyrics to try and make sense of them. After a couple of minutes, it dawned on me that Shakur was articulating many of the theories I was learning in class. I could hear clearly in his lyrics the concepts of differential association, rational choice, and inner and outer containment. This was my aha moment. Not only was I able to better understand deviance theories, but that I could identify them through the works of my favorite hip hop artist was mind-blowing. At this point, I decided that when I became a teacher, I would infuse hip hop into my courses as a means to convey theories to students in a manner that would help them understand the material. Part 1 of this book is a step in that direction, as it provides an overview of some of the unique histories of hip-hop music and culture and how it can be used to understand societal ills.

It is well known that the roots of hip hop stretch into the streets of the Bronx in New York City and are represented in the artistry created, primarily, by Black men and women. The lesser-known story of hip hop's emergence includes accounts of the contributions of non–African Americans to the field. Part 1, "Hip Hop Beyond the Stereotype," extends our understanding of who some of the early contributors to hip hop were. Most of the artists discussed in this section have been historically overlooked, but their role in the development of the art remains noteworthy. In "Gender Politics of Hip-Hop and Hip-Life Music in New York and Ghana," Tara Jabbaar-Gyambrah focuses on "the ways in which women in hip-hop and hip-hop life navigate a male-dominated music genre by embracing cultural strategies of global liberation." While she critiques the role of women in hip hop in New York City, her work expands our understanding of the ways women in Ghana use hip hop to make substantive changes in their communities.

In "Afro-Latin Soul and Hip-Hop," Alejandro Nava extends our understanding of the contributions of non–African American hip hop pioneers by reflecting on Latin artists. Nava introduces the reader to some of the major Latin hip hop artists and demonstrates how they molded the art in their country to address concerns in their communities. In many respects, he suggests they were using hip hop as a method of communicating their society's ills to the broader community in the same way that Public Enemy leadman Chuck D viewed hip hop in America as the "CNN of Black America." By combining the strong religious tradition of Catholicism with an understanding of hip hop, the author demonstrates how music can have a positive impact on and possibly improve a society.

"From A-Town to ATL: The Politics of Translation in Global Hip Hop Culture" by Holger Droessler also gives one insight into the development of hip hop outside the United States. Droessler examines how groundbreaking Tanzanian rapper Gsann's experience during a televised cipher was a missed opportunity to show an American audience how the art is practiced in his country. Producers for Black Entertainment Television (BET) translated his rhymes into English instead of respecting his craft and that led to a backlash from hip hop fans in the African nation. Through an examination of Gsann's career, the author informs the reader on Tanzanian and other African hip hop artists and how they have been pressured to mold their art into packages suitable for consumption by American fans. Collectively, the articles in Part 1 provide the groundwork for an understanding of the international impact and relevance of hip hop.

Gender Politics of Hip-Hop and Hip-Life Music in New York and Ghana

By Tara Jabbaar-Gyambrah

INTRODUCTION

Over the last thirty years, hip-hop has become a national phenomenon that was cultivated out of the youth resistance movement that emerged in the South Bronx of New York during the 1970s. It ultimately transformed its segment of popular culture into a worldwide entity. Known as the headquarters of hip-hop, the South Bronx continues to serve as its birthplace. It is a community where Black and Latino Youth used their creative voices of expression to speak out against poverty and inequity in American society through emceeing, djing, breakdancing and graffiti. Several factors set the stage for hip-hop's emergence in the seventies, including, but not limited to: job loss, cutting of music programs, migration of Black middle class from the Bronx, white flight, the building of the Cross Bronx Bridge Expressway, increased drug trafficking, and the rapid building of housing projects that did not provide families with a good quality of life. Although hip-hop started as an underground movement that spread from the South Bronx community to other areas of New York, one song on the radio spurred its international growth.

In 1979 the Sugar Hill gang's song "Rappers Delight" put hip-hop on the map as a new innovation of popular culture. While there were other hip-hop artists who were notable contributors to its success—the God Fathers of hip-hop: Gil Scot Heron, DJ Kool Here, Afrika Bambaata and Grandmaster Flash—their music was not selected to be played on the radio. The late Gil Scot Heron was famous for his song "The Revolution Will Not Be Televised" which critiqued the mass media for its representation of the Black community. DJ Kool Here was known for his signature song "Apache" and the invention of the break-beat. Afrika Bambaata formed Zulu Nation, a group named after the film *Shaka Zulu* (1964) to represent the uniting of gangs in the South Bronx community. Grand Master Flash was known for the quick mix theory and the song "The Message." Hip-Hop had a powerful impact on youth across New York, New Jersey, California, and several other states. Each community had their own cause to fight and resist. By the late eighties and early nineties, police brutality became the center of discussion. NWA's "F*** the Police" (1988) addressed excessive force in the Compton community of California with its own unique style. It was not long before hip-hop became a global phenomenon in the 1980s spreading to France, Japan, Ghana, South Africa, and Nigeria.

Although many people are aware of the transformative nature of hip-hop in New York, most are unaware of the transnational influence of the New York-born musical subculture in the continent of Africa. One such genre emerged in the early 1990s in Ghana—hip-life. It is the combination of African American style hip-hop (e.g., rapping) and highlife music created by Ghanaian youth. It is not just a blend of other forms of music, but it is a combination of local rhythms like the Adowa,[1] instruments such as Kpanlogo drums[2], xylophones, flutes, thumb pianos, and samples of old highlife favorites like Alhaji Frimpong, Abrechieba Kofi Sammy, CK Mann, Gyedu Blay Ambolley, Amakye Dede, Nana Tufour, and A.B. Crenstil. Reggie Ossei Rockstone,[3] a famous Ghanaian musician, introduced hip-life music to Ghanaian youth by infusing styles and lyrics with traditional African music when he returned from London in 1994. Rockstone not only transferred hip-hop's style to Ghana, but he integrated it into Ghanaian cultural music for the youth. In hip-life, hip-hop's cultural values remained intact, such as the social consciousness to engage in political struggle, the wearing of various fashion trends, and the style of rapping. Hip-life music gained its popularity through television, radio, nightclubs, music videos, local drinking spots in Ghana, and through the circulation of newspapers, CDs, and cassettes.

------

1   The *adowa* is a local rhythm that has several different meanings that can be used in the musical and the-atrical concept. It is connected to the cultural heritage of the Ga people of southeastern Ghana. It is a body of songs and/or dance that is utilized as a rite of passage for all Ga people which are performed by women. For example, a particular dance form may be named after a drum, and an *adowa* would be an example of this.

2   The *kpanlogo* drum is a musical instrument that is used to signify the culture of the Ga people in Ghana's Accra region. It is used for marking the rhythm for traditional *kpanlogo* dance performances. It is a hand crafted drum made of *tweneboa* wood, with a calfskin drum head attached to wooden pegs with round ropes. Although it is derived from the Ga people of Ghana it is popular throughout West Africa because of its defined characteristics (e.g. deep and loud sound).

3   Although Reggie Rockstone invented hip-life music in the early 1990s, he did not release his first com-mercial album until 1997. His album *Maaka Maka (If I said so I said it)* was produced by Ghanaian Michael Coalhouse Horthman, who was familiar with Britain. Rockstone was finally recognized internationally in March of 2001 for his creation of hip-life in *The Source Magazine* in the United States. Other Ghanaian artists such as Freddie Funkstone, Lord Kenya, Michael Cook, Talking Drum and Panji Anoff of Pidgen music soon followed suit by releasing their own albums.

JJC, a Nigerian hip-hop artist created a four-part documentary entitled *Afropop: The Rise of African Hip-Hop,* focusing on how hip-life has given youth a new type of African identity. Through a series of interviews with producers, DJs, artists, music talk show host Bola Ray and Reggie Rockstone, he explores the cross-cultural connections of hip-hop and its African roots. At the core of hip-hop is the West African tradition of storytelling, which is often passed down through the griot in an oral history form. It is this African culture that was brought to America, grew during the slavery plantation era and was re-created in the form of hip-hop in the [South] Bronx in the 1970s. Ironically, this same tradition traveled back home to Africa in the 1980s but with an African American and New York influence. Panji Anoff, the first producer of hip-life of Ghana, furthers this argument as he believes that hip-hop is derived from a traditional African tradition that has been reinvented in America. According to Anoff, "The source of hip-hop is an African tradition, an ancient African tradition of freestyling, which is spontaneous poetry to a rhythmic pattern."[4] One of the core connections between hip-hop and hip-life music is rapping, which is the art of sharing one's story. In this way, hip-hop globally adapted to cultural expressions of each region it encountered and served as a platform for a variety of voices in collaboration and in competition with its original message.

Although they have often been overshadowed by their male counterparts, women played a key role in the founding moments of hip-hop. In New York, women artists and emcees such as MC Lyte, Salt-N-Pepa, Lauryn Hill, Nikki Minaj, Lil' Kim, Foxy Brown, and the Real Roxanne illustrate how hip-hop culture is infused with various meanings and cultural strategies. These strategies are not gender neutral but take on the message of the emcees. For women emcees, this can be read as both lessons of liberation and tales of caution.

This [reading] examines the ways in which women in hip-hop and hip-life navigate a male-dominated music genre by embracing cultural strategies of global liberation. By focusing on the similarities and differences of experiences women in these different geographic contexts, I address the following questions: (1) What is the relevance of the birth of hip-hop in New York to its various global transformations and hip-life in particular? (2) How do the roles of women in hip-hop and hip-life music industries differ based on their locations in Ghana as compared to New York-based artists? What are women's roles in hip-hop and hip-life music?

---

4 "Accra Reclaims Hip-Hop", BBC News, accessed February 13, 2015, http://news.bbc.co.Uk/2/hi/africa/3241007.stm

NEW YORK ORIGINS AND GLOBAL TRANSFORMATIONS

The music of the Black Atlantic world was the primary expressions of cultural distinctiveness in which populations in New York and other areas across the African Diaspora seized upon and adapted to its new circumstances. Black and Latino youth used these separated, but converged musical traditions of the Black Atlantic world to create itself anew as a conglomeration of communities as a means to gauge the social progress of spontaneous self-creation. All of this was cemented together by the endless pressures of economic exploitation, political racism, displacement, and exile.

In his book *The Black Atlantic: Modernity and Double Consciousness* (1995), Paul Gilroy indicates that as music travels across the Diaspora it adapts to new ascribed conditions to which it is subjected, thus creating a space whereby traditions are upheld and creatively sculpted to fit the location, time, socio-cultural factors, and the individual and communal life experiences of the people. It is through these factors, the transatlantic flow of Black music via the Diaspora, that creative expressive culture is reborn. I posit that hip-hop and hip-life[5] music are two forms of music that have traveled across the Black Atlantic and embody Gilroy's definition and are representative of "Sankofian Diasporic" connections.[6] Furthering this idea, in *Dangerous Grounds: Popular Music, Postmodernism and the Poetics of Place* (1997), Lipsitz states: "hip hop and other forms of Diasporic African music participate in constructing these local identities, but they bring to them a global consciousness."[7] In other words, when music travels across the diaspora, it is sort of like a butterfly—it goes through a metamorphism that creates a hybrid form, sculpted to its particular locations, culture, politics, and economic status.

Hip-hop and hip-life music industries are two Diasporic communities where there are complex and contradictory hierarchies centered upon socio-cultural histories (i.e., colonialism, cultural reproduction of youth identity, etc.) that are continually reproduced through lyrics and music videos that create a patriarchal illusionary image of women. Gender inequity in both of these male dominated music industries stems from societal views and cultural influences from different groups of people that have been reproduced to fit today's world.

---

5   It is a combination of African American style hip-hop (i.e., rapping) and highlife music.

6   The literal meaning of sankofa is *"se wo were ft na wosan kofa a yenki "* (it's not a taboo to go back and fetch what you have forgotten). The Sankofian Diasporic connection is the way in which hip-hop and hip-life music participates in constructing cultures and identities by traveling from locality to another.

7   George Lipsitz, *Dangerous Grounds: Popular Music, Postmodernism and the Poetics of Place* (New York and London: Verso, 1997), 33.

In his book, *Hip-Hop Generation* (2003), Bakari Kitwana says that the gender problem between Black men and women are related to the generational divide between the Civil Rights generation and what he calls, the hip-hop generation, those born between the years of 1965–1984, which essentially boils down to the older vs. younger generation ideology. Disparities in housing, education, health care, mortgage loan programs, public policy, and the negative portrayal of Blacks in the media have led to increased tensions within the community that have turned into misdirected anger towards Black women.[8] Misrepresentations of the Black community, especially women in hip-hop music videos sparked some of the conflict between the older and younger generation. And, Byron Hurt unpacks this in his film, *Hip-Hop: Beyond Beats and Rhymes* (2006) that explores issues of masculinity, violence, and sexism in hip-hop music, ultimately finds that hip-hop is a reflection of American society's view on gender roles.

Even though hip-life's historical location are firmly placed in Ghana, it was born out of the cultural history of Ghanaians and African Americans through migration. In this sense, factors such as the generational divide in West African communities and the African Americanisms in hip-hop culture have shaped hip-life. Studying these elements will help us understand the ways in which hip-life artists represent themselves in the music industry. As a result, some hip-life artists emulate some forms of African American hip-hop culture in the music genre while others uphold a strong Ghanaian cultural heritage through their music. In other words within the hip-life music industry there are two primary forms of expression:

1.   Hip-life artists imitate African American culture (e.g., hip-hop). Musicians do this by using similar messages in their lyrics, adopting dress code values of hip-hop, hairstyles, and using African American slang in their music.
2.   Hip-life artists maintain strong Ghanaian cultural traditions through their music. Hip-life artists symbolize and preserve their culture through the types of clothing that they wear, hairstyles, the production of metaphorical "creative" messages in their songs that addresses socio-cultural and political issues of the Ghanaian community and the use of native languages and/or dialects.[9]

The above examples show that there are West Africanisms in hip-hop and African Americanisms in hip-life. There is a reciprocal relationship between hip-hop in the United States and hip-life music in Ghana. However, these connections do not mean that one hip-life artist cannot possess cultural representations of both African Americans and Ghanaians. For example, Sidney, a popular hip-life artist in the Ghanaian song

---

8   Bakari Kitwana, *The Hip Hop Generation* (New York: BasicCivitas Books, 2003), 87.

9   Tara Jabbaar-Gyambrah, "Hip-Hop, Hip-Life: Global Sistahs" (PhD diss., University of Buffalo, 2007)

"Abuskeleke"[10] degrades women by using misogynistic lyrics and making fun of the newest sexualized Western fashion style of wearing half shirts."[11] By imitating the language used in African American hip-hop, Sidney is expressing his disapproval of the Ghanaian female fashion that was adopted from Western culture in the 1990s. In another song called *"Scenti No,"*[12] he plays the role of revolutionary who speaks about corrupt behavior in the government system that goes against Ghanaian ethical values. Both songs send two different messages which fall into two categories—"negative" and political. Within the hip-life industry, themes ranging from social, cultural, political, and African/Black feminist perspectives have emerged. The categories discussed above do not exempt the continual emergence or integration of other musical forms or cultural ideologies into hip-life.

THE BRITISH POST-COLONIAL EFFECTS ON HIP-LIFE MUSIC

Although hip-life is a genre of protest music that emerged from Ghanaian youth expressing themselves, some British colonial influences have appeared in the genre which creates a contradiction of cultures. Many historians such as Adu Boahen, Jean Allman, Victoria B. Tashijian, Amina Mama and others have studied and researched economic, political, social structure and religion on West African countries, but do not explore the impact of colonialism on hip-life music. Kofi Agawu believes that scholars have "ignored" colonialism's impact on music because it is such a complex area to study. According to Kofi Agawu, "... unlike political history, with its kingdom wars, migrations and inventions, music-an art of sound and a performing art in an oral culture-leaves different, more complex and elusive traces on the historical record, which may explain why historians of Africa have ignored its music."[13]

In other words, according to Agawu, music is a creative form that is bound by complicated oral histories where only traces are left behind to be examined on record. Music includes a wide variety of styles and practices that continuously re-invents itself through

---

10   The translation could mean mini skirt, or short dress that women wear that show body parts that are not to be seen in public according to Ghanaian cultural values.

11   John Collins, "A Social History of Ghanaian Popular Entertainment Since Independence" (unpublished paper presented at the Ghana Historical Society, August 2005). To be published in *Transactions: Journal of the Ghana Historical Society* in 2006–2007.

12   The translation literally means smell and signifies something is rotten or not good in reference to Ghanaian government politics.

13   Kofi Agawu, "Colonialism's Impact," in *Representing African Music: Postcolonial Notes, Queries, Positions,* ed. Kofi Agawu, 1–22 (New York: Routledge, 2003), 2.

migrations. Colonialism has produced a complex musical society in Africa. Similar to the way Black music in the United States has been shaped by structural forces of slavery and Jim Crow, in contemporary Africa a bewildering diversity of inter-and intracontinental musical influences have shaped hip-life. Agawu urges us to consider that these 'foreign' modes of expression sometimes retain their original forms in the new environment, at other moments they transform indigenous forms. As we think about the place of hip-life music and the legacy of hip-hop in Africa, postcolonial Africa is thus best characterized as a *constellation* of musical practices.[14]

One example of these "constellations" at work in postcolonial Africa is a specific music form called highlife, "a blend of traditional Akan rhythms and melodies with European musical elements, such as the European instruments and harmony. It encompasses a variety of artistic expressions: music, dancing, storytelling, and theater."[15] Highlife music origins reside in English speaking West African countries of Liberia, Sierra Leone, Ghana, and Nigeria.[16] These influences evolved from contact with soldiers stationed on the Guinea Coast, African American seamen, centuries of church music, and adaptations of Western ballroom music. In its modern form, highlife music includes traces of African American blues, Caribbean reggae, pop and rock music all blended in a unique African style. Similar to hip-hop, highlife music is a multi-ethnic and cultural blend of music that represents a constellation of traditions across the Diaspora.

As Gilroy argues extensively in *The Black Atlantic*, there are no pure forms of Black music. There are distinctive attributes of Black cultural forms that are "modern" because they are hybrid and have origins in the West and Creole. Gilroy states:

> They [Black cultural forms] are modern because they have struggled to escape their status as commodities and the position within the cultural industries it specifies, and because they are produced by artists whose understanding of their own position relative to the racial group and of the role of art in mediating individual creativity with social dynamics is shaped by a sense of artistic practice as an autonomous domain either reluctantly or happily divorced from the everyday life world.[17]

---

14   Ibid., 22.

15   Sjaak Van Deer Geest and Nimrod K. Asante-Darko, "The Political Meaning of Highlife Songs in Ghana," *African Studies Review* 25 no. 1 (March 1982): 27–35.

16   John Collins, "The Early History of West African Highlife Music" *Popular Music*, 8 no. 3 (October 1989): 222.

17   Paul Gilroy, The *Black Atlantic: Modernity and Double-Consciousness* (New York and London: Verso, 1993), 73.

In the end, Gilroy argues that the Black cultural forms derive their power from Western and modern ideals and that a doubleness of locality comes along with them, where in fact the music is being produced with unique attributes produced by their experiences.

Extending Gilroy's argument related to the presence of hip-hop in Ghana, I believe that hip-life follows a similar trajectory, whereas there is a distinct Ghanaian cultural dynamic embedded within the music, related to an artist's experiences and creativity. There are significant cultural markers and societal themes such as gender roles, economic, political, social, and cultural issues that have been influenced Ghanaian society are evidence in new cultural forms of the music.

Facing similar commercial scenarios that hip-hop and Black cultures have historically encountered in the United States, aspects of Ghanaian popular culture have also struggled to escape commoditization. This is an important and integral theme in hip-life music that makes it worthy of comparison to hip-hop. There has been a steady shifting of power between artists and record companies that, as they have in the United States, have the ability to influence the production of the music and its meaning as they filter life experiences and socio-cultural histories through various media. Elements of African traditional music often resurface in the face of the rebirthing process of highlife and hip-life bringing together events, location, time, language, traumatic events (e.g. slave trade experience and colonialism) and space. Hip-life music was birthed out of this very process of remixing Diasporic voices of African American hip-hop, highlife music, and Ghanaian youth, to confront the effects of British colonialism.

ROLES OF WOMEN IN HIP-HOP AND HIP-LIFE MUSIC

Ghanaian and African American women often face challenges when addressing sexuality in their songs. This is frequently met with backlash from the media and community. The globalization of hip-hop has brought a variety of images that continues to transform the perceptions of Black women in Africa and the African Diaspora. In her work, *Black Feminist Thought,* Hill-Collins, discusses the irreparable damage of the jezebel, mammy, matriarch, and hot momma plays in the United States against Black women. These images did not grow over night, but has historically been developed for hundreds of years through the pre-colonial, colonial, and Jim Crow eras.

The perpetuation of Black women's beauty, sexuality, and personas have manifested through various media forms, including but not limited to commercial ads, films, and music videos. It is not the fact of these being developed and shown to the global world that makes them so powerful, but how others perceive Black women through media experiences without knowing their true character and how the development of the self-fulfilling prophecy drives the identity of so many young Black women in society today.

Self-fulfilling prophecy is the idea that when one is presented with the same image over and over again, they begin to take on those characteristics. Now, while I love hip-hop culture and the socio-cultural movement that grew out of resistance, I cannot deny the fact that over the last 10 years, I have grown to question the ways in which women's bodies are canvassed and utilized in music videos to shape their identity. But it has become an intricate web that points to the complexity of economics, privilege, and how colonial history has shaped our perceptions of Black women's body, beauty, and sexuality.

Hip-hop is no stranger to the discussion of derogatory lyrics and music videos that subject the Black female body into submission through the power of patriarchal ideals. Nelly's received backlash from Spelman College students in 2004, when he released his explicit music video "Tip Drill" which displayed Black women in various comprising positions. In one scene, a credit card was swiped down the buttocks of a young African American woman, signifying that her body can be bought. More than this, the ideology itself connects to aggressively sexual behavior that was displayed during slavery, thus emerging through the stereotypical image—jezebel. As time has passes by, I have tried to unpack the multidimensional representations of Black women in media, namely hip-hop videos, and the benefit that we receive as Black women, and the greater international community.

In the U.S., artists like Salt-N-Pepa, Lil' Kim and Foxy Brown set the stage for Black women expressing their sexuality in music videos through their dress and lyrics. Salt-N-Pepa's "Push It" (1986) was one of the first songs to express Black women's sexuality from their perspective. Nearly ten years later, under the mentorship of Biggie Smalls, Lil' Kim released her album *Hardcore* (1996) which took the idea of Black womanhood to another level of expression. While on one hand, Lil' Kim challenged the notion that African American women did not have control over their bodies. On the other hand, her crass but explicit lyrics, fed into patriarchal illusions and fantasies of men about Black women's bodies and sexuality. Sut Jhally's *Dreamworlds 2* (1995) considers how these narratives are shaped through a narrow set of myths of gender and sexuality in music videos, sometimes blurring the division between reality and fantasy. Consequently, the emotional ride given by the male viewer can often times lead him to believe that all women want to be engaged in their sexualized fantasies, thus erupting in more sexual assaults and rapes in American society.

Black women who encounter these personas and attempted to engage broader themes in the African Diaspora face significant challenges. In Ghana, hip-life artists like Mzbel have used their music to address gender issues such as sexual violence and harassment under the shadow of colonialism. Mzbel's career began in 2002 with Hush Studios but skyrocketed after the release of her two most controversial albums *Awoso Me* (Give It To Me) (2004) and *16 Years* (2006). In between the releasing of these albums, Mzbel

(2005) was brutally attacked[18] and sexually assaulted.[19]

The first incident occurred in October of 2005 Mzbel was invited to perform on campus of Kumasi Nkrumah University of Science and Technology (KNUST) in Kumasi in celebration of Art Society week at the college. Mzbel was dressed in a "white unzipped long-sleeved mini-jacket; a glittering pink bra, a pair of white 'track' trousers and a pair of white sneakers"[20] Mzbel was accompanied by her female dancers who wore "red-checkered mini-skirts." She performed three songs solo, one being a hit, with hip-life artist Castro, *Awoso Me* (Give It to Me); a song about two lovers who create a dialogue about their intimacy with one another. Core themes of the video are freedom of female expression, reclaiming sexuality, and the ability to assert sexual desires. In one of the verses, Mzbel provides directions to her lover Buk Tye and warns him against infidelity:

> That's how it is, let's do it as it is
> It's so sweet, very sweet
> Can you? No, don't rush. Take it easy
> Don't be busy like a player
>
> I'm about to give you flavor
> Something sweet which you can never stop eating
> Give it to me[21]

During the performance the two hip-life artists play the role of lovers who create a dialogue about their sexual experiences and pleasures. Mzbel gave a compelling

---

18 "Mzbel Sues KNUST 600m," Ghanaweb, accessed February 13, 2015, http://www.ghanaweb.eom/GhanaHomePage/entertainment/artikel.php?ID=98252

19 "Mzbel: Standing Strong," Modern Ghana, accessed February 13, 2015, http://www.modemghana.com/music/3393/3/mzbel-standing-strong.html; "Mzbel*s Attackers escape from police custody," GhanaWeb, accessed February 13, 2015, http://www.ghanaweb.eom/GhanaHomePage/lQewsArchive/artikel.php?lD=114962; "Mzbel rape story turns dramatic Laptop Found in Hairdressing Salon," GhanaWeb, accessed February 13,2015, http://www.ghanaweb.eom/GhanaHomePage/entertainment/artikel.p hp?ID=l 92612; "Goodies Hits back at Mzbel,"GhanaWeb, accessed February 13, 2015, http://www.ghanaweb.eom/GhanaHomePage/entertainment/artikel.php?ID= 192790; "Mzbel was not raped," GhanaWeb, accessed February 13, 2015, http://www.ghanaweb.eom/GhanaHomePage/NewsArchive/artikel.php?lD=l 10552; and "Mzbel Damns Manager," GhanaWeb, accessed February 13,2015, http://www.ghanaweb.eom/GhanaHomePage/entertainment/artikel.phn?lD= 192780

20 "Mzbel Sues KNUST 600m," Ghanaweb, accessed February 13, 2015, http://www.ghanaweb.eom/GhanaHomePage/entertainment/artikel.php?ID=98252

21 This part of the song was originally sung in Twi and translated into English by Hannah Essien of Indiana University.

performance with many of the students demanded an encore but she was unable to comply because other artists were waiting to perform. Nothing could prepare her for what happened next. A riot erupted, with audience members lurching forward stripping Mzbel naked citing her refusal to comply with the demands of the crowd. Although some students tried to carry her off to safety, there were others who blatantly assaulted her by ripping fondling her breasts and buttocks. Ultimately, three students at Kumasi Nkrumah University of Science and Technology (KNUST) were implicated in the molestation charge of Mzbel, Alex Dapaah, Aaron Adusah-Poku and Theodore Djokoto. Each of the students was suspended from the university for one year.

The second incident occurred in September of 2006 Mzbel and her dancers were attacked, raped, and robbed at her home in Accra, Ghana. According to news reports from ghanamusic.com, Joy FM and myzongo.com, thieves stole items such as DVD players, laptop computers, jewelry and clothes. While there is still a debate as to whether Mzbel and her dancers were raped, Mzbel reported verbally in an interview with Joy FM that she was in fact raped. Although the experience was horrifying Mzbel continued to write and sing her music. Is it because of the way that she dresses? Or, is it because she has chosen to voice her opinion as a Ghanaian woman?

In her article, "African Women, Fashion, and Scapegoating," Audrey Wipper talks about controversy surrounding "appropriate" dress of African women in East and Central parts of Africa. In the excerpt below Wipper explains how the wearing of mini-skirts sparked a massive riot in Ethiopia:

Mini-skirts were blamed for widespread rioting in Ethiopia in which 50 persons were injured, 100 vehicles destroyed, and schools closed for two weeks. There has been vigilante mob action. 'Offending' women have been jeered at, physically assaulted and stripped of their clothes in public by youth wingers and college students.[22]

Many of these types of attacks have occurred in Kenya, Uganda, Malawi and Zambia. These attacks are as a result of the deep-rooted social changes that urban Africa has been experiencing over the last several years and African women are being used as targets of aggression to symbolize the strains of these changes.[23]

Mini-skirts in particular provoked the government to put a ban on wearing short skirts and dresses that were deemed "inappropriate." As Wipper states, "in Zambia, President Kenneth Kaundra ruled that all skirts must be at least three inches below the knee. And one of the most authoritarian of all heads of state, Dr. Banda, forbade women to use lipstick, straighten their hair, paint their fingernails, and wear trousers

---

22   Audrey Wipper, "African Women, Fashion, and Scapegoating," *Canadian Journal of African Studies* 5, no. 2 (1972): 329–330.

23   Wipper, "African Women, Fashion, and Scapegoating," 330.

or shorts."[24] African women who wore Western fashions, make-up, wigs, and lightened their skin were ridiculed because they were moving away from being "African." Some African countries, in an attempt to preserve "traditional" African culture banned such items from being used.[25]

Mzbel has used the site of the concert as a form of resistance in which she challenges African traditional roles subscribed to women in the community by using dress. According to Allman:

> Dress and fashion have been centrally implicated in the forgoing of a distinct African modernity, through slavery and freedom, colonialism and conversion, ethnicity and nation, gender, and generation, hybridity and cosmopolitanism, state-building and state authority, subjecthood, and citizenship. Moreover, as part of their agenda of liberating modernity from Eurocentric paradigms, they dismantle the tradition vs. modernity binary by demonstrating that tradition does not exist either prior to or in opposition to the modern.[26]

In other words, is it possible to be "modern" and "traditional" at the same time? Mzbel has been cited for being dressed inappropriately, and not serving as an "appropriate" role model for young girls in the community. In the end, there is a merging of African and Western culture ideologies through Mzbel's song *Awoso Me.* Through the influence of colonialism, Ghanaian women were encouraged to wear clothing that did not reveal their breasts or butts [bottoms?], as they were thought of as "sexual beasts."

In 1957 under Kwame Nkrumah's presidency, Hannah Kudjoe, a woman's rights activist, began to campaign for women to wear European style clothing. Her purpose appeared to be different from that of Ghana's former colonial master, Britain, because she wanted to "uplift" women and create an atmosphere of self-reliance. It is however ironic that her leadership role to empower women mirrored that of colonial guidelines given Britain's influence on Ghana. There has been a complex merging of African patriarchy and Western ideologies that continues to resurface in Ghanaian society. Mzbel resists both African and British patriarchy by straying away from the "norm" by wearing mini-skirts, dresses, halter tops, and shorts.

Dress is important because it has been influenced throughout Ghana's colonial history with Britain. Dress can be used as a form of power and it is deeply embedded in economic, political, the gendered perspectives of the British and culture. The ways in which women dress in the community gets played out in these areas because it is a complex

---

24   Ibid., 335.

25   Ibid., 331.

26   Jean Allman, "Introduction" in *Fashioning Africa: Power and the Politics of Dress* (Indiana University Press: 2004), 5.

realm of socio-cultural realities. Over time it has become a hybrid form that either resists African patriarchy or plays into Western ideologies about African women. For example, the British attached the way in which women dressed in African communities to their sexuality. Through the use of educational services, missionary groups such as the Basel and Wesleyan Mission encouraged and promoted the idea of wearing European clothing, suits for the men and flowery long dresses for the women.

The current debate surrounding young girls and women's choices to be more "sexy" in the way that they dress is said to be moving away from the more "traditional" forms of dress in Ghana towards Western fashions. However, is it possible that women are reverting back to Ghanaian traditional forms of dress prior to colonialism? Or, is the way in which young girls or women choose to dress a reflection of the shift in gendered perspectives of Ghanaians as a result of colonialism? The patriarchal relations in Ghanaian society disregard the significance of women's experience which suggests that violence against women in Ghanaian societies is deeply rooted in "gender power relations, identities, and social institutions."[27] Inevitably, young women are violated to maintain systems of oppression that subordinate their roles in society.

Riot outbursts are not just limited to economic and political concerns. There are other factors such as gender inequities and women's public invisibility, which partially emerged as a result of British colonialism. The attack on Mzbel at the KNUST concert in 2005 emerged as a result of complex social and cultural contradictions. What transpired at this concert and at other similar events over the last several years in Ghana are traceable to the influence of British colonialism. For example, the way in which Ghanaian women dressed became associated with her sexuality during colonialism. Wearing little or no clothing for the British symbolized a "loose woman." The ideology that women are to wear clothing that covers their entire body emerged during colonial rule and has been internalized in Ghanaian culture. The young women who were at the concert stepped out of roles that have been inscribed by British colonialism and that are continually carried out as a "norm" of Ghanaian society. By wearing clothing that revealed "sacred" parts of the body they resisted British and Ghanaians subscribed roles. While dress may seem to be a big part of the issue, it is only part of the equation. Dress was used to create subscribed gender roles for Ghanaian women in the community.

Similar to its American counterpart, hip-hop, hip-life is often characterized by male aggression with women largely absent in the industry. When women are present, their ability to articulate authentic critiques of serious societal issues is muted by hyper masculine sexual objectification of their bodies and music. This aggression has serious

---

27   Ibid, 166.

consequences in a transnational context that have been more carefully scrutinized in the United States than abroad.

The riot at Mzbel's concert emerged as a result of a complicated web stemming from Ghanaian society's transitions between the economic, social, cultural, and political sectors. Mzbel who was attack at the concert at KNUST in 2005, then, serve as "scape-goats" for the real issues that plague Ghanaian society such as high unemployment rates, the meshing of Ghanaian and British patriarchal views of women, and subscribed gender roles.

CONCLUSION

Comparing the impact of hip-hop culture on hip-life artists in Ghana, several important issues become apparent. Music is not simply a passing culture form relegated to the aesthetic realm but rather it becomes a conduit for political, cultural, emotional, and sexual trauma. From the experiences of Mzbel and others we can see how the remix of hip-hop in a West African context both challenged and confirmed traditional roles assigned to women in West African societies. As a platform hip-life has great potential to challenge Western patriarchal stereotypes about a "woman's place," however it also can exhibit and amplify the same misogynistic and anti-feminist qualities that characterized aspects of the subculture in the United States

Despite these contradictions, understanding hip-life as a strategy of liberation for women is important for a variety of reasons. First, it broadens our understanding of the power of Black music by engaging the international dimensions of its appeal. We see a New York form that was developed to address a certain socio-political context taking on new forms to challenge colonial and patriarchal systems of power. While much has been discussed about how African American youth have interpreted hip-hop music as a venue for their political affirmation, we also see that Ghanaian women can engage the music and the culture as a platform with the same fervor. We should carefully consider the connection of regional and cultural influences in New York to a broader conversation about gender, power, class, and culture. Instead of thinking of New York as a separate microcosm, we can use stories of trauma and musical performance to interrogate patriarchy and violence directed against women on a global scale.

Afro-Latin Soul and Hip-Hop

By Alejandro Nava

Only in his music has the black man been able to tell his story.

—James Baldwin[1]

With his murals, Rivera fashioned a vision of the outsized humanity pulsing within the common Mexican laborer. ... What the world needs now is a rapper who can do for the common man and woman verbally what Diego Rivera was able to do with a paint brush and a blank wall.[2]

James Baldwin's famous remark about music in black history largely holds true for Latin American cultures as well: music has been the central platform for their display of personality, style, and aesthetical character. "Is it even remotely clear to most students of English," writes music critic Timothy Brennan, "that African-based popular music plays a similar role in Latin America and the Caribbean that literature does in Europe and the United States? Is it appreciated that the popular and national sense of self is bound up with musical expertise, musical style, the power of exerting musical influence that seems to be every bit as strong as the urge for political dominance, scientific prowess, or literary skill?"[3] If it's true that musical prowess has been a defining feature of Latin American and Caribbean identities, any study of these traditions should begin by listening to their musical signatures. In letting music act as our guide, we might catch certain themes and sonorities often overlooked by standard European accounts of the New World, certain pulses that give us an alternative history of the Americas, told at a sonic level in the beats of a drum, a base line, a chant, or a grunt. As Gustavo Perez Firmat once said about the mambo, there can be greatness and eloquence in a simple grunt, a whole record of human experiences and beliefs contained in such compacted sounds.[4] To the right ear, noises that seem like so much babble can represent untold stories of cultural life and can reveal truths that are only available through the beauty of sound.

The great Cuban novelist, musician, and architect of magical realism Alejo Carpentier clearly understood the revelatory importance of music in Latin America: His classic study *Music in Cuba* puts the theme of music in Latin American cultures front and center, as a necessary prelude to any opus dealing with the Americas. In his telling, music has not only shaped many of the distinctive patterns of culture in the New World; it has also prefigured the future when it comes to race relations, as if it were a blind seer compelled by sounds and stories more than by colors of skin.[5] As early as the sixteenth century, music in Hispaniola outran the other arts and sciences when it came to cooperation and intermingling among Africans, American Indians, and Europeans, with oppressed groups experiencing spaces of freedom here while they were still corralled and caged elsewhere.[6] In these open plains of musical creativity, *mestizaje* (cultural miscegenation) came alive in the New World like a new breed of the human species, blending different rituals and sounds into a thick, curvaceous aesthetics of culture.

In the following centuries the mix thickened, as festivals such as Día de los Reyes and Corpus Christi added African "native tongues"—Yoruba hymns, sacred drums, and ritual dances—to Catholic processions to produce a distinctly American and baroque extravaganza of ritual, music, dance, and sexuality. One can see why Carpentier, or more recently Jacques Attali, considers music a harbinger of change and subversion.[7] As an auditory revelation, felt in the sinews and muscles of the body, or deeper in the rhythmic contractions of the heart, music has proven to be far more supple and sinuous than some of the other arts, changing and whirling with the times and venturing into forbidden regions of experience. In some cases, when music has been attuned to the gusts of the spirit in history, it has breached the repressive barriers of society like a hurricane, leaving not only shards and debris in its wake, but also the opportunity for a fresh start. Unlike in other arts, especially those with the authority of the written word, many of the breakthroughs in American music have come from the bottom rungs and peripheries of the modern world, from those cultures on the margins of the literary and political centers of Western power. In emerging from the cracks and fissures of the modern world, many of the greatest achievements in American music have subtly but undeniably challenged prejudices that consigned non-European traditions to a cultural backwater. In too many cases to count, as David Tracy has written, the West used the custody of writing as a sign of cultural superiority and consequently demeaned, if not silenced altogether, nonliterate and nonalphabetic traditions, considering them stagnant inlets of history, with no current or flow.[8] The ability to manipulate the sacred aura of writing often allowed the educated and lettered classes of Europe and America—the *letrados* in Latin American societies—to use grammatology as an instrument of empire, especially in largely illiterate contexts. (Aptly put, Nebrija's classic book of grammar, *Gramática sobre la lengua castellana* [1492], called written language "the companion of empire.")[9]

In this tired narrative of Western evolutionary development, with the proprietors of the written word at the apogee of culture and politics, the study of music, folklore, dance, ritual, or ceremony has the potential to alter, even overthrow, these glaring biases. With their surging, rocking, cresting sonic waves, the blues, jazz, rock and roll, soul, hip-hop, *son*, salsa, and so many other American sounds are proof of a riotous potential that can batter and break many of our barriers of prejudice.[10] In terms of race relations in the New World specifically, music has frequently been the occasion for an exchange of ideas and sounds that has brought together various cultures, transforming conflicting and clashing relations into harmonious streams of sound. Among the many examples of such synthesizing arrangements, African and Spanish fusions have a venerable history. For Ted Gioia, these fusions have been so plentiful and fecund in the Americas that he imagines a lasting and haunting influence from the Moorish age in Spain: "Indeed, in the area of music alone, the number of successful African and Latin hybrids (including salsa, calypso, samba, and cumbia, to name a few) is so great that one can only speculate that these two cultures retain a residual magnetic attraction, a lingering affinity due to this original cross-fertilization."[11] According to Gioia, lingering affinities from medieval Al-Andalus have been the inspiration for African and Spanish conjunctions and collaborations in modern times and have resulted in novel, hybrid inventions, everything from salsa and samba to funk and hip-hop. Before considering hip-hop in particular, I take a quick look at the cultural soil of Latin America to appreciate the roots and branches of African and Spanish blends in the New World.

THE CATHOLIC BAROQUE IN THE AMERICAS

Catholicism played a key role in the baroque culture of the New World. When contrasting the respective roles of Protestantism and Catholicism in the Americas, it is fair to say that each had its own logic and aesthetic values. At the very least, we can say that their evangelization proceeded in different ways, with Iberian and Catholic cultures assuming a more accommodating stance when it came to African and Native peoples, and North American Protestantism generally practicing a policy of separation and segregation, keeping non-Christian cultures at a greater distance. Each had its own glaring, titanic sins, colossal in scale, when it came to the African slave trade or treatment of Native peoples, but the Catholic baroque model—with its penchant for visual excess, folkloric richness, and indulgent syncretism—seems to have been better able to acclimatize its mind to the strange new myths, gods, and narratives that it encountered in the Americas. Even in the face of official warnings and censures, the Latin baroque soul swelled and expanded to make room for the pantheon of gods and cultures in the New World. By "baptizing" American "pagan" traditions, a new Catholic baroque was created, *el indio barroco*, which brought together various religious and cultural fragments—African,

European, and indigenous—into a fresh concert of sound, flavor, and belief specifically for the Indies: a *concierto barroco* (incidentally, the title of one of Carpentier's novels).[12] Faced with improbable juxtapositions and fantastic combinations, Latin American dictionaries and vocabularies reeled in the effort to name the creatures of this hitherto unmapped world. A ravishing lexicon of brownness was the result, as Richard Rodriguez has observed: "Mexico has for centuries compiled a ravishing lexicon of brown because in Mexico race is capricious as history is capricious. For the colonial era, the verbal glamour of Mexico has been to entertain a spectrum of brown—of impurity—as rich and as wet as a Hollander palette: *mestizo, castizo, alvina, chino, negro torno atras, morisco, canbujo, albarrasado, tente en el aire, canpa mulato, coyote, vorsino, lobo.*"[13] Like the arabesque lines of a baroque church, or the verbal abundance of baroque rhetoric, words multiplied and proliferated to find the right adjectives and descriptions for the dizzying variety of New World identities. In this restless odyssey searching for the right word, the lexicon of the Indies has a way of overwhelming the human mind's compulsion to define and classify, reminding us of the sheer incommensurability of human identity. Racial nomenclature in Latin America accordingly has been a profusion of metaphors and anthropomorphisms, thick with nuances, gradations, accents, and puzzles. As the names of God in mystical traditions did, metaphors and labels have multiplied, if only to remind us that human identity, like God, is wholly other. In lieu of emptiness as metaphor, the baroque piled together confused, frenetic, and vertiginous lines and images, with borders that gyrated and zigzagged, crisscrossed and meandered in search of the perfect design that would encapsulate the wonder of the world. If we contrast this "Hollander palette" of identity with North American categories for race, the latter come across as unusually thin and pale, especially when conceived in black and white, with straight lines and stark borders separating them, as if the categories mimicked the simple lines of a Shaker table.

For the purposes of this [reading], we can see and hear evidence of the baroque imagination in the music of the Americas, all the way up to the hip-hop scene. The music of Latin America is proof of the carnival-like identity of Latin America, with African and indigenous cultures surviving and even thriving in the Caribbean and Latin America, while largely disappearing from Protestant North America. In Cuba, Haiti, and Brazil, African cultures transplanted themselves and put down deep roots, eventually becoming part of Latin America's religious and musical soil. African cultural and religious traditions in the United States, by contrast, rarely survived the violence of the Middle Passage, falling on hard, rocky soil when they came ashore, or worse, encountering concerted efforts to uproot and exterminate any traces of these traditions.[14]

Of course there are many explanations for the survival of African culture in the Caribbean and Latin America—especially given the greater number of first-generation slaves in those settings—but certainly one factor was the part played by the Catholic theater of saints, martyrs, festivals, and theologies in keeping African memories and rituals alive.[15]

In the words of Albert Raboteau, "The nature of Catholic piety with its venerations of saints, use of sacramental and organization of religious fraternities among the slaves offered a supportive context for the continuity of African religious elements in recognizable forms."[16] The color and religious bars were more unclear and malleable in Latin America, so Catholicism and African religions entered into secret pacts and covenants, resulting in a version of soul that was a colorful mask of heterogeneity, animated by a multitude of spirits. While many U.S. evangelical Protestants regarded such unions as evidence of Catholic promiscuity, debauchery, and the idol-making faculty of the Catholic mind, Catholic thought assumed that grace was generously and universally diffused in the diverse array of human cultures. Seen through eyes aided by grace, all tribal ancestors and graven images—say, Quetzalcoatl and Tonantzin in Mexico, or Elegua and Shango in Cuba—had sacramental value and were worthy of communion with Christian belief and practice.

AFRO-LATIN SOUL IN THE AMERICAS: THE *SON*

Many of these features of Catholicism in the New World are evident in the development of Afro-Latin religion and music. On the stage of the eccentric world of the Americas, religion underwent a metamorphosis as startling as anything else that occurred on the continent. After making contact with African and indigenous traditions, Catholicism would not be the same. Evangelization worked both ways, injecting African and Native religions with a Christian element while converting Old World Catholicism into a new American variety, replete with pagan rites, gods, and stories. As Carpentier sees it, in this way American cultures added exotic colors and flavors to an already rich rainbow in baroque Catholicism. "The altars, the accessories surrounding the cult of worship, the images, the religious garments, were crafted to seduce souls strongly attracted by a sumptuous world of rites and mysteries. Deep down, of course, it did not mean that the ancient gods of Africa were renounced. Ogún, Changó, Eleguá, Obatalá, and many others continued thriving in the hearts of many."[17] Catholicism's "sumptuous world of rites" found a place for these gods even if they were unofficially recognized and concealed under the façade of Catholic icons, saints, and festivals. Wedded to these Catholic figures, African deities continued to thrive in the hearts of many and reappeared in countless fiestas and ceremonies.

Music and dance in particular were conduits for these appearances of the Orishas (African ancestors and deities), bursting into time and space through the charged, throbbing currents of the drums. In the language of vibrations and beats, only intelligible to the initiates, the African *batá* drums would summon the Orishas and plead for their intercession in the lives of the people. With the repetition of certain words, or the precise sequence of beats alone, the Orishas would descend into the participants and take possession of their bodies and spirits. (The expressions *bajar al santo,* "to make the saint descend," and *subirse el santo,* "to have the saint rise through you," describe these experiences.)[18] When these percussive qualities were joined with Spanish and Arabic musical legacies, a ravishing symbiosis of New World religion and sound was created—the Cuban *son* was one of these products, a child of these synchronicities.

As a result of the migration of African slaves to Cuba from San Domingo in the 1790s in the aftermath of the Haitian revolution, African-based rhythms arrived in force, seducing and converting more and more Cubans. Suddenly the sediments of Haitian French traditions filtered into the wide river of Spanish-Arabic music from Andalusia and Cuba. Unlike the *contradanza,* a French salon dance and musical style performed with an orchestra, the *son* developed in the lowest strata of Cuban society, among Spanish settlers, freed slaves, mulattos, and *cimarrones* (runaway slaves).[19] Some critics trace its origins to the eastern mountain regions of Cuba around 1860, where greater permissiveness seemed to prevail in relations among settlers from Spain, freed slaves (many Bantu and Dahomeyan), and mulattos. (The term *son montuno,* "son of the mountain," reveals its rural origins.)[20] Carpentier, however, traces the roots of the *son,* particularly its narrative and poetic components, back further into the mists of time, to the slum songs of the eighteenth century that delighted in puns, humor, and libidinous allusions (derived from the *chuchumbé*).[21] Whatever its exact origins, the *son* supplemented the Spanish *canción* and other European melodies with a battery of African percussion, thus creating a prototypical Afro-Latin genre. (The *son* usually was played in an ensemble of the guitar, tres, güiro, bongos, marímbula, maracas, and claves.)[22]

In this vein, Samuel Feijóo speaks of the *son* as "heated-up rhythm, with its percussion section of neo-African instruments and its extraordinary folkloric literary sense."[23] For our purposes, the folkloric sense of the *son* is important, as it introduced popular ballads, social satire, political commentary, and religious hymns and incantations to the remarkable variety of African drums. If we add the music of the carnival parades *(comparsas),* with their totemic echoes of Yoruba gods and hymns as well as invocations to the Virgin and the saints, we get an idea of the various currents and waves of emotion and rhythm that inundated the island like a tropical storm. Because the *son* traversed a wide spectrum, it disturbed artificial categories of the sacred and profane. In this respect, *son*'s polyrhythm—its signal achievement in Carpentier's view—represents in music the wider spiritual and cultural climate of Afro-Latin America.[24] In its rhythmic variation and spontaneity, *son* gave voice to the vibrant, vertiginous *mestizaje* of the New World just as jazz would later articulate key principles of North American culture.

As *son* infiltrated forbidden domains, however, it acquired detractors among the ruling white elites in Cuba, the zealots of a monotone version of Cuba. For Jory Farr, *son* has a subversive history: "As it spread across the island, it became a dangerous music, a shout of defiance, a fluming of raw, mixed-race sensuality that disrupted the tight controls enforced by Cuba's light-skinned ruling class. The early history of *son* has tales of repression and harassment, of police destroying instruments and jailing 'lewd' musicians."[25] Accusations of its diabolical character emerged as an index of its perceived danger from those fearing an outbreak of wild poly-rhythm, uncontrolled polyphony, and cultural miscegenation. Just as the blues, jazz, soul, and hip-hop have been sullied and demeaned with indictments of their devilish character, *son* faced similar charges, accused of prodigality and sensual extravagance. Heedless of high and low cultural boundaries, or sacred and profane classifications, *son* borrowed from disparate sources and produced sounds that brought together classes, races, and religions into a bacchanalia of jubilation. Like the *zarabanda* of the sixteenth and seventeenth centuries, *son* had lowly and disreputable origins but would eventually prove delicious and irresistible to cultured elites. Fernando Ortiz makes this point about the *zarabanda:* "But there is also the art born below that climbs from class to class, from the puddles to the mountain tops, adjusting itself to the atmosphere at every level, until it finally converts itself, thanks to its beauty, into an art whose gestation and early upbringing are utterly forgotten. ... This was true of the *zarabanda,* that sprang to life in a scandalous and diabolical impropriety among black conjurers and witchdoctors of the Congo, and then, with the passing of time, was danced at the royal courts."[26]

In the case of *son,* not unlike the *zarabanda,* its origins are impossible to disentangle from the circumstances of slavery. One song in this tradition, related to the *nengón,* is a plaintive, haunting lament about the plight of a slave. Like the blues in North America, the *son* could swing low and strike notes of sorrow and anguish, and then, just as suddenly, become jubilant and humorous; tragedy and festivity are hardly irreconcilable in the music. When channeling a bolero, *son* is typically mournful; when approximating the mambo, a later development of the *son,* it can be fast-paced, aggressive, and lascivious. Gustavo Perez-Firmat puts it this way: "The bolero is a medium for bemoaning unhappiness in love, for questioning the injustice of fate. If the mambo is about conquest, the bolero is about loss. If the mambo is copulative, the bolero is disjunctive. The mambo grunts, the bolero moans."[27]

Grunts and moans, conquests and losses, copulations and disjunctions: everything from the wide world of human experience can appear in the sublime cathedral of emotion known as *son.* Following is a well-known *son,* "Cajón de Muerto":

> Solo ambicion de fatiga yerto
> Cansado ya de fatiga guerras
> Y al acostarme en mi cajón de muerto
> Dormir en paz debajo de la tierra.
> My only ambition, exhausted
> and tired of the enduring war,
> is to lie down in my box of death,
> to sleep in peace underneath the earth.[28]

Like a bolero, the song bemoans the relentless banality of war and pleads for eternal peace beneath the earth. The plain meaning of the song is obvious here, but since the reference to *cajón,* coffin, can also be to the wooden boxes used in Afro-Cuban music and religion (used as percussion, for calling the Orishas), there is a hidden religious meaning as well. The singer thus spreads out his emotions in various directions, aiming at the sacred as much as the profane, at the sky as much as the earth.

At the table of this spacious imagination, Cuban musicians often find a place for the sacred even in moments of sensual indulgence. For such artists, the beats of the *batá* drum strike chords much deeper than the pleasures of the body. The beats may trigger the quivering vibrations of the flesh, the rush of the blood through the veins, and the gloss of sweat on the body, but they also stimulate spiritual faculties and mystical chords of memory. They can represent the thunderous sound of the coming of Shangó/Santa Barbara or the passage of Eleguá/San Antonio into the crossroads of the world. The drums invoke the ancestors in Afro-Cuban music the way ancient Greek poets and musicians invoked the muses with the lyre. When describing these revels in Cuban music and religion, Jory Farr offers this testimony: "At a jazz club in Havana one night, explosions of bebop horns and electric guitars, all building into climax after shuddering climax, suddenly gave way to chants of the Abakuá, a men's secret leopard society, and the sacred rhythms of the *batá* drums. At Casa de la Música, I saw the lead singer of Cuba's all-girl, twelve-member Chicas del Son go from a lusty bump-and-grind to the rapturous ritual dance of her *Orisha,* suggesting that sex, rhythm, harmony, and divine resonance were one and the same."[29] In these examples, music plays loosely with a wide range of ecstasies, sacred and secular alike. Whether in sacred rhythms or profane climaxes, these ceremonies charge the body electric with spiritual and physical energies and enrapture the listener with music "heard so deeply that it is not heard at all, but you are the music while the music lasts."[30]

Transports and elevations of this kind are of course abundant in African American music of the United States, [...] but the echoes of African and Latin traditions grow fainter in the North American context and recede into the background of mainstream music. It becomes more difficult to determine the sources of the sound, to identify what role African ancestors or Latin rhythms played in the evolution of black music. The average listener to hip-hop knows very little, if anything, of fusions and collaborations among African and Latin traditions.

On the eve of hip-hop's delivery into the Bronx in the 1960s, however, Afro-Latin alliances were palpable parts of the atmosphere, setting the stage for musical innovation. Juan Flores calls attention to one case, the movement known as "Afro-Latin soul," sometimes called the boogaloo: "The bawdiness, the strong presence of funk and soul music, the abrupt break with some tradition-bound conventions of Latin style, all figure centrally in most boogaloo and point more clearly to the musical influences that set the stage for that brief yet dramatic transition in Latin music of the mid-1960s period."[31]

Afro-Latin soul emerged with the Latin-funk fusions of the 1960s in North America and soon gave way to hip-hop. Though there was already a long tradition of interplay between jazz and Latin music in North America, the decades of the 1960s–1970s took the affiliations of Afro-Latin and Afro-American styles in new directions, especially with the rising tidal waves of R & B, soul, and funk.[32] The symbolic rapport of black and Latin revelry continued in these decades, but increasingly picked up new sensibilities, becoming harder, grittier, and funkier, a reflection of the brutal exigencies of American ghettos. Since Latinos and blacks often shared the beleaguered spaces of U.S. ghettos (Puerto Ricans in New York, Mexicans in Southern California, Haitians and Cubans in New Orleans and Florida), it was natural for them to cooperate in the production of new styles and sounds. Hip-hop is a product of these interactions, as Afrika Bambaataa once said: "Wherever hip hop was, and the Blacks were, the Puerto Ricans, and other Latinos were, too."[33]

AFRO-LATIN HIP-HOP IN THE AMERICAS

Besides the well-known contributions of Latinos in the areas of break-dancing and graffiti, it is clear that Latinos contributed greatly to the music of hip-hop. In particular, it is well established that hip-hop copped the percussion beats from Afro-Latin music (a descendant of the *batá* drums).[34] One of the pioneers of hip-hop beats, Jimmy Castor, is a case in point: "From watching or hearing records of Latin musicians like Tito Puente, Chan Pozo and Cal Tjader," writes David Toop, "he learned to incorporate authentic Afro-Cuban rhythms and percussion, adding timbales to his vocal and multi-instrumental abilities."[35] Besides appropriating some of these rhythms (as in his "Block Party," 1972), Castor introduced the dozens and jive talk into his music with songs like "Hey Leroy, Your Mama's Callin'," "Say Leroy, the Creature from the Black Lagoon Is Your Father," and "Dracula." At a minimum, he is a bridge figure who straddles the world of soul, funk, and Latin music, on the one hand, and the budding rap game, on the other.

Beyond the example of Jimmy Castor, the close encounters between Latin and African American music in New York in the 1960s–1970s created a climate that was positively saturated with hybrid sounds and styles; Castor was a microcosm of a larger, multicolored cosmos that included contributions from Latin America, the Caribbean, and elsewhere. (The Caribbean roots of some of the founding figures of hip-hop, like DJ Kool Herc and Afrika Bambaataa, have long been acknowledged.) At this stage in hip-hop studies, appreciation for the pluralistic history of rap's origins seems well established, but it is worth recalling the transnational and intercultural influences that coalesced, condensed, and heated up to produce the big bang explosion of hip-hop. Because so many North Americans think of the U.S.–Mexican border as a mental wall as much as a political demarcation, this recognition of a common musical heritage throughout the Americas is frequently overlooked and even denied.[36] Whether in musical theory or cultural studies, the building of insurmountable fences between various nation-states or ethnic nationalities has a way of obscuring the mad combinations and riotous arrays of musical and cultural influences that produced black music in the Americas. And this holds true in hip-hop studies, in which so many voices, rhythms, and loops are echoed, sampled, faded in and out, and scratched over, as much as in anything else.

It is equally true, however, that rap music created something authentically new in the Bronx, something quite different from Latin musical conventions. Though there were many forerunners of rap in Latin America—*decimas* (dueling and mocking verses); *plenas* and *corridos* (news reports and folk stories chanted or sung); and carnival conventions of satire, parody, obscenity, and saturnalia—there is no doubt that rap music in North America reconfigured and remixed various sources into a unique and singular creation.[37] Without denying the importance of the creole complexity of New York in the 1970s, hip-hop was surely a breakthrough of African American youth, as Imani Perry has maintained.[38] Though African American youth drew from a crazy variety of musical heritages, they emerged from the laboratory of invention with a previously unheard style, fresh and original.

Many Latinos who were in earshot of this new sound greeted hip-hop like a newly discovered truth, with a shock of recognition, like falling in love. Because of this new beloved, Latinos in the United States saw the traditions of their ancestors interrupted and amplified by African American styles and flows, making for new identities for these Latinos in the diaspora. In my case, the mariachi music that my parents adored was passed on to me in the milk of my mother, but I was also nursed on the music of Grandmaster Flash, the Gap Band, Run DMC, Rakim, Tupac, Nas, and others. As Gustavo Perez Firmat once said about mambos, mariachi music will not be forever.[39] And the fact that mambos and *corridos* have given way to hip-hop for many Cuban and Mexican youths only illustrates the inevitability of change for Latinos dispersed in this "first world" America. In both the United States and Latin America, hip-hop has challenged traditional Latin music for the right to speak for the barrios.[40]

And yet at the same time the converse is true: Latino hip-hop has also challenged the mainstream scene in the United States. By adding their own intonations and themes to North American rap, many Latin rappers indigenize their music with a *sabor Latino,* inserting their own piquancy and kick into the soul food of hip-hop. For this reason alone, the relationship of Latino hip-hop with U.S. rap is usually dialogical rather than simply mimetic, a critical exchange rather than plain imitation. While U.S. hip-hop has clearly worked its magic on these cultures, Latin America has also spoken back with some of its own charms.

In the remainder of this [reading] I consider some of the distinctive themes in Latin hip-hop throughout the Americas, assessing first its "third world" context, then its sampling of African religion, and finally its connection with indigenous histories.[41]

The "Third World" Context of Afro-Latin Hip-Hop
[O]ne of the great MCs of hip-hop, Chuck D, used his furious, apocalyptic-inspired tongue to decry American-sponsored violence against blacks in the United States. However, I neglected to mention that he can be equally tough on the state of the hip-hop industry today. As a key witness to the rise and success of hip-hop, Chuck D has expressed deep concern about how it has aged: a child once so fresh and so clean, a child of endless promise, it is now in danger of losing its soul, "talkin about popping locks, servin rocks and hittin switches, now she's a gangsta rollin with gangsta bitches, always smokin blunts and gettin drunk."[42] Though Common penned these lines, Chuck D has long been warning the hip-hop nation of these dangers, of the ruinous incursions of venal materialism and crass hedonism in the soul of the rap game.

Besides changing the message of hip-hop—preferring the themes of booty, blunts, and bling over prophetic indictments of grinding poverty, racist legacies, and spiritual emptiness—more recent developments in the business of hip-hop have had the effect of severely shrinking the range of its voices and perspectives. Now an artist must secure a corporate imprimatur in order to get any play, and this process has clearly blunted the prophetic edge. As in biblical prophecy, when a prophet works for the king and is a part of the courtly retinue, he becomes the voice of the king, not the voice of God. Something like this, according to Chuck D, has happened in hip-hop: "In the first ten to twelve years of rap recordings," he states, "rappers rapped for the people, and they rapped against the elite establishment. In the last ten or so years, rappers rap for their companies and their contracts, and they're part of the establishment now. It's two diametrically opposed ideas."[43] Because of this sea change in hip-hop, the tides have frequently turned against the most artistic and dissident voices. We are left, as Immortal Technique, Chuck D, and Brother Ali suggest, with a civil war for the soul of the nation of hip-hop.[44]

Given these concerns about hip-hop's survival in a culture of self-gratification, Chuck D began to look to other parts of the world for alternatives to U.S. rap. During a visit to South Africa in 2011, he spoke with excitement about what he was experiencing there, as if he had traveled through a wormhole and returned to the state of hip-hop in its "livest" infancy. "The world has parity now," he wrote, "and has surpassed the USA in all of the basic fundamentals of hip hop."[45] For those disenchanted with the current status of hip-hop in the United States, voices from the global periphery offer refreshing alternatives; they are more urgent, more timely, and more relevant to the convulsions and distresses of communities throughout the world. These voices give us glimpses of hip-hop at its most resourceful and cunning, in which beats and rhymes are diamonds mined out of the ruins of poverty and social crisis, and a concern with "ends" runs deeper than "money, hos, and clothes." Instead of eliding or reinforcing the massive inequalities of the global capitalist order, these rappers raise their voices against the powers that benefit from this discriminatory state of affairs. And when necessary, they target all those in hip-hop who are untroubled and complacent about these realities, all the perpetrators of hip-hop, those too faded on chronic to notice the depths of global suffering.

The study of hip-hop's global dispersion has other benefits as well. I see it as decentering and challenging the North American ego about supremacy in art and culture, reminding us of the unconscious (and sometimes blatantly conscious) prejudices that elevate this ego like a sacred chalice at the moment of consecration. As Paul Gilroy insists, there is a glaring "American-centrism" in a lot of hip-hop, and when this attitude prevails, it tends to be silent about the struggles of anyone outside the United States, whether south of the border, across the Atlantic, or throughout the African continent.[46] When turning our attention to the global underground, not only do we get a different spin on hip-hop, but we are also exposed to a more heterogeneous and chameleon-like version of "blackness" than portraits in the United States, "blackness" as the color of pariahs and outcasts, as a symbol of various stripes and hues of oppression.[47] Since the majority of blacks in the western hemisphere reside in Latin America (approximately 37 percent live in the United States), by expanding our field of vision in hip-hop studies, we encounter a new vista of the African diaspora, one that can shed light on the unions, blends, and combinations between Africa and various Spanish and Portuguese cultures, the Afro-Latin hybrids. True to the spirit of hip-hop, when we flip the script on the prevailing state of hip-hop in the United States, we may begin to see things with fresh eyes, fixing our sight on previously unseen things.

Many Cuban hip-hop artists, I argue, embody this construction of faith, in which the poor of their country are suddenly made visible and their voices are given a hearing. Consider EPG's simple description of their mission: "We rap about the conditions of our lives, the fact that our people, the poor, continue to get poorer while the rich get richer."[48] Or Anónimo Consejo on a similar note: "Rap is something that is born here in your heart, with the idea of combatting injustice perpetrated by the government against immigrants, African Americans and Latinos."[49] For many Cuban rap groups—add Obsesión, Hermanos de Causa, Gente de Zona, Daymé Arocena, and the Orishas to this list—hip-hop remains a revolutionary struggle, a voice of protest and peace. This engaged vision of hip-hop comes up a lot among Latin American rap groups, as if they feel obliged to mark their territory with a distinct demarcation from the commercially popular rap of North America, more in keeping with a pedagogy of the oppressed than a pedagogy of ballin'. In one of their raps, "Tengo," Hermanos de Causa describe their griefs and grievances as follows:

> Tengo una palmera, un mapa sin tesoro
> Tengo aspiraciones sin tener lo que hace falta. ...

Tengo una raza oscura y discriminada
Tengo una jornada que me exige y no da nada
Tengo tantas cosas que no puedo ni tocarlas
Tengo instalaciones que no puedo ni pisarlas
Tengo libertad entre un parenthesis de hierro
Tengo tantos derechos sin provechos, que me encierro
Tengo lo que tengo sin tener lo que he tenido.
I've got a palm tree, a map without a treasure
I've got aspirations without having what I need. ...
I've got discrimination because I'm black
I've got a job that demands and gives nothing
I've got so many things that I can't even touch
I've got all these places I can't even step foot in
I've got freedom in a parentheses of iron
I've got so many rights without any benefit that I feel confined
I've got what I have without having what I've had.[50]

As Alan West-Durán and Sujatha Fernandes note about this song, it is riffing on the classic poem by Nicolás Guillén, "Tengo" ("I Have"), about many of the achievements of the Cuban Revolution of the 1950s: "Tengo que ya tengo donde trabajar y ganar lo que me tengo que comer. / Tengo, vamos a ver, tengo lo que tenía que tener." (I have, now, a place to work and I can earn what I have to eat. / I have, let's see, I have, what was coming to me.)[51] In adopting this trope from the Cuban Revolution, Guillén cast his lot with the promises and dreams of the new regime. Typical of the hip-hop generation, however, this song by Hermanos de Causa interrupts complacency about the revolution's noble ideals with a disillusioned note of complaint, protest, and dissent. In line after line the song accumulates these gripes until the regime appears deficient and defective, fragmented by the weight of these social problems, humbled by the conspicuous cracks that appear in the façade of Cuba's state apparatus. By using irreverent parody and ridicule in their raps, Hermanos de Causa hold the revolution accountable for not making good on its promises, for writing checks with no bullion in the bank (the attitude of U.S. rappers toward "civil rights" is similar). Though this attitude does not lead the group to disown the revolution, they also refuse to muzzle their barking at the poverty and racism that continue to hound Afro-Cubans.

In the same manner, the song targets material and consumer values: "No confundas tener más con tener cualidades" (Don't confuse having more with being better), or "Mientras más tienes más quieres y siempre más querrás. / Mientras más tú tengas más ridículo serás" (The more you have, the more and more you want. / The more you have, the more ridiculous you'll be). The group uses the Cuban style of *choteo*—a style of signifying—as a way of censuring and "dissing" anything that presumes innocence and sanctity, anything that claims for itself an infallible eminence, be it socialism, capitalism, or any other triumphal ideology.[52]

It's important to note here that Guillén's poetry was inspired by the rhythms and flows of Afro-Cuban *son;* therefore, what appears in Hermanos de Causa's rap is the *son* remixed for the hip-hop generation. (In a very interesting example of black and Latin exchanges, according to Arnold Rampersad, it was Langston Hughes who first encouraged Guillén to make use of *son* in his poetry, as Hughes had done with the blues.)[53] Many of the group's songs rework the *son* in this manner, such as in another rap, "Lagrimas Negras" ("Black Tears," the title of a classic *son* by the famous composer Miguel Matamoros). The persistence of racism in Cuba is its topic:

> Siento odio profunda por tu racismo
> Ya no me confundo con tu ironía
> Y lloro sin que sepas que el llanto mío
> Tiene lágrimas negras como mi vida.

> I feel profound hate for your racism
> I am no longer confused by your irony
> And I cry without you knowing that my cry
> Has black tears like my life.[54]

In this rap, the group has changed its focus from romantic abandonment and mourning, in Trio Matamoros's original version, to the legacy of racism. The song follows the plaintive and gentle tone of Matamoros's song (true to a classic Cuban bolero), but the lyrics are delivered with the anger and edginess of a hip-hop activist, someone who has simmered and simmered until finally reaching a boiling point. The black tears represent so much more than the agony of love; they are traces and symptoms of centuries of dishonorable behavior toward Afro-Cubans, tears that have calcified into rage and distrust.

In the Brazilian hip-hop scene, also, many of these themes—race, religion, poverty, and violence—are almost always the scaffoldings on which musicians build their houses of language and music. Derek Pardue suggests that the youth movements of the late twentieth century in Brazil—responses to the military dictatorship that ruled from 1964 to 1985—were used in these ways and infused rap music in Brazil with a revolutionary spirit.[55] In Pardue's account, hip-hop is the voice of the *periferia,* the voice of slums and abandoned neighborhoods, in which outlaws and the destitute live together in a common struggle. Brazilians use the perfectly apt term *quebradas,* broken or cracked, to designate these communities, as if everything here is inoperative, wrecked, and failed, as if there is a fissure or fault line running through their hoods, ready to swallow them. One of the best known hip-hop groups in Brazil, Racionais MCs, raps about life in these dilapidated and broken circumstances. In their early work in a compilation titled *Consciência Black,* and in the subsequent albums *Holocausto Urbano* (Urban Holocaust, 1990), and *Sobrevivendo no Inferno* (Surviving in Hell, 1997), they present harrowing portraits of life in the *periferia,* with lyrics laced with both distress and determination, lyrics that are threads of light guiding the listener through the mazes of their hoods. "Diaro de um detento" is a song about the smothering darkness of prison life, from the album *Sobrevivendo no Inferno*:

Hoje, tá difícil, não saiu o sol
Hoje não tem visita, não tem futebol. ...
Gracias a Deus e á Virgem Maria
Faltam só um ano, três meses e uns dias.
Tem uma cela lá em cima fechada
Desde terça-feira ninguém abre pra nada
Só o cheiro de morte e Pinho Sol.

It's hard today, the sun has not come out
There is no visitation, there is no soccer. ...
Thank God and the Virgin Mary,
There is only one year, three months and some days left.
There's a cell block upstairs that is closed.
Since Tuesday, nobody opens it.
There is only the smell of death and Pine Sol.[56]

In this song and others by this group, the raps move freely between the sacred and the profane, the spiritual and the social, stitching together a composite quilt of many emotions and concerns. As if they are wringing from their souls bitter poisons that would sink them in despair if they were held in, the group's appeals to God and the Virgin Mary give them strength and grace to face the darkness without succumbing to the self-destructive temptations of drugs, violence, and nihilism. The reference here to Mary is particularly noteworthy given the importance of Marian devotion in the Caribbean and Latin America (associated with Yemanjá in Brazil and Yemayá in Cuba). Like a touch of tenderness in an otherwise hard and violent life, the image of Mary is an enlivening presence in the song, the smell of roses in an environment that reeks of death and Pine Sol.

It seems to me that these songs, in a world far from the Bronx, are true to the original spirit of hip-hop that once broke loose and electrified the ghettos of the world. While the form and flow of the rap—the distinctive lyrical cadence, timbre, timing, tone, poetry, rhythm—are as essential to the music as the content and substance of what is said, I nevertheless insist that the dominant beat of Latin American hip-hop is meant to match the tough and impoverished predicaments of urban life, and that it's meant to be, to quote K'naan, "the new poor people's weapon."[57] In Latin American hip-hop's efforts to produce music that summarizes the cultures, spirituality, and social injustices of the global periphery, it has the potential of being the refrain and requiem for our postmodern age, reminding us of the desperate need in our world today for sounds and lyrics that are attuned to the ghettos of the world, for music that rides low and close to the streets, a music that has a steely, asphalt edge to it, a music with the metallic polish of a lowrider.

Afro-Latin Religion and Hip-Hop

The sampling of African religion has been an essential feature of Latin American music and culture, thanks in no small part to the Catholic societies and guilds *(cabildos)*. Almost from the beginning of their arrival on the shores of the Americas, the *cabildos* coupled African beliefs, music, and dance with Catholic rites to produce a new flavor of belief, a rich, polyglot gumbo of religion and culture. Though they existed in fifteenth-century Seville (there were *cabildos* for gypsies, African slaves, and many other groups in Spain), those of the New World surpassed in number the Old World guilds and increasingly acquired African features, with secret ceremonies, hermetic languages, and special musical signatures. "Isuama's *cabildo*," one researcher remarks, "preserved the chants, songs, and dances of the original Carabalí slaves."[58] It is remarkable that these guilds could conserve such fragile treasures in oral and fleshly forms, passing on these rites in many cases without written records. Like curators of a dazzling heritage of sound, the *cabildos* built living museums to these memories and styles and had an impact on the entire history of music in the Americas. The *cabildos* did nothing less than ransom the spirits of the ancestors so that they could continue to live, dance, and sing in a new land, an example of the surprising, indomitable capacity of uprooted cultures to thrive in oppressive and inhospitable circumstances.

In the cases of *son* and salsa, incantations to African gods and ancestors were frequent themes. We see this in *cantos* to the Orishas by Roberto Fonseca, Chucho Valdés, Celina González, Machito, Mercedes Valdez, Willie Rosario, Tommy Olivencia, Los Van Van, and numerous others. In Olivencia's version of "Chango 'ta Beni" (Shango is coming), for example, the sound and lyrics capture the threatening, apocalyptic expectations of Shango, a dream that once fired the Haitian revolution:

> Chango 'ta beni, Chango 'ta beni, Chango 'ta beni.
> Con el machete en la mano, mundo va acabar, tierra va temblar.

> Shango is coming, Shango is coming, Shango is coming.
> With a machete in his hands, the world is coming to an end,
> The world will tremble. [the rhyming words acabar/temblar don't quite work in English][59]

Like the mysterious writing on the wall of the Babylonian palace in the book of Daniel—hieroglyphic words that spelled doom for the arrogance of empire—the rhymes and incantations here are highly charged with political significance and spell the end to all empires built on the backs of slaves and the poor. The desperate pleas for Shango here, repeated like a liturgical chant, strike an apocalyptic tone and are ill omens for the masters of history. Replete with warning and eschatological expectation, the song combines threat and promise, envisaging a transformation that will redeem the lives of the degraded and disenfranchised.

For many Afro-Latinos, hip-hop continues this legacy. With the dead still haunting the young votaries of hip-hop, music becomes an idiom of rebellion and a portent of danger. The retrieval of the past is a subversive act, taking the community forward, not backward. Consider one of EPG's raps: "We are creating hip hop using our roots. / Giving you these ancestral rhythms, uncovering your mind with my fountain, showing you clearly that on my island there is a branch of hip hop that rises like a stairwell."[60] For EPG, hip-hop surely represents a break with older generations, but there is a stronger note of continuity with the past than in much of U.S. rap, a resolve to constantly renew one's homage to "ancestral rhythms." In group after group, we encounter similar attitudes, such as in the song "Muralla," by the Cuban rap group Cuarta Imagen: "Entiendan que la voz de siete rayos ya llegó / Yoruba soy Yoruba lucumí / Desde Cuba suba mi llanto Yoruba / que suba el alegre llanto / Yoruba que sale de mí." (Understand, the voice of Nsasi has arrived / I'm Yoruba, Yoruba lucumí / may my Yoruba tears rise up from Cuba / may the joyful Yoruba weeping rise out of me).[61] In addition to the heartfelt description of joy and sadness in this song ("joyful weeping"), the rapper joins his voice with the chorus of the gods from the Palo religious traditions of the Congo (the reference to the Nsasi is from the Reglas de Palo). His rap is thus a link in a far-reaching chain that reverses the direction of the Middle Passage and takes his listeners back to Africa, hoping to be a remedy for the maladies of cultural loss and forgetfulness. Rap in this conscious vein is a reproach to all "booty-ass, no grass-roots-having-ass MCs," as Bahamadia puts it, and a prime instance of her claim that the "divine beings got the true sound of hip-hop."[62]

As their name suggests, the most famous Cuban rap group, the Orishas, also join these refrains. In their song "Represent," reference is made to the rich blend of musical and religious heritages in Cuba: "Ven que te quiero cantar de corazón así / la historia de mis raíces / rumba, son, y guaguancó, todo mezclado. ... / Represento a mis ancestros." (You'll see that I want to sing from my heart the history of my roots, rumba, son, and guaguancó, all blended together. ... / I represent my ancestors.) This song ends with a litany of praise: "Hey bro Elegua, Changó, Obatalá, Yemayá, Ochún ... que mi canto suba pa' la gente de mi Cuba, mis ancestros, todos mis muerto, todo eso represento." (Hey bro Elegua, Changó, Obatalá, Yemayá, Ochún ... I pray that my song will rise and represent the people of my Cuba, my ancestors and all the dead.)[63]

It should be obvious that in this sacred hymn, African gods, largely dead to U.S. rappers, remain alive among this new generation of Latin American youth, as if they refuse the promises of the future if pursuing them means betraying the spirits of the past. If Protestant North America belongs to the future, and Latin America to the Catholic past, hip-hop in Latin America is a curious negotiation between or conciliation of the two, bearing truths and beats that are simultaneously ancient and yet new. Among the Cuban rap groups that I have noted, these truths are multicultural and multicolored, like light seen through a stained-glass window; the cult of the saints, the black Madonna, and African spirits all shine through the mosaic patterns of their music. In one of the most explicit examples, a song by the Orishas, "Canto a Elewa y Changó" (Chant to Elewa/ Elegua y Shango), highlights these religious themes:

> Hijo Elewa, mi santo Elewa, mi vida Elewa
> Mafareo, el rey de los caminos
> La ley de mi destino, rojo y negro como el tinto vino
> Quien me abre los caminos con su garabato. ...

> Yo como un rayo digo loco lo que siento
> Mi voz que ruge como el viento
> Blanco y rojo represiento
> Changó virtuoso gordete como un oso.

> Bien perezoso, jocoso, fogoso,
> Santa Bárbara bendita es tu Changó
> Guía por el bien camino a tus hijos como yo
> Dale la luz señora de virtud. ...

> Tonada para los Orishas
> Que llevo en el corazón con amor
> Pido que me den salúd e inspiración
> Y también la bendición. ...

> Recordarás mi voz, antes que reces,
> Antes que reces, reces.

> Son Elegua, my saint Elegua, my life Elegua,
> All power to you, king of the (cross)roads
> The law of my destiny, red and black like red wine
> Who opens every road for me with his cane. ...

> Like the lightning, I say madly what I feel
> My voice roars like the wind.
> I represent white and red
> Shango, masterful and powerful like a bear.
> Indolent, playful, passionate.
> Holy Saint Barbara is your Shango
> Guide your children, like me, on the right track.
> Give them light, Lady of Virtue. ...

A melody for the Orishas
That I carry in my heart with love
I ask that they give me health and inspiration
And their blessings as well. ...

You'll remember my voice before you pray,
Before you pray, pray.[64]

First, note the reference to the union of Shango and Santa Barbara; the song takes for granted their shared identity and bond. (Their feast day is celebrated together on December 4, one of the most important festivals of the year in Cuba.) As the master of lightning and fire, master of percussion-driven ritual and music, and master of dance and passion, Shango is the epitome of the flashy lover of life, the exuberant performer and artist.[65] Upon first glance, it seems peculiar that he would be associated with a Catholic female saint, but if we consider the ways in which Santa Barbara was celebrated in Spanish traditions—in fiery, rapturous, reveling festivity—the connection is not so remote. During the feast day of Santa Barbara and Shango the two figures converge in carnivals of dance and music, with certain jerky, fulgurating dance moves simulating the path of lightning from heaven to earth characteristic of both Shango and Santa Barbara. (Santa Barbara was the patroness of those who worked with explosives, those who harnessed the power of lightning.)[66] The fantastic legend of Santa Barbara—a faithful Christian woman who met a martyr's death but was eventually avenged by a bolt of lightning—seems to have been perfectly arranged to turn these figures into strange bedfellows, with Shango's command of lightning now given credit for avenging Santa Barbara's death, as if Shango would assail with his lightning and fire anyone who would do her harm. In connubial embraces, with Santa Barbara and Shango rubbing, clutching, and dancing with each other, it becomes difficult to tell the two apart, an allegory perhaps of a wider process of cultural eroticism and syncretism. Whatever the case, the product of this union is an eccentric, quixotic marriage of ideas and beliefs, the meeting of Yoruba and Catholic traditions at the crossroads of Hispaniola.

As I mentioned previously, such cross-cultural encounters inevitably affect each tradition brought into the mix: the cultures of master and slave, colonizer and colonized. With oblique allusions to Christian ideas and virtues in this song—the triad of faith, hope, and love is mentioned—it is clear that Christianity steals up on African culture here, changing its cast of mind to include biblical values and virtues. Given this transfiguration, the revolution that is being broadcast by the Orishas is primarily an upheaval of values rather than anything political, perhaps something in the spirit of W. E. B. Du Bois when he claimed that the stranglehold of poverty and injustice would be broken "not so much by violence and revolution, which is only the outward distortion of an inner fact, but by the ancient cardinal virtues: individual prudence, courage, temperance, and justice, and the more modern faith, hope, and love."[67] I suggest that this vision of revolution, cultural more than political, rings true for a great number of rappers throughout the Americas.

Perhaps more striking about this song, however, is that Shango is plainly feminized by his contact with his other half in Santa Barbara. Now Shango is colored with the virtues associated with the goddess traditions of Catholicism. In his female avatar, in other words, he is the "Lady of Virtue," a term that is unmistakably related to the female saints and of course to the Virgin Mary in her many apparitions in the Americas.

At the same time, the influence of the African side is also obvious. After her contact with Shango, Santa Barbara emerges from the ashes of her death as a liberator of African slaves, a fabulous and spectacular metamorphosis to say the least. As Roger Bastide has argued about the Brazilian case, Catholic saints underwent something like a transvaluation in the New World: they became confidants, protectors, and liberators of Africans.[68] Similar to the way in which Guadalupe was indigenized in Mexico, Santa Barbara became a patroness of many Afro-Cubans, lending her protection to the important guild Sociedad de Socorros Mutuos Nación Lucumí de Santa Barbara. Whether St. Benedict the Moor in Salvador, Bahia; or St. James the Elder in Haiti; or the Virgin of Regla (associated with Yemayá), the Virgin of El Cobre (associated with Ochún), the Virgin of Mercy (associated with Obatalá), and Saint Barbara, all in Cuba, the Catholic saints underwent an apotheosis that enthroned them on every Afro-Cuban altar that was dedicated to the struggle for humanity and justice in the Americas.

With Shango's features superimposed on Santa Barbara, furthermore, it is clear that both males and females can wield power. Hence another line in the song appeals to the sword of Santa Barbara, cutting through the obstacles and obscurities of life to light the path of virtue. In this construction, she is strong and brave, a shield and safeguard for weary workers and downtrodden communities; she is anything but a submissive, timid figure. Even with her beatific, feminine countenance, she appears in this tradition as a thunderous threat to the status quo, a lightning bolt against injustice; she appears as a figure of human rights, deft with the sword, perhaps something like the biblical Judith (who famously wields the sword against Holofernes): "For thy power stands not in multitude nor thy might in strong men," Judith prays, "for thou art a God of the afflicted, a helper of the oppressed, an upholder of the weak, a protector of the forlorn, a savior of them that are without hope" (Jth. 9:11).

In this betrothal of Santa Barbara and Shango, then, a religious imagination dedicated to the oppressed and forlorn is fashioned out of the crosscurrents of African religion and Catholicism. Even when Cuban rappers are summoning the Orishas in their raps, calling on them with a ritual-like cadence, the acoustics of their world are clearly Catholic, and this creates a fusion of sound and image that could be the sound track of the New World. This encounter is like a vibrant painting in watercolor, suddenly sodden with rain so that there are smudged borders, blended pigments, amalgamated colors, jumbled images, dripping dyes, and puddled paints. In this postdiluvian view of culture, the original image is irretrievable, but what remains is nonetheless resplendent.

Considering these Afro-Cuban religious influences on the rap scene in Cuba, I suggest in summary that Cuban *raperos* know when to play the trickster, á la Elegua; when to channel Shango's fiery dances and percussion-driven hymns; when to add Spanish and Arabic flourishes; and finally, when to engage and battle with North American sounds. In playing with such combinations, the best of these artists create a feast of meaning that combines the sacred and the profane, the spiritual and the political. Alan West-Durán nicely sums up these various themes in his reading of the Hermanos de Causa song "Tengo." His exegesis concerns the following lines: "Tengo de elemento, tengo de conciente, tengo fundamento." (I've got some funky elements, but I don't scare, I'm politically aware, I've got the initiation, got the foundation.) West-Durán writes: "Both *conciente* and *fundamento* have philosophical, educational, and political meanings, with *conciente* referring to political or social consciousness and *fundamento,* speaking not only to foundations of knowledge, but also of being a *santero.* Hence, in three short lines, Hermanos de Causa reveal their situated knowledge: they 'drop science' from street experience, from their educational training, their politico-philosophical background and their religious dialogue with the Orishas."[69] In claiming *conciente* and *fundamento,* Hermanos de Causa embrace a higher order of knowledge in which there is no contradiction among street smarts, social consciousness, and spiritual wisdom—each plays its part in this science of the soul.[70]

Exile and Indigenous Motifs

When compensating for the relative invisibility of indigenous struggles in U.S. rap, Latin American rappers tend to give considerable, even primary, weight to American Indian voices. Especially in parts of Latin America where the indigenous presence is most conspicuous, hip-hop has frequently modified its accent and cadence to resonate with Native histories and beliefs. In bringing these communities into bold relief, Latin hip-hop exhibits a constant preoccupation, almost an obsession, with the subjects of mass displacement, exile, and migration ("Latin hip-hop" here is inclusive of Latin Americans and U.S. Latinos). Music is transformed into a site of aesthetical experimentation in the face of social traumas and disturbances: violence and conflict, poverty and inequality, oppression and incarceration, migration and diaspora, and so forth.[71] Among U.S. Latinos in particular, hip-hop has been the medium for many immigrants and their children to verbalize feelings of disaffection and alienation in the promised land of North America. In making so much of these themes, Latin rappers often wrap themselves around their countries of origin like a flag worn to a soccer game and transform their music into a network of identification and alliance with slum dwellers south of the border. With their music spinning on an axis of cultural nationalism—interrupted by the scratches, breaks, and ruptures of life in the United States—rap in the Latin style often seems frenzied in its compulsion to find a sense of belonging to center their disoriented souls. A connection with American Indian histories has often been a remedy in this regard, a balm to ease the disorientation.

Given the prominence of indigenous themes in Mexican history and culture, it should not be surprising that many rappers in this tradition travel across the U.S.–Mexican border in search of native roots. The names of some of these groups demonstrate the connection: the Funky Aztecs, Kinto Sol (an Aztec reference to the fifth sun), Ñengo el Quetzal, Aztlan Underground, the Mexakinz, and Ozomatli (Aztec god of dance, fire, and music). And whether or not they have such names, many Latin groups appeal to the indigenous heritage of Latin America as a symbol of solidarity with colonized communities. This is certainly true for Immortal Technique, the Peruvian-American rapper and self-identifying "Zapatista," and for Jaas, the Mapuche *mestiza* from Chile, and for Mare, the wonderful Zapotecan rapper from Oaxaca, and for Cypress Hill in their "Los Grandes Éxitos en Enspañol." Almost without exception, these musicians employ hip-hop as a medium for narrating indigenous memories and struggles and for "transnationalizing" the hip-hop community.[72]

For Kinto Sol, for example, these themes are pervasive. One song, "Hecho in Mexico," radiates indigenous pride: "Soy Azteca, Chichimeca, Zapoteca, (y adentro) soy Indio, Yaqui, Tarasco, y Maya."[73] The Spanish legacy of Kinto Sol's Mexican identity is hardly acknowledged in this song, as the group gives the listener a roll call of tribal filiations. In prioritizing Indian blood in this way, the group strikes a rebellious pose and derides middle-class and elite Mexicans who claim Spanish ancestors while ignoring or downplaying their native roots. Kinto Sol mocks this legacy, calling these types *malinchistas* after La Malinche, the famous interpreter and mistress of Hernán Cortés. There is of course plenty of hyperbole in this attitude (the group consists of *mestizos,* after all, the children of La Malinche *and* Cortés), but the rhetorical excess in the song is a response to centuries of tortured memories and violent histories that have consistently belittled Indian blood. If the group's position is inflated and overstated in this identification with Native America, it is clearly for a prophetic purpose, scathing in the manner of Bartolomé de Las Casas (himself notoriously profligate with words).

In this same signifying, mocking tone, a song by the Funky Aztecs, "Prop 187," ridicules those Mexican-Americans who suddenly become super-patriotic when it comes to the influx of new undocumented immigrants, largely comprised of the poorest and most indigenous of Latin Americans. In solidarity with the stranger and the vulnerable, the group berates the prevailing racism in North American society, so widespread that it creeps into the hearts of every person regardless of color. With Mexicans cast in the role of illegal alien, dope-dealer, rapist, or gang member (descriptions widely used in the election of Donald Trump), the song "Prop 187" castigates everyone active or complicit in the racism:

> A message to the coconut: no matter how much you switch,
> here is what they think about you:

cactus frying, long distance running,
soccer playing, shank having, tortilla flipping,
refried beans eating, border crossing, fruit picking,
piñata breaking, lowrider driving, dope dealing,
Tres Flores wearing, green card having, illiterate gang-member,
go the fuck back to Mexico.[74]

Proposition 187 in California would have denied citizenship to U.S.-born children of undocumented immigrants, as well as access to health services, public schools, and other public services. In this song the Funky Aztecs unroll a long scroll of grievances about this proposition and similar initiatives, leading up to a witty collection of racist epithets that have been hurled at Mexicans and other Latinos.

In another cut by Kinto Sol, "Los hijos del Maíz" (Children of maize), these themes continue, but now with a relentless mantra that adds up the agonies and atrocities endured by Native peoples, until the hymn slowly seeps into the listener's blood. Since the narrative relates many of the hardships of the poor and tries to extract meaning out of the misfortunes endured by the common Mexican laborer, it's not surprising that the group resorts to myth as a means of grappling with the perplexities of life. When the mind and spirit have reached an impasse, when reason is at a loss to explain or justify tribulation, myth is often the most creative means for producing order out of chaos, and in this case for bestowing dignity on the "children of corn."[75] In combining poetry, prophecy, and myth, Kinto Sol's rap does verbally "what Diego Rivera was able to do with a paint brush and blank wall" (cited in the epigraph to this [reading]).

In this particular song, the lyrics swing between a prophetic demand for action and social change on the one hand and a more tragic sense of disappointment and despondency on the other. (The melancholic guitar chords and the refrain of women's voices, in particular, give the song a dirge-like feel.) Just as the group's name has apocalyptic echoes (like the four preceding ages, the age of the fifth sun appears to be coming to a catastrophic end), this particular song is mournful and nostalgic, dejected and eschatological. The rap bleeds with aggrieved memories, from the painful struggle for survival of the rapper's Tarascan grandfather in Mexico to the plight of all *hijos del maize* in diaspora:

Esclavo del hambre, miseria, violencia,
Trabajos no hay, dinero esta escaso
Politicos con feria no nos hacen caso
Esto es un fracaso cada día que paso
Un nuevo partido es otro madrazo
Le llaman democracia, me causa gracia
Pero mas dolor y me deja un mal sabor
Yo a la muerte le he perdido el temor

No se si morir sea el remedio major
Nuevas caras nuevas leyes, falsas ilusiones
He pasado tanto tiempo que he llegado a conclusions
Atencion los hijos del maize.

500 años escondida la verdad
5 generaciones en la oscuridad
Llego la luz termino la tempestad
El gigante dormido vuelve a despertar
El alma del Che me aconseja
Villa me dice mochales la oreja
Por fin esta lucha se encuentra pareja
Con gusto termino con toda la nobleza. ...
Llego la estapa spiritual.

Slave of hunger, poverty and violence,
There are no jobs, money is scarce
Politicians with money don't pay us any attention
Every day that passes is a disaster
A new political party is another blow
They call it democracy, makes me laugh
More pain, and it leaves me with a bad taste in my mouth
I've lost all fear of death,
Perhaps dying is a better solution
New faces, new laws, false illusions
It's been a long time since I've had any answers
Listen to me, children of maize.

For 500 years, the truth has been hidden
5 ages in darkness
The light has arrived, the storm has ended
The sleeping giant will awaken again
The soul of Che guides me
Villa advises me to slash ears
Finally this struggle is fair
I will finish it with nobility. ...
The spiritual era has arrived.[76]

The song covers a broad spectrum of emotions, seeming despairing at one end and then suddenly inspired at the other. At one moment the rapper seems resigned and melancholic, ready to commit his spirit to the earth, but then the light of Che Guevara and Pancho Villa comes to him and rallies his flagging spirit. In this valley of dry bones on earth, he suddenly visualizes a renewal and promise of justice, with the wounds of the conquest healed and equality bestowed on the children of the sun, with the same superabundance of the sun over the Sonoran desert.

As buoyant as hope appears in the song, it hardly obviates the tragic motifs. Unlike the prophetic vision, in which hope remains in the capacity for social reform, here the tragic attests to the losses and troubles that haunt every human effort. [T]his tragic sensibility is present in much of hip-hop, marking the movement's distance from the prophetic orientation of the civil rights generation. In this specific case, Kinto Sol assumes this tragic mood, in which poverty seems ineradicable, ignorance and darkness are pervasive, and death is a "better solution." Like a nightmare in which one is running and going nowhere, history seems to be running to stand still, beset on all sides by forces that impede advancement. With its invocation of Villa and Che, Kinto Sol wants to believe that the revolution can drive the "locomotive of history" forward (Marx's famous metaphor) and wants to believe in a spiritual age that will flood the world with a light of parity and truth. The conflict in the song, however, is between what the rapper's mind perceives about history—that it is a stalled locomotive going nowhere—and a mythological dream of a more just and humane future. The rap moves across these various borders of thought, starting with the tragic, where misery seems crushing and falls on Native peoples like a leaden, winter sky, and then suddenly, when things seem bleakest, the heavens open up and let in rainbows of light that illuminate the earth with brilliant, colorful rays.

Notice that the dream of revolution is described here in spiritual terms, not as political acts of violence. The war waged against racism and colonialism is understood to be a war of words, a strategy of music, poetry, dance, art, and prayer. More like a modern shaman than a modern politician, Kinto Sol uses mythical images, tight loops, bass lines, and spell-like words to restore its patients to their lost dignity, allowing the ceremony to wash over them like a cleansing rain and rumbling thunderstorm. If we recall that the shaman, at least for many romantics, was a poet, myth-reciter, and performance artist, Kinto Sol nicely fits the description.[77] With the rapper playing the role of shaman and soul artist, Kinto Sol and others in this tradition call upon myth, poetry, religion, and music in the struggle to preserve the defeated memories of the past. The group Anonimo Consejo also strikes this note: "Here I go: silencing mouths of jealous people who want us to change. I know what I have to do. We feel the support of our dear people. In the footsteps of the Taino. ... America, discovered by our indigenous people, who suffered three hard blows of the New World. When Columbus arrived, slaughter, slavery and oppression also arrived. Kokino is here though you forgot me, honoring study like Don Fernando Ortiz."[78] In addition to this intriguing reference to the pioneering scholar of Afro-Cuban culture and music Fernando Ortiz, the group leaves no doubt that it is following the trails of tears and long walks taken by many black and indigenous communities throughout the Americas, and that rap music is bread and wine for the journey, a new shamanistic medium for an ancient struggle.

For Anonimo Consejo and many others, hip-hop is a return to the sweaty and sublime roots of soul. In preserving the sacred and profane inflections of soul, rap in this tradition does its part to counter the modern dilution and thinning of soul. By considering the needs and trials of the soul from the perspective of ghetto dwellers, migrants, and colored folks—the way the soul is constantly migrating, shifting, adapting, amalgamating, scattering, hiding, fleeing, and doing whatever it takes to carry on—hip-hop gives expression to the ills of time (to recall Nas again) and to the many travails that the soul must endure in the wastelands of the modern world.

But hip-hop also resists these ills. In the forms we have examined, the music mixes bitterness with sweetness, adding the taste of anguish when needed and the taste of solace and joy when the former is overpowering. Religion, myth, and folklore play a key role in endowing the music with this balance and harmony of contrasts. By embracing religious and mythical ligatures that bind them to an ancient past, Latin rappers work with an understanding of myth that is older and richer than what appeared in the Age of Reason, that is even older than Plato and is closer to Homer and Hesiod. In their retrieval of myths from Yoruba, Aztec, Taino, and other indigenous traditions, rappers employ an understanding of *mythos* that is a vehicle of *alethea* (truth), a truth that is a gift of the divine. "In the *Odyssey*," writes Talal Asad, "Odysseus praises poetry—asserting that it is truthful, that it affects the emotions of its audience, that it is able to reconcile differences—and he concludes his poetic narration by declaring that he has recounted a *mythos*."[79] For many of the rappers whom I have discussed, the same is true: myth provides them with a poetic language that reconciles the contradictions of their lives and touches some deep part of truth that eludes the purview of scientific knowledge, some deep part of themselves, some deep part of this astonishing universe. Far from being a lie, myth lights the path of human quests for truth, sometimes in small doses like "matches struck unexpectedly in the dark," and at other times in glaring, raging illuminations.[80] For many of these rappers, myth and religion are employed to deconstruct the dogmas that modern men and women ascribe to the free market, progress, reason, science, and European civilization; they use *mythos* as an alternative narrative to the standard portrait of European hegemony, and they use *mythos* as a way of shoring up the soul against the ruinous and oppressive conditions of modern history.

One might say, borrowing from Aristotle on tragic poetry, that rap music effects a catharsis of artist and listener in this regard, a metamorphosis of pain into pleasure, whereby the drops or even torrents of suffering are channeled into tributaries that can nourish the soul and prevent it from corroding and rusting. As dire and distraught as some of these rap songs seem, the sheer act of composition, the pure creative achievement in making this music, is surely an act of resistance against the demons of destruction, a spell against the most fatal curses. However hip-hop expresses this resistance—in bombast or boast, mourning or festivity—what consistently beats through it all is the ever-resilient pulse of life, the throbbing, flowing movement of blood through the veins. In riding the wave of these sounds and surfs, hip-hop robs death of its tyranny, as joy and love prove stronger than the abyss, more powerful than the grave. When this happens, the music offers the listener a high that is far more profound and lasting than anything a blunt can provide: dope beats, tight lyrics, and spiritual feelings so intoxicating that they allow us to lose ourselves and gain something bigger and better. Something like this happens in Ozomatli's exuberant, boisterous song, "Cumbia de los muertos" (The dance of the dead). Though the lyrics do very little to convey the richness of the song—which requires full band sound of percussion and horns, guitars and accordions, Latin cajónes and tablas, and hip-hop mixers and flows—a small piece of the song is caught in the words that follow:

> Aqui no existe la tristeza, sole existe la alegrias
> El baile de los queridos, de los queridos del pasado
> Mira como baile mi mama, bailando con mi hermano del pasado
> Sus espiritus se juntan bailando, lleno de alegria y gozando.

> Here, sadness doesn't exist, only joy
> The dance of loved ones, the loved ones of the past
> Look how my mother dances, dancing with my dead brother
> Their spirits joined in dance, filled with joy and delight.[81]

For this East L.A. rap group, hip-hop celebrates an impossible, spiritual vision, in which music finds the still point of the turning world and binds us—in the ancient sense of *religare*—to the community of the dead: "At the still point of the turning world. Neither flesh nor fleshless, neither from nor towards; at the still point, there the dance is."[82]

NOTES

1   James Baldwin, "Many Thousands Gone," in *Notes of a Native Son* (Boston: Beacon Press, 1983), 24.

2   William Jelani Cobb, *To the Break of Dawn: A Freestyle on the Hip Hop Aesthetic* (New York: NYU Press, 2008), 35.

3   Timothy Brennan, *Secular Devotion: Afro-Latin Music and Imperial Jazz* (London: Verso Books, 2008), 9.

4   Gustavo Perez Firmat, *Life on the Hyphen: the Cuban-American Way* (Austin: University of Texas, 1994), 102.

5   Alejo Carpentier, *Music in Cuba,* trans. Alan West-Durán (Minneapolis: University of Minnesota Press, 2001), 95.

6   Ibid., 84.

7   Jacques Attali, *Noise: The Political Economy of Music,* trans. Brian Massumi (Minneapolis: University of Minnesota Press, 1985), 4–5.

8   David Tracy, "Writing," in *Critical Terms for Religious Studies,* ed. Mark C. Taylor (Chicago: University of Chicago Press, 1998), 391–92.

9   See Angel Rama, *The Lettered City,* trans. John Charles Chasteen (Durham, NC: Duke University Press, 1996), 24–25.

10 See Hisham Aidi, *Rebel Music: Race, Empire and the New Muslim Youth Culture* (New York: Pantheon Books, 2014), for a discussion of music in various anticolonial struggles across the globe.

11 Ted Gioia, *The History of Jazz* (Oxford: Oxford University Press, 1997), 6.

12 Alejo Carpentier, *Concierto Barroco* (Mexico City: Editorial Lectorum, 2003).

13 Richard Rodriguez, *Brown: The Last Discovery of America* (New York: Viking Books, 2002), 132.

14 The only exception to this would be among Afro-Latin Catholics of New Orleans and New York, who clearly brought Haitian vodou and Cuban *santería/lukumí* to North America, as Zora Neale Hurston shows in her classic study, *Mules and Men.* In part 2 of *Mules and Men,* Hurston travels to New Orleans for her study of voodoo in African American folk culture. As she notes, the vast majority of figures associated with voodoo continued to consider themselves Catholic. See *Mules and Men* (New York: Harper Perennial, 2008).

15 Many factors contributed to the loss of African culture in North America: the smaller number of African slaves in relation to white Americans in the United States allowed for tighter control and supervision over African customs than in Latin America; the emphasis on reproduction in North America versus importation in Latin America led to a larger number of second- and third-generation of slaves in the United States; and the greater number and concentration of free black communities in Latin America, organized in various guilds and *cabildos,* proved beneficial for the survival of African gods and customs. See George Reid Andrews, *Afro-Latin America: 1800–2000* (Oxford: Oxford University Press, 2004), 3, 13, 40.

16 Albert Raboteau, "Death of the Gods," in *African American Religious Thought: An Anthology,* ed. Cornel West and Eddie Glaude (Louisville, KY: Westminster John Knox Press, 2003), 274.

17 Carpentier, *Music in Cuba,* 81.

18 Ibid., 261–65.

19 "Once confined to the slave barracks and dilapidated rooming houses of the slums," writes Carpentier, "*son* eventually revealed its marvelous expressive resources, achieving universal status." See ibid., 228.

20 See Danilo Orozco, "El son: ¿ritmo, baile o reflejo de la personalidad cultura cubana?" *Santiago* 33 (March 1979): 87–113. See also Maya Roy, *Cuban Music,* trans. Denise Asfar and Gabriel Asfar (London: Markus Wiener, 2002), 120ff.

21 Carpentier, *Music in Cuba,* 155.

22 Similar to a guitar, the tres has three doubled strings; the güiro is made from a gourd or calabash and scratched with a stick; the marímbula is a bass instrument, consisting of metal strips arranged on a sounding board and mounted on a box; the bongo is a drum of Bantu inspiration, held between the knees; the maracas is a pair of gourds, filled with seeds and shaken for

rhythm; and the claves are small percussion instruments, made of small, cylindrical pieces of wood struck together.

23 Brennan, *Sacred Devotion,* 60.

24 Carpentier, *Music in Cuba,* 229.

25 Jory Farr, *Rites of Rhythm: The Music of Cuba* (New York: Regan Books, 2003), 31–32.

26 Brennan, *Sacred Devotion,* 101.

27 Firmat, *Life on the Hyphen,* 150–51.

28 Quoted in Farr, *Rites of Rhythm,* 39–40.

29 Ibid., 3.

30 T. S. Eliot, "The Dry Salvages," in *The Four Quartets* (New York: Mariner Books, 1968).

31 Juan Flores, *From Bomba to Hip Hop: Puerto Rican Culture and Latino Identity* (New York: Columbia University Press, 2000), 87.

32 As Juan Flores suggests, songs like "Danzón Boogaloo," "Guaguancó in Jazz," "Azucaré y Bongo," "Richie's Jala Jala," "Colombia's Boogaloo," and "Stop, Look and Listen" were examples of the rich sense of kinship of Afro-Cuban sounds with African American music. See Flores, *From Bomba to Hip Hop,* 84.

33 See Nelson George, "Hip Hop's Founding Fathers Speak the Truth," in *That's the Joint: Hip Hop Studies Reader,* ed. Murray Forman and Mark Anthony Neal (London: Routledge, 2012), 49.

34 "Many of the bass patterns heard in today's hip hop and classic funk were nicked from Afro-Cuban bands," writes Jory Farr in *Rites of Rhythm,* 7. And William Eric Perkins says the same thing in an early critical volume on hip-hop, *Droppin' Science: Critical Essays on Rap Music and Hip Hop Culture*: "I contend that the introduction of percussion beats in the dance music of the 1970s and in early hip hop were products of Latin music's powerful influence on New York and New Jersey popular culture." See Perkins, *Droppin' Science,* 6.

35 David Toop, *Rap Attack #3* (London: Serpent's Tail, 2000), 24.

36 Brennan, *Sacred Devotion,* 9.

37 In his study of Cuban festivals, Roberto González Echevarría explores the idioms and customs of carnival in Cuba: the mocking and satire of decorum, the insults and parodies of the ruling classes, the language games of *choteo,* and so forth. See Echevarría, *Cuban Fiestas* (New Haven, CT: Yale University Press, 2012).

38 Imani Perry, *Prophets of the Hood: Politics and Poetics in Hip Hop* (Durham, NC: Duke University Press, 2004) 13.

39 Firmat, *Life on the Hyphen,* 17.

40 In speaking of Brazil, Hisham Aidi argues that the hegemony of samba has been dethroned by hip-hop as the voice of the favelas. See Aidi, *Rebel Music,* 32–33.

41 For a discussion of Latin influences on hip-hop origins, see Flores, *From Bomba to Hip Hop*; Raquel Rivera, *New York Ricans from the Hip Hop Zone* (New York: Palgrave Macmillan, 2003); Pancho McFarland, *The Chican@ Hip Hop Nation: Politics of a New Millenial Mestizaje* (Lansing: Michigan State University, 2013).

42 Common, "I Used to Love H.E.R.," on *Resurrection,* Relativity Records, 1994.

43 Quoted in S. Craig Watkins, *Hip Hop Matters: Politics, Pop Culture and the Struggle for the Soul of a Movement* (Boston: Beacon Books, 2005) 127.

44 S. Craig Watkins, *Hip Hop Matters: Politics, Pop Culture, and the Struggle for the Soul of a Movement* (Boston: Beacon Books, 2005), 137–38, 242. See Immortal Technique, feat. Brother Ali and Chuck D, "Civil War," on *The Martyr,* Viper Records, 2011.

45 See Aidi, *Rebel Music,* 255.

46 Paul Gilroy, "It's a Family Affair," in *Black Popular Culture,* ed. Gina Dent (Seattle: Bay Press, 1992), 307.

47 Manning Marable, "Race, Identity and Political Culture," in *Black Popular Culture,* ed. Gina Dent (Seattle: Bay Press, 1992), 302.

48 Quoted in the hip-hop documentary *Inventos: Hip Hop Cubano,* Eli Jacobs-Fantauzzi (Clenched Fist Productions, 2005). Quotes from this video are my translations.

49 Ibid.

50 Hermanos De Cause, "Tengo," Papaya Records, 2001.

51 Nicolás Guillén, *Yoruba from Cuba,* trans. Salvador Ortiz-Carboneres (Leeds: Peepal Tree, 2005), 122. See Alan West-Durán, "Rap's Diasporic Dialogue: Cuba's Redefinition of Blackness," *Journal of Popular Music Studies* 16 (2004): 20. See also Sujatha Fernandes, *Close to the Edge: In Search of the Global Hip Hop Generation* (London: Verso Books, 2011), 45.

52 See West-Durán, "Rap's Diasporic Dialogue," 20, for a good discussion of *choteo.*

53 This relationship between Langston Hughes and Guillén is discussed in Arnold Rampersad's biography, *The Life of Langston Hughes, Vol. 1, 1902–1941* (Oxford: Oxford University Press, 2002). See also Claudia Milan, *Latining America: Black-Brown Passages and the Coloring of Latino/a Studies* (Athens: University of Georgia Press, 2013), 90–91.

54 Hermanos de Causa, "Lagrimas Negras," Mixer Music, 2008.

55 See Derek Pardue, *Brazilian Hip Hoppers Speak from the Margins* (New York: Palgrave Macmillan, 2011), 39–43.

56 Racionais MCs, "Diaro de um detento," on *Sobrevivendo no Inferno,* Cosa Nostra Phonographic, 1997.

57 Quoted in Alastair Pennycock and Tony Mitchell, *Global Linguistic Flows,* ed. H. Samy Alim, Awad Ibrahim, and Alastair Pennycock (London: Routledge, 2008), 33.

58 See Farr, *Rites of Rhythm,* 215.

59 Quoted in Brennan, *Secular Devotion,* 114.

60 *Inventos.*

61 Cuarta Imagen, "La Muralla," High Times, 2005.

62 Bahamadia, "Spontaneity," and "Uknowhowwedu," on *Kollage,* Chrysalis/EMI Records, 1996.

63 Orishas, "Represent," on *A lo Cubano,* Universal Latino, 2000.

64 Orishas, "Canto Para Elewa y Chango," on *A Lo Cubano,* Universal Latino, 2000.

65 See David Brown, *Santería Enthroned: Art, Ritual, and Innovation in Afro-Cuban Religion* (Chicago: University of Chicago Press, 2003), 271, for an excellent discussion of Shango and other aspects of Afro-Cuban religion.

66 See ibid., 67.

67 W. E. B. Du Bois, *Black Folk, Then and Now* (Oxford: Oxford University Press, 2014), last page. See also Kwame Anthony Appiah, *Lines of Descent: W.E.B. Du Bois and the Emergence of Identity* (Cambridge, MA: Harvard University Press, 2014), 135.

68 See Roger Bastide, *The African Religions of Brazil: Toward a Sociology of the Interpenetration of Civilizations,* trans. Helen Sebba (Baltimore, MD: Johns Hopkins University Press, 1978), 114–16.

69 West-Durán, "Rap's Diasporic Dialogue," 24.

70 Another example of this is the previously mentioned group Obsesión. In their music, Yoruba chants are carefully layered with hip-hop beats and Afro-Cuban percussion, with an effect that seems contemporary and nostalgic, modern and traditional (such as in the song, "La llaman puta," in which Magia Lopez raps about the debasing and violent treatment of prostitutes in Cuba using a jazz vibe and Yoruba chant). In this group's case, it is clear that the barrio where the rap duo is from, Regla, has left its imprint on their music. Home of one of the very first secret Abakuá societies (a black male society with origins in Nigeria), Regla today remains a center for Afro-Cuban traditions and a very popular destination for Santería pilgrims, who go to visit La Santisima Virgen de Regla, the "black Madonna," in the town's colonial church.

71 George Lipsitz, *Dangerous Crossroads: Popular Music, Post-Modernism and the Poetics of Place* (London: Verso Books, 1994), 17.

72 Pancho McFarland, "Here Is Something You Can't Understand: Chicano Rap and the Critique of Globalization," in *Decolonial Voices,* ed. Arturo Aldama and Naomi Quiñonez (Bloomington: Indiana University Press, 2002), 308.

73 Kinto Sol, "Hecho en Mexico," on *Hecho en Mexico,* Disa, 2003.

74 Funky Aztecs, "Prop 187," on *Day of the Dead,* Raging Bull Records, 1995.

75 In speaking of the appeal of myth to literary modernists, specifically the Arab poet Adonis, Talal Asad expresses this exact point: "For Adonis, myth arises whenever human reason encounters perplexing questions about existence and attempts to answer them in what can only be a non-rational way, thus producing a combination of poetry, history and wonderment." See Asad, *Formations of the Secular: Christianity, Islam and Modernity* (Stanford, CA: Stanford University Press, 2003), 55. Sacvan Bercovitch also has a nice description of myth in *The American Jeremiad* (Madison: University of Wisconsin Press, 2012), xli.

76 Kinto Sol, "Los Hijos del Maize," on *Los Hijos del Maize,* Univision Records, 2006.

77 See Gloria Flaherty, *Shamanism and the Eighteenth Century* (Princeton, NJ: Princeton University Press, 1992), 74–75. In particular, writes Georgi, "the litany was one favored form because its rhythms and tones affected the body directly, without appeal to the higher faculty of reason." See also Asad, *Formations of the Secular,* 50.

78 Quoted in *Inventos.*

79 Asad, *Formations of the Secular,* 27.

80 This quote is from Virginia Woolf, *To the Lighthouse* (New York: Harcourt, Brace, Jovanovich, 1989).

81 Ozomatli, "Cumbia de los Muertos," on *Ozomatli,* Almo Sounds, 1998.

82 T. S. Eliot, "Burnt Norton," in *The Four Quartets* (New York: Mariner Books, 1968).

From A-Town to ATL
The Politics of Translation in Global Hip Hop Culture

By Holger Droessler

At the 2009 Black Entertainment Television (BET) Hip Hop Awards in Atlanta, Gsann, an emcee from Arusha, Tanzania, joined a cipha with such African American veterans as DJ Premier and KRS-1. Gsann's one-minute rap in Swahili made his African American colleagues nod their heads in agreement with his flow, although the content of his lyrics remained a mystery both to them and most of the viewers in front of the TV screens. Aware of the importance of language in Hip Hop, the BET producers sought to close the language gap and provided an English translation of Gsann's rhymes in subtitles.[1]

Taking Gsann's appearance at the BET Awards as a case study, this article explores the fundamental tension between Hip Hop's local roots and global routes. Gsann's Swahili rap, I argue, represents a miniature example of the unifying and dividing forces at work in contemporary global Hip Hop culture. On the one hand, Gsann uses Swahili to reflect on local issues to Tanzania such as religion, but also on his global travels that have led him to Atlanta. On the other hand, the BET producers translated his Swahili rhymes into English to make them intelligible to viewers in the United States and around the world. If Gsann's rap was an act of cultural and linguistic self-assertion, it also became quickly incorporated into the commercial spectacle of American Hip Hop on primetime television. The artistic journey of a Tanzanian emcee—from A-Town (Arusha) to ATL (Atlanta)—deserves a more thorough contextualization than the BET subtitles were able to provide.

WELCOME TO THE GLOBAL CIPHA

From 'J-Hop' in Tokyo to 'Nederhop' in Amsterdam and Aboriginal rap in Melbourne, Hip Hop has truly gone global—while staying firmly rooted in the local. Global Hip Hop

---

1   The video is available on youtube: <youtube.com/watch?v=TetSMSdxIqA> 1:34-2:18. Accessed Apr. 24, 2015.

today thrives in a creative tension between what historian Robin D. G. Kelley has called Hip Hop's fundamental "ghettocentricity"[2] and the hybrid process of adapting globalized cultural practices to local needs, often referred to as "glocalization."[3] Mohammed Yunus Rafiq, one of the founding members of the X Plastaz, described his view of the glocal hybridity of Hip Hop in a roundtable discussion with other artists: "We can be tribal, and at the same time, we can also be global."[4]

As Gsann's fellow crew member notes, the local and the global need not to be mutually exclusive in Hip Hop—particularly in its everyday practice. By contrast, the local and the global can enter into a dialogue in what global Hip Hop scholars James G. Spady, H. Samy Alim, and Samir Meghelli have called the "global cipha."[5] This global cipha can be seen as the extension of community ciphas on the micro level of Hip Hop culture: "In the same way that local Hip Hop artists build community and construct social organization through the rhyming practices involved in tha cipha, Hip Hop communities worldwide interact with each other (through media and cultural flow, as well as embodied international travel) in ways that organize their participation in a mass-mediated, cultural movement."[6]

As "an organic, highly charged, fluid circular arrangement of rhymers wherein participants exchange verses," the cipha represents Hip Hop culture on its molecular level.[7] The BET cipha—pre-recorded before the actual show in an empty factory building in Brooklyn—represents a conscious attempt to re-enact the atmosphere of an old-school cipha in the now antiquated visual aesthetics of black and white. The preproduced snippet was then played on screens for the live audience at the awards ceremony in Atlanta. In other words, Gsann's performance in the cipha was both spatially and temporally detached from the actual awards show, even though the viewers in front of the TV screens were made to believe that Hip Hop's past and present easily merged into one another.

---

2   Robin D. G. Kelley, *Race Rebels: Culture, Politics, and the Black Working Class* (New York, NY: Free Press, 1994), 212.

3   Roland Robertson, "Glocalization: Time-Space and Homogeneity-Heterogeneity," in: *Global Modernities*, edited by Mike Featherstone, Scott Lash, and Roland Robertson (London, UK: Sage Publications, 1995), 26.

4   Cristina Verán, "'Native Tongues: Hip-Hop's Global Indigenous Movement," in: *Total Chaos: The Art and Aesthetics of Hip-Hop*, edited by Jeff Chang (New York, NY: Basic Civitas Books, 2006), 281.

5   The English word "cipher" or "cypher" derives from the Arabic ṣifr, which means "zero" or "nothing." Hip Hop practitioners appropriated the term "cipha" with its circular representation in the Arabic number "0" to describe the community circles among freestylers, b-girls, and weed smokers.

6   James G. Spady, H. Samy Alim, and Samir Meghelli, *Tha Global Cipha: Hip Hop Culture and Consciousness* (Philadelphia, PA: Black History Museum Press, 2006), 11.

7   H. Samy Alim, Awad Ibrahim, and Alastair Pennycook, eds., *Global Linguistic Flows: Hip Hop Cultures, Youth Identities, and the Politics of Language* (New York, NY: Routledge, 2009), 1.

The BET cipha, in sum, offers a highly mediated and meticulously orchestrated performance stage that Gsann and the other emcees are using to showcase much more than simply their rhyming skills. In an interview after the show, Gsann acknowledged that his rhymes were not improvised: "It was a written verse taken from a new track 'Safari Na Muzik.' I just crafted it to the beat of 'The Funky Drummer' by James Brown, backspun by DJ Premier."[8] Beyond their mere verbal agility, the artists' membership in global Hip Hop culture is on display in the cipha.

GOD AS THE CAPTAIN OF GSANN'S SHIP

Gsann's rap can be read as an act of self-positioning of a Tanzanian emcee in Hip Hop's cultural center. His rap shows both his self-awareness as an African emcee among African Americans and draws attention to the global map of contemporary Hip Hop culture. In his rhymes, Gsann brings a uniquely global perspective to the BET cipha, which sets him apart from the local ghettocentricity of the African American emcees. Here are Gsann's Swahili rhymes (in italics) and their English translation as it appeared on the television subtitles (with literal translations in parentheses, when applicable):

Ni safari na musiki
It's a journey with music

Tunakwenda hatufik
We are traveling, but we are not getting there

Japokuwa tuna dhik bado tumekaza 'buti'
Despite all the difficulties we persevere
(Despite difficulties, still we tighten our boots)

Toka TZ nyumbani mpaka 'cipha' BET
From our home in Tanzania to the BET cipha

Mungu ibariki, tupo siku pita dhiki
God bless, one day we will succeed
(God bless, we are at the day of overcoming difficulties)

Nikipata riziki, hata kidogo sikatai
If I just can sustain myself, I am alright
(If I get blessings, even a little bit, I won't refuse it)

---

8 Thomas Gesthuizen, "Tanzanian Emcee in BET Hip Hop Awards Cipha," *AfricanHipHop.com*. Oct. 26, 2009. <http://www.africanhiphop.com/tanzanian-emcee-in-bet-hip-hop-awards-cypher>. Accessed July 31, 2014.

Popote naingia, hata kama sina 'tai'
I'm entering every spot, even when I don't wear a tie

Popote nina 'chana', hata kama hapafai
I will rap everywhere, even if it's the wrong place
(I light fire anywhere, even if it's not a suitable place)

Na popote ninakwenda pale njisinidai
And wherever I go, I won't pretend to be someone I'm not

Safari na musiki, piga teke usiogope
On this journey with music, don't be afraid to kick
(The journey of music, kick it, don't be afraid)

Unaweza ukafika pia unaweza usifike
You may arrive, but then again you may not

Unaweza ukasifika pia unaweza usisifike
You may be praised and you may not

Ukaaibika usiaibike; na ukachemsha usichemshe
You may be embarrassed and you may mess it all up
(You may be embarrassed or you may not, you may be boiled or you may not)

Kiongozi na Mlinzi wa jahazi ni Mwenyezi
God is the captain and the protector of this ship

XPs, TZ, Uholanzi, Brixton, Brussles, na Stockholm, na Olso, na Gabon, na Brazil
X Plastaz, Tanzania, Holland, Brixton, Brussels, Stockholm, Oslo, Gabon, and Brazil

Ni sisi na safari ya muziki ni asili.
It's us and the journey with music is the source.[9]

While Gsann does mention his home country of Tanzania twice, he goes on to index a set of localities in which global Hip Hop culture has taken root. Far from being arbitrary, Gsann's mapping of countries and cities on three different continents recounts the actual global journey of the X Plastaz over the years leading up to 2009.

As part of their first tour abroad, the X Plastaz performed in the Netherlands in 2001 and 2002. While touring through the Netherlands, the group was introduced to a Dutch-Ethiopian DJ and producer, DJ Precise, with whom they went on to record songs for their first album *Maasai Hip Hop*, which was released by the German label

---

9   English subtitles by BET: <youtube.com/watch?v=TetSMSdxIqA> 1:34-2:18. Accessed Apr. 24, 2015. Swahili transcription and literal English translation by Lowell Brower, Nkatha Kabira, and John Mugane.

OutHere Records in 2004. In 2003, they returned to Europe for a performanceat the Coleur Café Festival in Brussels as well as two shows in London. After attracting attention from European audiences and DJs, the X Plastaz continued their global journey in 2005 to Brazil and Scandinavia participating at festivals in Rio de Janeiro and Salvador as well as in Oslo and Stockholm. The following year, the X Plastaz performed at the Gabao Hip Hop Festival in Libreville, Gabon—the first East African Hip Hop group to do so in French-speaking Africa. Over the years, the X Plastaz have performed alongside such American Hip Hop bands as The Roots and Public Enemy, as well as Senegalese world music superstar Youssou N'Dour. In his rhymes, Gsann proudly recalls this journey around the world, illuminating the truly global contours of today's Hip Hop culture.

The recurrent metaphor of the *journey* that frames Gsann's rap highlights both his individual journey from A-Town to ATL as well as the global flows of Hip Hop culture, in general. Using the metaphor of the journey—*safari* in Swahili—Gsann not only structures his rhyme flow, but, more importantly, also captures the spatial and cultural mobility of Hip Hop. Several verbs that Gsann uses help to reinforce the centrality of mobility and travel: "We are *traveling*, but we are not *getting* there," "I'm *entering* every spot," "wherever I *go*," "You may *arrive*," "God is the *captain* and the protector of this *ship*." The first and last of these examples are of particular interest. The line "We are traveling, but we are not getting there" invokes an unspecified subject in the plural—Gsann and his crew, Gsann and his fellow emcees in the cipha, or Gsann and the entire global Hip Hop community—that is "traveling," but "not getting there."

This tension between the act of communal travel and the failure to arrive at the desired destination can be read in different ways. On the most immediate level, Gsann could be referring to the global travels that he and his crew have completed over the last few years, without fully achieving the commercial and artistic success they were aiming for. On a more abstract level, the verse could also be understood as an analogy to life, in general, that keeps us on a continuous journey without the guarantee of safe arrival at the places we intend to go. Yet despite our awareness of the contingency of successful traveling, Gsann continues, "we persevere." This connection between the trope of mobility and the contingency of success resurfaces again when Gsann's staccato rhymes explore the competitive character of a cipha: "You may arrive, but then again you may not / You may be praised and you may not / You may be embarrassed and you may mess it all up."

The fundamental openness of success—in a Hip Hop cipha as in life—eventually dissolves into another set of metaphors of motion: "God is the *captain* and the protector of this *ship*." No matter how uncertain his life journeys appear to be, Gsann suggests, God's stewardship and protective hand will guide our way. The religious theme of the concluding line, in particular, sets Gsann's rhymes apart from the more traditional battle rhymes of the other emcees. The verse powerfully foregrounds Gsann's belief in God and his inherent goodness. Gsann remains true to his earlier statement that he will not "pretend to be someone [he is] not" when he makes his religious faith explicit in a setting that does rely on something like divine inspiration, but traditionally is as far removed from the realm of the sacred word as Arusha is from Atlanta.

While religion does figure prominently in the music of many Hip Hop artists in the United States and has even sparked entire subgenres, verbal battles are rarely arenas where the confession of one's religious faith is deemed appropriate, let alone helpful to win the battle.[10] As Gsann's emphasis on his religious beliefs illustrates, Hip Hop outside of the United States does not only adapt its musical grammar to local languages, but, perhaps even more importantly, also incorporates local issues and concerns. Religion is one of the most salient examples of Hip Hop culture's localization in Africa. Significantly, it is not only African Hip Hop artists who incorporate their spiritual concerns into their music, but African immigrants arriving in the United States, too, bring along their religious beliefs and are knitting networks of spiritual exchange across the Black Atlantic.[11]

Gsann's presence within the core of an art form traditionally associated with African Americans cannot be understood without taking into account the crucial context of African immigration to the United States. The claims by some African Hip Hop artists that the cultural origins of Hip Hop do not lie in the North American inner city, but in the griot and rhythmic poetry traditions of Western and Eastern Africa, are paralleled by discussions about who counts as "black" in the age of Obama.[12] Just as recent African immigrants complicate monolithic notions of black solidarity in American society, creating new sites of conflict as well as cooperation among people of color, so does Gsann

---

10   To be sure, there are also spiritual battle raps among adherents of the subgenre of explicitly religious Hip Hop, but none were present in Gsann's BET cipha. For examples of the burgeoning literature on the intersection of religion and Hip Hop, see Eric Dyson, *Between God and Gangsta Rap: Bearing Witness to Black Culture* (New York, NY: Oxford University Press, 1996); Anthony B. Pinn, ed., *Noise and Spirit: The Religious and Spiritual Sensibilities of Rap Music* (New York, NY: New York University Press, 2003); Imani Perry, *Prophets of the Hood: Politics and Poetics in Hip Hop* (Durham, NC: Duke University Press, 2004); Felicia M. Miyakawa, *Five Percenter Rap: God Hop's Music, Message, and Black Muslim Mission* (Bloomington, IN: Indiana University Press, 2005); Daniel White Hodge, *The Soul of Hip Hop: Rims, Timbs, and a Cultural Theology* (Downers Grove, IL: IVP Books, 2010).

11   Jacob K. Olupona, and Regina Gemignani, eds., *African Immigrant Religions in America* (New York, NY: New York University Press, 2007).

12   Eric S. Charry, "A Capsule History of African Rap," in: *Hip Hop Africa: New African Music in a Globalizing World*, edited by Eric S. Charry (Bloomington, IN: Indiana University Press, 2012), 3f. On emcees as modern griots, see Patricia Tang, "The Rapper as Modern Griot: Reclaiming Ancient Traditions," in: *Hip Hop Africa: New African Music in a Globalizing World*, edited by Eric S. Charry (Bloomington, IN: Indiana University Press, 2012), 79–91.

challenge the historically grown cultural hegemony of African American artists within Hip Hop culture. Like other African immigrants to the United States, Gsann (who was living in Chicago in 2009) brings new issues to American debates about race, class, gender, religion, and empire.

The BET producers made sure to present Gsann's performance within the all-African American cipha as a "natural" extension of global Hip Hop culture. And yet, the fact that his rap was subtitled into English points to tensions within the linguistic contact zone of the cipha that reflect broader tensions between the African American community and newer waves of African immigrants. Just as some voices within the African American community are concerned about protecting their perceived discursive monopoly on such issues as the memory of slavery and the continuing reality of racism, the globalization of Hip Hop has complicated the neat narrative of its origins among African American inner-city youth in the late 1970s South Bronx. To these cultural gatekeepers, Hip Hop from Africa poses not only a conceptual, but, more importantly, also an identity problem. What does it mean, after all, for young urban African Americans when Canadian-Somali emcee K'Naan counters the glorification of violence in American gangsta rap by saying that "in my country, everyone is in that condition?"[13] Gsann, it seems, is not the only African emcee with translation problems in the United States.

No less significantly, Gsann reintroduces the metaphor of the ship—*jahazi* in Swahili—in this age of global air travel. It should be obvious to all who are watching Gsann's performance that he has not arrived at the BET Hip Hop Awards in Atlanta by ship. Gsann's use of the metaphor, however, evokes a host of historical associations. As Paul Gilroy has suggested, the metaphor of the ship conjures up violent as well as liberating images for people in the African Diaspora. For Gilroy, the ship signifies, on the one hand, the violence and death of the Middle Passage that African slaves had to endure. On the other hand, it also denotes the transatlantic cultural flows that sustained slaves and continue to sustain their descendants across the Black Atlantic.[14]

The history of Gsann's land of birth, Tanzania, forces us to expand Gilroy's privileging of the Atlantic Ocean to incorporate the various economic, cultural, and linguistic influences that Arab, Indian, Chinese, and European ships have brought to the eastern seaboard of Africa. In Swahili, the word *jahazi* is generally used to describe a large sailing ship, traditionally used for trading goods across the Indian Ocean. These trading ships not only brought back goods, ideas, and people from other parts of the Indian Ocean world,

---

13   Alastair Pennycook, and Tony Mitchell, "Hip Hop as Dusty Foot Philosophy," in: *Global Linguistic Flows: Hip Hop Cultures, Youth Identities, and the Politics of Language*, edited by H. Samy Alim, Awad Ibrahim, and Alastair Pennycook (New York, NY: Routledge, 2009), 31.

14   Paul Gilroy, *The Black Atlantic: Modernity and Double Consciousness* (Cambridge, MA: Harvard University Press, 1993), 4.

but they also exported Swahili culture abroad. Seen in this light, Gsann's performance in the BET cipha parallels the historical role of the *jahazi* connecting Swahili cultures with faraway places.

Furthermore, Gsann's referencing of the *jahazi* provides a powerful semantic contact zone between his Tanzanian background and the cultural memory of his African American co-performers. However, Gsann does not make the physical violence and cultural repression that European ships brought to Tanzania explicit in his rhymes; an elision that further distinguishes him from the traditional battle rhymes of his African American colleagues.[15] In Swahili, the term *jahazi* is usually not used to denote ships of European origin and the violence they brought with them. On the contrary, *jahazi* is an indigenous symbol and a source of pride among coastal Tanzanians. In the metaphor of the ship, then, Gsann's local *roots* in Tanzania connect with the global *routes* of contemporary Hip Hop culture.[16] At the same time, Gsann's use of the metaphor also exposes the limits of cultural translation since the ship mobilizes different historical and cultural registers within his American and African audience. Even though it was not a ship that has transported Gsann physically into the BET cipha, the historical richness of the metaphor of the ship allows him to join the imagined community of African American Hip Hop.

The geographical as well as cultural mobility that Gsann foregrounds in his rap also reflects the broader cultural realities of East Africa, both past and present. For centuries, Tanzanians have been travelling both within their country and beyond looking for a better life. In their quest for opportunity, the ship has been one of the foremost modes of transportation for Gsann's migrating fellow countrymen. As historian Sidney Lemelle has noted, the concept of *msafiri* (traveler) continues to play an important role in Swahili folklore and popular culture.[17] Thus, the pervasiveness of the theme of travel and mobility in Tanzanian culture grounds Gsann's metaphor of the ship in the concrete realities of his home country's past and present, lending his rhymes cultural authenticity.

Finally, the dynamics within the BET cipha deserve a closer analysis. It is noteworthy that there are no women among the participating emcees nor among the Hip Hop

---

15   This violent past becomes more explicit in Gsann's crew name. Echoing Malcolm Little's name change, the letter "X" in "X Plastaz" draws attention to the unknown numbers of African victims of slavery, Euro-American colonialism, and continued capitalist exploitation.

16   African linguist Katrina D. Thompson makes a similar point about the X Plastaz' attempt to occupy a place between their Tanzanian roots and international popularity. Cf. Katrina D. Thompson, "Reality and Representation in Maasai Hip-Hop," *Journal of African Cultural Studies* 20:1 (2008): 39.

17   Sidney Lemelle, "'Ni Wapi Tunakwenda': Hip Hop Culture and the Children of Arusha," in: *The Vinyl Ain't Final: Hip Hop and the Globalization of Black Popular Culture*, edited by Dipannita Basu, and Sidney Lemelle (London, UK: Pluto, 2006), 231.

emcees in the background. While this absence could be justified given the underrepresentation of popular female Hip Hop artists today, some of the earliest pioneers in the United States were female emcees such as Roxanne Shante and Sister Souljah. Likewise in Tanzania, female artists such as Zay B and Nakaaya are breaking down long-standing gender prejudices with their powerful music, especially in urban centers.[18] One of the members of the X Plastaz, Gsann's sister Dineh, is a skilled emcee in her own right and contributes a significant part to their mesmerizing stage performances.[19] If the conscious re-enactment of the old-school cipha at the BET Awards was aiming for historical accuracy, at least a few female emcees should have been included.

However, gender constructions are at play also in the lyrics of the emcees. Echoing on-going debates in the United States, there is a fierce debate raging in contemporary Tanzanian Hip Hop over the use of sexually explicit, if not outright misogynist, song lyrics. The centrality of Islam in most Swahili rap contrasts sharply with misogynist representations of women by some Tanzanian gangsta rappers such as Dully Sykes, whose 2001 release 'Nyambizi' (slang for a voluptuous woman), was too sexually explicit for Tanzanian radio stations to play.[20] Despite (or rather because) of this public outcry, Sykes sold quite a few singles of the song. Beyond religious concerns, most Tanzanian emcees also share a general didactic purpose on the microphone, which prompts them to tone down overly sexual and violent lyrics.

As Kenyan ethnomusicologist Mwenda Ntarangwi notes, the "most defining attribute of Hip Hop is its increased localization, where it not only represents local realities in local languages but also follows local structures and expectations of social decorum."[21] Sexually explicit or overly violent Hip Hop lyrics are a case in point. In many East African countries where religion—particularly Pentecostal Christianity and Islam—plays a central role in ordering society the fact that some American Hip Hop artists liberally rap about sex, drugs, and violence, has triggered a heated debate about the limits of cultural translation. Some Tanzanian Hip Hop groups (including the X Plastaz) define their music in contrast to mainstream Hip Hop reaching their airwaves from the United States. Tanzanian emcee Dola Soul illustrates this representational gap when he says

18   Alex Perullo, "Imitation and Innovation in the Music, Dress, and Camps of Tanzanian Youth," in: *Hip Hop Africa: New African Music in a Globalizing World*, edited by Eric S. Charry (Bloomington, IN: Indiana University Press, 2012), 207 n18.

19   Katrina D. Thompson, "Bongo Flava, Hip Hop and 'Local Maasai Flavors': Interviews with X Plastaz," in: *Native Tongues: The African Hip Hop Reader*, edited by P. Khalil Saucier (Trenton, NJ: Africa World Press, 2011), 291.

20   Lemelle, "Hip Hop Culture and the Children of Arusha," 240.

21   Mwenda Ntarangwi, *East African Hip Hop: Youth Culture and Globalization* (Urbana, IL: University of Illinois Press, 2009), 21.

that "Hip Hop shouldn't be all about 'I shot your mom...' People are dying out there in the streets, people are executed in countries. We want to bring out messages in our rap and tell the people what is going on and how we can change the world to make it a better place to live in."[22] X Plastaz' political project aims to avoidstatements that denigrate women or glorify violence.[23]

The refusal by many Tanzanian emcees to imitate gangsta rap rhetoric from the United States can be further traced back to the stylistic conventions of ancient Swahili poets. According to historian José Arturo Saavedra Casco, these ancient Swahili poets "believed that their works should contribute positive messages to the community through sophisticated prosodic rules and an elegant use of the language."[24] Pre-colonial Swahili poets incorporated local themes and social concerns into their works and participated—like Gsann centuries later—in composition contests (*mashindano*) that were staged during public festivities: "Contenders had to compose verses replying to what their opponents previously said."[25] The custom of reciting improvised verses at weddings and similar celebrations has survived until the present day. As this historical background shows, Gsann's participation in the BET cipha is part of a long cultural tradition in Tanzania dating back to pre-colonial times.

THE POLITICS OF TRANSLATION: SWAHILI RHYMES IN ATLANTA

Gsann's presence within the core of an art form traditionally associated with African Americans raises the question of translation. After his performance, Gsann reflected on his own positionality in the linguistic contact zone between English and Swahili:

> Many people were blown away with what I did and asked me why I rhymed in Swahili, 'cause they wanted to understand. I was just like "English is not my first language, I speak it, I love it, but you will be able to mess me up if I rhyme in English." There were emcees from all over the world in one setting, and I was happy to represent for Africa. I wasn't star struck, just glad to showcase what I did and could do with my American counterparts. I mean, think of it,

---

22 Cit. in ibid.

23 See, for instance, Katrina D. Thompson, "Bongo Flava, Hip Hop and 'Local Maasai Flavors': Interviews with X Plastaz," in: *Native Tongues: The African Hip Hop Reader*, edited by P. Khalil Saucier (Trenton, NJ: Africa World Press, 2011), 274.

24 José Arturo Saavedra Casco, "The Language of the Young People: Rap, Urban Culture, and Protest in Tanzania," *Journal of Asian and African Studies* 41, no. 3 (2006): 235.

25 Ibid.

we really have the same names, just one word changes, African American and African, do you understand what that means?[26]

Unfortunately, Gsann has not directly commented on his involvement in the English subtitles, but it is likely that he was consulted by the BET producers.

Since the founding members of the X Plastaz, including Gsann, were born and raised in Arusha in northern Tanzania where Swahili is the dominant language of commerce and everyday life, Gsann's use of Swahili is hardly surprising.[27] It was not until 1997 when Maasai singer Merege joined the crew that the X Plastaz started incorporating Maasai lyrics, musical traditions, and dressing styles into their performances.[28] Like in many other parts of the world, pioneering Tanzanian emcees, too, started introducing the new musical style of Hip Hop by rapping in English before adapting the American original to their local circumstances and linguistic particularities.[29] Some early innovators, such as Saleh J, then began to take the English rhymes they encountered on imported mixtapes and translated them into Swahili.[30] In contrast to the urban working-class origins of American Hip Hop, this original act of translation from English to Swahili was made possible by the fact that the majority of the early Tanzanian Hip Hop fans and practioners came from middle-class backgrounds, understood English, and had the financial means to buy American records or even travel there.[31] These Tanzanian Hip Hop pioneers served as the first generation of translators who paved the way for Hip Hop culture to take root in eastern Africa.

The use of Swahili, however, has also to be seen as a political move in the context of the role of Swahili in Tanzanian history and Tanzania's official policy of English-Swahili bilingualism. After independence in 1961, Tanzania's first prime minister Julius Nyerere promoted a socialist project known as *ujamaa* (family hood), which made Swahili the

---

26   Gesthuizen, "Tanzanian Emcee in BET Hip Hop Awards Cipha."

27   In a 2006 interview with applied linguist Katrina D. Thompson, Gsann said that Swahili is his first language before he learned Haya, Maa, and English. Katrina D. Thompson, "Bongo Flava, Hip Hop and 'Local Maasai Flavors': Interviews with X Plastaz," in: *Native Tongues: The African Hip Hop Reader*, edited by P. Khalil Saucier (Trenton, NJ: Africa World Press, 2011), 264.

28   Alex Perullo, "Imitation and Innovation in the Music, Dress, and Camps of Tanzanian Youth," in: *Hip Hop Africa: New African Music in a Globalizing World*, edited by Eric S. Charry (Bloomington, IN: Indiana University Press, 2012), 190.

29   Alex Perullo, *Live from Dar es Salaam: Popular Music and Tanzania's Music Economy* (Bloomington, IN: Indiana University Press, 2011), 164f.

30   Lemelle, "Hip Hop Culture and the Children of Arusha," 236.

31   Ibid.

basis of national culture.[32] Due to the long history of Swahili as the *lingua franca* of central and eastern Africa, the rhymes of the X Plastaz can today be understood throughout the region. This, at least, partly accounts for the regional success of *bongo flava* rap in Tanzania, both in its more party-oriented, sexually explicit, and commercial variants and the more socially conscious and politically informed Hip Hop of the X Plastaz.[33]

And yet, Tanzanian emcees, like their counterparts across Africa, are confronted with a linguistic paradox, as ethnomusicologist Eric Charry has noted: "The more they shape the genre to reflect and express their own experience, the more they rely on African languages and the less their chances of being understood by an international audience."[34] Despite the exceptional status of Swahili as a language with more than a hundred times more non-native speakers than native speakers, the approximately 100 million Swahili speakers worldwide remain predominantly located in central and eastern Africa, even though recent emigration to North America has increased the Swahili-speaking diaspora outside of Africa.[35] Swahili Hip Hop groups can, thus, rely on a rather large audience in close proximity, but are confronted with a linguistic barrier beyond eastern Africa. The decision of the BET producers to provide English subtitles for Gsann's Swahili rhymes illustrates this language gap.

Seen in historical perspective, the English subtitles expose a tension between the political uses to which Swahili and English have been put over the course of Tanzanian history. On the one hand, the use of Swahili can be read as a political and cultural act of empowerment on the part of Tanzanian rappers. Over the course of the 1990s, "Swahili became the more powerful language choice within the Hip Hop scene because of a desire among youth to build a national Hip Hop culture that promoted local rather than foreign values, ideas, and language."[36] Even though not explicitly included in anthropologist Kelly M. Askew's groundbreaking study of the relationship between music and Tanzanian national identity, Hip Hop played a vital part in performing the Tanzanian

---

32 For an overview of the history of Swahili, see Alamin M. Mazrui, and Ibrahim N. Shariff, *The Swahili: Idiom and Identity of an African People* (Trenton, NJ: Africa World Press, 1994).

33 Gsann clearly distances himself and his crew's music from *bongo flava*. Cf. Katrina D. Thompson, "Bongo Flava, Hip Hop and 'Local Maasai Flavors': Interviews with X Plastaz," in: *Native Tongues: The African Hip Hop Reader*, edited by P. Khalil Saucier (Trenton, NJ: Africa World Press, 2011), 265. On *bongo flava*, see Koen Stroeken, "Immunizing Strategies: Hip-Hop and Critique in Tanzania," *Africa: Journal of the International African Institute*, 75, no. 4 (2005): 488–509.

34 Eric S. Charry, "Music for an African Twenty-First Century," in: *Hip Hop Africa: New African Music in a Globalizing World*, edited by Eric S. Charry (Bloomington, IN: Indiana University Press, 2012), 292.

35 John M. Mugane, *The Story of Swahili: Identity and the Geopolitics of Language* (Athens, OH: Ohio University Press, forthcoming), iii.

36 Alex Perullo, and John Fenn, "Language Ideologies, Choices, and Practices in Eastern African Hip Hop," in: *Global Pop, Local Language*, edited by Harris M. Berger, and Michael Thomas Carroll (Jackson, MS: University Press of Mississippi, 2003), 33.

nation.[37] If, according to Askew, "the continual accommodation of foreign elements" is a "key Swahili trait," then Tanzanian Hip Hop culture is one of the best illustrations for its inclusive character.[38]

Over time, as ethnomusicologists Alex Perullo and John Fenn have noted, Tanzanian emcees have grown adept at using English to rap about the positive aspects of life—including their own skills—and Swahili to highlight the social problems in Tanzanian society.[39] Swahili's historical development into a widely used language of economic, religious, and cultural exchange has made it highly malleable and adaptable to new influences.[40] In many ways similar to English, Swahili's flexibility provides an ideal linguistic platform for a global, heterogeneous, and dynamic cultural practice such as Hip Hop. Indeed, Saleh J, the winner of the *Yo! Rap Bonanza*, held in Dar es Salaam in 1990, won this first national rap competition by rapping partly in Swahili.[41]

On the other hand, however, the English subtitles can be seen as an attempt to reclaim Gsann's Swahili rhymes for a primarily American audience. English, after all, was not only the language of the former British colonizers of Tanzania, but also remains the dominant language of American Hip Hop and globalization. The act of translation from the original Swahili to English thus violently breaks up a cluster of cultural memories about language and power.[42] If the use of African American Vernacular English by African American Hip Hop artists mobilizes a specific historical and cultural register in American society, the use of Swahili in Tanzanian Hip Hop conjures up the specters of European colonialism and American cultural hegemony. In a sense, every act of translation can be seen as an act of conquest.[43] While translating Hip Hop lyrics from outside of the United States into English necessarily does violence to the original language with its peculiar vocabulary,

---

37   Kelly M. Askew, *Performing the Nation: Swahili Music and Cultural Politics in Tanzania* (Chicago, IL: University of Chicago Press, 2002).

38   Ibid., 66.

39   Alex Perullo, and John Fenn, "Language Ideologies, Choices, and Practices in Eastern African Hip Hop," in: *Global Pop, Local Language*, edited by Harris M. Berger, and Michael Thomas Carroll (Jackson, MS: University Press of Mississippi, 2003), 20.

40   Mugane, *Story of Swahili*, 17.

41   Eric S. Charry, "A Capsule History of African Rap," in: *Hip Hop Africa: New African Music in a Globalizing World*, edited by Eric S. Charry (Bloomington, IN: Indiana University Press, 2012), 15.

42   Alastair Pennycook, *Global Englishes and Transcultural Flows* (New York, NY: Routledge, 2007), 107.

43   Among the first, Nietzsche described the practice of ancient Roman poets who translated Greek works as yet another Roman conquest: "In those days, indeed," he wrote in *Gay Science* in 1882, "to translate meant to conquer [...] And all this was done with the very best conscience as a member of the Roman Empire without realizing that such action constituted theft." Cit. in Rainer Schulte, and John Biguenet, eds., *Theories of Translation: An Anthology of Essays from Dryden to Derrida* (Chicago, IL: University of Chicago Press, 1992), 69.

tempo, and style, the specific relationship between English and Swahili in Tanzanian history makes the BET subtitles a special case of linguistic re-conquest.

More specifically, the English subtitling hearkens back to the historical connections of the African American community with Swahili. As linguist John Mugane reminds us, Swahili has exerted considerable influence on the cultural imagination of African Americans, from Maulana Karenga's invented tradition of *Kwanzaa* to the late LeRoi Jones's name change to Amiri Baraka to the use of Swahili as a code language by African American street gangs.[44] Seen against this historical backdrop, the performance of a Tanzanian emcee freestyling in Swahili alongside African Americans highlights the complicated relationship between African and African American cultural production. If African Americans' long-standing fascination with Swahili represents a crucial context for Gsann's presence at the BET Hip Hop Awards, the decision to translate his Swahili rhymes into English can only partly be explained by concerns about the language barrier, but reveals more about the cultural politics between African and African American artists at large. Given the long-standing African American fascination with Swahili culture, it seems hardly a coincidence that the first African emcee to appear at the BET Hip Hop Awards raps in Swahili.

Significantly, Gsann's rap made use of the standard form of Swahili taught in Tanzanian schools. In contrast to the linguistic mix of various East African languages, Arabic, and English that other Tanzanian and Kenyan emcees use in their lyrics, Gsann refrains from inserting lexical markers in English that might help his audience better understand him. The idiosyncratic and highly dynamic mixture between Swahili and English, also known as "Swanglish," is prevalent among young urban Tanzanians, many of whom also participate in Hip Hop culture. As cultural historian Maria Suriano has shown, young Tanzanian Hip Hop artists "contribute to the spread of new slang terms, and 'Swanglish' words [...], while on the other hand [adopting] street language in their hits [...], and in this way [contribute] to its 'institutionalization'."[45] The X Plastaz do have recorded songs in which they creatively mix different languages (English, Swahili, and Maa) and linguistic codes (street Swahili, urban slang, and standard Swahili).

Given the group's linguistic diversity, Gsann's use of standard Swahili in the BET cipha stands out as a conscious act of cultural self-positioning. As he himself explained in an interview after the awards ceremony, Gsann is fluent in English as well as in the more urban forms of Swahili prevalent among east African Hip Hop practitioners, but in the cipha with African American emcees he chose to rap in Standard Swahili. In an earlier interview, Gsann had already stressed the importance of language when performing

---

44 Mugane, *Story of Swahili*, 145ff.

45 Maria Suriano, "'Mimi Ni Msanii, Kioo Cha Jamii': Urban Youth Culture in Tanzania as Seen Through Bongo Fleva and Hip-Hop," *Swahili Forum* 14 (2007): 210.

abroad: "When we are in foreign countries we have to use extra energy in order to please and satisfy our fans" because most listeners could not understand Swahili.[46] This insistence on the use of a "pure" Swahili can be read as a reaction against BET's attempt to protect the cultural hegemony of African Americans over the art form of Hip Hop.

CONCLUSION

To be sure, the inclusion of the non-American emcee Gsann within the commercial spectacle and cultural navel-gazing of the BET Hip Hop Awards attests to a growing awareness of Hip Hop's global reach. But at the same time, Gsann's self-awareness of his unlikely presence and peripheral position in Hip Hop's cultural center allows him to successfully elude the centripetal force of American Hip Hop. Even though the BET producers probably welcomed Gsann's rhymes in his exotic yet somewhat familiar native tongue of Swahili, rapping in English would certainly have helped Gsann to bring his message across to the worldwide audience watching the show. With his decision to use his native tongue of Swahili, Gsann marked off his own turf in the African American cipha and put his native Tanzania on the map of contemporary global Hip Hop culture.

Gsann's use of Swahili combined with his emphasis on religion and his global travels disrupts the grand narrative of Hip Hop's birth in the South Bronx and its subsequent diffusion throughout the world. Gsann's rap uncovered the local roots of "African Hip Hop from the cradle of civilization: Arusha, Tanzania, East Africa," as the X Plastaz' website proudly proclaims. As this case study of an artist from Tanzania has shown, Hip Hop's global journey has united Hip Hop artists around the world, but the linguistic conflicts of the past and the commercial imperatives of the present remain. If there is power in diversity, this power needs to be directed more forcefully against the homogenizing forces of the marketplace. The X Plastaz, for their part, are trying to resist the demands of the Tanzanian music industry and refuse to pay bribes to radio deejays and television hosts to play their songs.[47] Even though Gsann's performance within the African American cipha was presented as a natural extension of American Hip Hop, the fact that his rap was translated into English raises broader questions about the contested politics of translation in global Hip Hop culture. The 2009 BET cipha, in the end, illustrates the

---

46   Katrina D. Thompson, "Bongo Flava, Hip Hop and 'Local Maasai Flavors': Interviews with X Plastaz," in: *Native Tongues: The African Hip Hop Reader*, edited by P. Khalil Saucier (Trenton, NJ: Africa World Press, 2011), 265.

47   Katrina D. Thompson, "Bongo Flava, Hip Hop and 'Local Maasai Flavors': Interviews with X Plastaz," in: *Native Tongues: The African Hip Hop Reader*, edited by P. Khalil Saucier (Trenton, NJ: Africa World Press, 2011), 266.

creative ways in which a Tanzanian emcee made sense of his cultural and linguistic journey from A-Town to ATL.

BIBLIOGRAPHY

Alim, H. Samy, Awad Ibrahim, and Alastair Pennycook, eds. *Global Linguistic Flows: Hip Hop Cultures, Youth Identities, and the Politics of Language.* New York, NY: Routledge, 2009.

Askew, Kelly M. *Performing the Nation: Swahili Music and Cultural Politics in Tanzania.* Chicago, IL: University of Chicago Press, 2002.

Casco, José Arturo Saavedra. "The Language of the Young People: Rap, Urban Culture, and Protest in Tanzania." *Journal of Asian and African Studies* 41, no. 3 (2006): 229–48.

Charry, Eric S. "Music for an African Twenty-First Century." In: *Hip Hop Africa: New African Music in a Globalizing World*, edited by Eric S. Charry, 283–315. Bloomington, IN: Indiana University Press, 2012.

————. "A Capsule History of African Rap." In: *Hip Hop Africa: New African Music in a Globalizing World*, edited by Eric S. Charry, 1–25. Bloomington, IN: Indiana University Press, 2012.

Dyson, Michael E. *Between God and Gangsta Rap: Bearing Witness to Black Culture.* New York, NY: Oxford University Press, 1996.

Gilroy, Paul. *The Black Atlantic: Modernity and Double Consciousness.* Cambridge, MA: Harvard University Press, 1993.

Gesthuizen, Thomas. "Tanzanian Emcee in BET Hip Hop Awards Cipha." *African Hip Hop.com.* October 26, 2009. <http://www.africanhiphop.com/tanzanian-emceein-bet-hip-hop-awards-cypher>.

Hodge, Daniel White. *The Soul of Hip Hop: Rims, Timbs, and a Cultural Theology.* Downers Grove, IL: IVP Books, 2010.

Kelley, Robin D. G. *Race Rebels: Culture, Politics, and the Black Working Class.* New York, NY: Free Press, 1994.

Lemelle, Sidney. "'Ni Wapi Tunakwenda': Hip Hop Culture and the Children of Arusha." In: *The Vinyl Ain't Final: Hip Hop and the Globalization of Black Popular Culture*, edited by Dipannita Basu, and Sidney Lemelle, 230–54. London, UK: Pluto, 2006.

Mazrui, Alamin M., and Ibrahim N. Shariff. *The Swahili: Idiom and Identity of an African People.* Trenton, NJ: Africa World Press, 1994.

Mugane, John M. *The Story of Swahili: Identity and the Geopolitics of Language.* Athens, OH: Ohio University Press, forthcoming.

Ntarangwi, Mwenda. *East African Hip Hop: Youth Culture and Globalization.* Urbana, IL: University of Illinois Press, 2009.

Olupona, Jacob K., and Regina Gemignani, eds. *African Immigrant Religions in America.* New York, NY: New York University Press, 2007.

Miyakawa, Felicia M. *Five Percenter Rap: God Hop's Music, Message, and Black Muslim Mission.* Bloomington, IN: Indiana University Press, 2005.

Pennycook, Alastair. *Global Englishes and Transcultural Flows*. New York, NY: Routledge, 2007.

Pennycook, Alastair, and Tony Mitchell. "Hip Hop as Dusty Foot Philosophy." In: *Global Linguistic Flows: Hip Hop Cultures, Youth Identities, and the Politics of Language*, edited by H. Samy Alim, Awad Ibrahim, and Alastair Pennycook, 25–42. New York, NY: Routledge, 2009.

Perry, Imani. *Prophets of the Hood: Politics and Poetics in Hip Hop*. Durham, NC: Duke University Press, 2004.

Perullo, Alex. "Imitation and Innovation in the Music, Dress, and Camps of Tanzanian Youth." In: *Hip Hop Africa: New African Music in a Globalizing World*, edited by Eric S. Charry, 187–207. Bloomington, IN: Indiana University Press, 2012.

_____. *Live from Dar es Salaam: Popular Music and Tanzania's Music Economy*. Bloomington, IN: Indiana University Press, 2011.

_____, and John Fenn. "Language Ideologies, Choices, and Practices in Eastern African Hip Hop." In: *Global Pop, Local Language*, edited by Harris M. Berger, and Michael Thomas Carroll, 19–51. Jackson, MS: University Press of Mississippi, 2003.

Pinn, Anthony B., ed. *Noise and Spirit: The Religious and Spiritual Sensibilities of Rap Music*. New York, NY: New York University Press, 2003.

Robertson, Roland. "Glocalization: Time-Space and Homogeneity-Heterogeneity." In: *Global Modernities*, edited by Mike Featherstone, Scott Lash, and Roland Robertson, 25–44. London, UK: Sage Publications, 1995.

Schulte, Rainer, and John Biguenet, eds. *Theories of Translation: An Anthology of Essays from Dryden to Derrida*. Chicago, IL: University of Chicago Press, 1992.

Spady, James G., H. Samy Alim, and Samir Meghelli. *Tha Global Cipha: Hip Hop Culture and Consciousness*. Philadelphia, PA: Black History Museum Press, 2006.

Stroeken, Koen. "Immunizing Strategies: Hip-Hop and Critique in Tanzania." *Africa: Journal of the International African Institute*, 75, no. 4 (2005): 488–509.

Suriano, Maria. "'Mimi Ni Msanii, Kioo Cha Jamii': Urban Youth Culture in Tanzania as Seen Through Bongo Fleva and Hip-Hop." *Swahili Forum* 14 (2007): 207–23.

Tang, Patricia. "The Rapper as Modern Griot: Reclaiming Ancient Traditions." In: *Hip Hop Africa: New African Music in a Globalizing World*, edited by Eric S. Charry, 79–91. Bloomington, IN: Indiana University Press, 2012.

Thompson, Katrina D. "Bongo Flava, Hip Hop and 'Local Maasai Flavors': Interviews with X Plastaz." In: *Native Tongues: The African Hip Hop Reader*, edited by P. Khalil Saucier, 253–297. Trenton, NJ: Africa World Press, 2011.

———. "Reality and Representation in Maasai Hip-Hop." *Journal of African Cultural Studies* 20:1 (2008): 33–44.

Verán, Cristina. "Native Tongues: Hip-Hop's Global Indigenous Movement." In: *Total Chaos: The Art and Aesthetics of Hip-Hop*, edited by Jeff Chang, 278–90. New York, NY: Basic Civitas Books, 2006.

DISCUSSION QUESTIONS

1. Why were many early contributors to hip hop excluded from narratives of its origin and developing years?

2. Compare and contrast hip hop as practiced in the United States and globally.

3. What did Chuck D of Public Enemy mean when he stated that hip hop was the "CNN of Black America?"

2

Global Hip Hop

By Keri Eason

I first was introduced to rap in high school after basketball practices. In the early 2000s, I enjoyed the music production from Dr. Dre, Pharrell Williams, Timbaland, and Jermaine Dupri. I could not keep myself from becoming energized when I heard their beats and synthesized sounds. Putting my headphones on and popping in Jay-Z's *Black Album*, T. I.'s *Trap Muzik*, or 50 Cent's *Get Rich or Die Tryin'* became a ritual for me before basketball games. This ritual didn't stop with basketball. I listened to rap during workouts and practices for golf and tennis, too. Over time, I began listening closely to the lyrics. Jay-Z, T. I., and 50 Cent not only were putting words together in a rhythmic fashion so that their lyrics would sound nice to people's ears, but they were also writing and talking about real issues like racism, oppression, and the culture and conditions of different Black communities in New York City and Atlanta. This was something very new to me.

As a South Korean adoptee, I grew up in a predominantly white community of lower- to middle-class residents. Most people living in the community were socially and economically privileged, including myself. White people in my community never talked about racism. It is possible, and even likely, that for some community members, their interactions with me were their only experiences with a person who was not white and heterosexual. I experienced racism and sexism along with the stereotypical jokes about being Asian and a member of the LGBTQ+ communities. For example, people often made comments to me about Chinese food, being good at math and science, nail salon shops, and lesbianism. Until I started listening to hip hop, however, I never had thought about racism, sexism, classism, and oppression on a systemic level.

I started searching for hip hop/conscious rap emcees like Tupac Shakur, Biggie, Black Star (and followed both Mos Def and Talib Kweli as solo artists), Nas, Common, and then later Lupe Fiasco. I learned that Black female emcees had unique social positions, perspectives, and experiences that influenced their lyrics, including some that resonated with me. I loved the way Lauryn Hill, Lil' Kim, and Missy Elliott offered their style of social commentary through their music. I began to recognize and appreciate how hip hop allowed these artists and fans to express themselves; comment on social, economic, and political conditions of Black and Brown communities; and serve as a form of protest. Eventually, the acts of putting on my favorite hip hop CDs and later scrolling through my iPod helped me not feel so alone in a community where there were few members of other marginalized groups. The music and lyrical content gave me strength when white people were making fun of my eyes or arguing that colleges should not give me admission preference over them simply because I was a South Korean adoptee. Hip hop gave me the courage to make new friends in college, including domestic and international students of different races, genders, and classes.

While an undergraduate, I learned about K-pop, or Korean popular music, when I became friends with several second-generation South Korean students. They introduced me to groups like Super Junior and Big Bang. There was no denying the appeal of the preppy pop sound of the music. I could understand why young fans enjoyed these groups as they presented what Westerners would expect in a wholesome family friendly image. K-pop music producers seemed to combine what one might hear in an NSYNC song of the time with beats and basslines that were reminiscent of American hip hop. The groups also featured one or two members who would serve as rappers on songs designated for them to perform.

Until I learned about K-pop, I never had thought of hip hop as a global artform. South Korean and American hip hop collaborations are some examples of how artists around the world are transforming hip hop into a global phenomenon. In 2003 Missy Elliott and G-Dragon, Big Bang's main rapper, collaborated and performed in Los Angeles on *M Countdown*, the South Korean version of MTV's *Total Request Live*. In 2010 K-pop group JYJ, a band that at the time included rapper Yoochun, collaborated with Kanye West and Malik Yusef on the track "Ayyy Girl." In the past, I would have said Korean emcees were imitating American emcees. After seeing the performance, however, it was apparent that Korean emcees like G-Dragon were "doing hip hop" in their own unique ways. Today, new emcees like Keith Ape, Zico, and CL illustrate how South Korean hip hop has changed and evolved over the years. For example, the hip hop platform allows South Korean emcees to talk about what would be taboo topics in their country, like sex, wealth, drugs, and their journeys to becoming entertainers.

The evolution of South Korean hip hop is only one example among many of countries outside of the United States where artists have created and practiced their own hip hop culture. Globally, hip hop has become the most influential form of pop culture today. Nevertheless, most Americans still consider only artists from the United States as legitimate when discussing new hip hop trends and history. Increasingly, however, there is a growing recognition that hip hop beyond the United States is equally as innovative, entertaining, and powerful in fighting social inequality and injustice globally. Part 2, Global Hip Hop, includes articles that directly demonstrate the ways hip hop culture and art are practiced in other countries outside of the United States.

"So I Choose to Do Am Naija Style: Hip Hop, Language, and Postcolonial Identities" by Tope Omoniyi is an analysis of frameworks that have been previously used when critiquing global hip hop. Omoniyi notes that some scholars have framed music produced outside the United States as imitative or replicating the sounds of Western producers and emcees and offers a contrasting perspective that views hip hop as a site of contested identities in a global context. Through this lens, global hip hop is viewed as a product of cultural exchange as opposed to the mere imitation of Western artists. This cultural exchange framework supports and acknowledges how global hip hop has contributed and continues to contribute to hip hop.

"Respect for Da Chopstick Hip Hop: The Politics, Poetics, and Pedagogy of Cantonese Verbal Art in Hong Kong" by Angel Lin examines the intersection of sociolinguistics and hip hop studies. The author explores Cantonese youth identities, the politics of the Cantonese language, and the processes of both globalization and localization. Lin begins the article with a discussion of Cantopop, the Cantonese pop genre that has dominated the Hong Kong airwaves since the mid 1970s, to show how Cantonese pop artists were using their art to express the conditions of "ordinary working-class people's plight" (Lin, 2008). Cantopop allowed artists to comment on social inequalities that working-class youth, and this genre provided a means to protest their social conditions as well as other areas of their lives, including friends, family, and existential philosophy.

Since the 1990s, Cantopop has moved away from a focus on working-class issues to creating good-looking idols who sing pop ballads about love. During this time, however, underground artists like LMF (Lazy Mutha Fucka) emerged to return the art to its protest and resistance themes that had originally been prevalent in early Cantopop. Audiences again were receptive to these themes and lyrics commenting on the experiences of working-class youths. LMF has paved the way for other hip hop artists in Hong Kong, and Lin introduces a few here, including FAMA and MC Yan. The brilliance of this essay is how the author shows how these emcees use hip hop as a form of protest in their fight for human rights by providing an in-depth analysis of their Cantonese lyrics. In many ways, Lin argues, these artists are engaging in socially conscious rap through their native tongue, Cantonese, in the tradition of American artists like Public Enemy and other pro-justice performers.

"Doin' Damage in My Native Language: The Use of 'Resistance Vernaculars' in Hip Hop in France, Italy, and Aotearoa/New Zealand" by Tony Mitchell completes the Global Hip Hop section. The author focuses on the localized global implications of hip hop in countries outside of the United States. He analyzes indigenous non-English languages and rap lyrics from artists in Zimbabwe, Switzerland, France, Italy, and Aotearoa/New Zealand to examine how the resistance narrative prevalent in many hip hop songs, especially during the early years of Western hip hop, are now found in the works of artists across the world. These global artists, he finds, use the resistance narrative as inspiration to make changes for improved conditions and quality of life for people in their countries.

Mitchell concludes that global hip hop artists have adopted American artists' carefully crafted resistance language. While some people across the world do not completely understand the resistance language created by American hip hop artists, the Western resistance vernacular is growing and has motivated and influenced many global hip hop artists to engage in similar works. These global artists have employed components of Western resistance language to create their own unique dialects, and the result is that global hip hop has given these artists and youth a voice to express themselves and a platform to discuss their experiences, concerns, and social issues arising from their own experiences.

▌REFERENCE

Lin, Angel. (2008). Respect for Da Chopstick Hip Hop: The Politics, Poetics, and Pedagogy of Cantonese Verbal Art in Hong Kong. In H. S. Alim, A. M. Ibrahim, & A. Pennycook (Eds.), *Global linguistic flows: Hip hop cultures, identities, and the politics of language* (pp. 159–177). Mahwah, NJ: Lawrence Erlbaum.

"So I Choose to Do Am Naija Style"

Hip Hop, Language, and Postcolonial Identities[1]

By Tope Omoniyi

INTRODUCTION

Let us begin with a brief initial explanation of the frame imposed on this discussion by the chosen title. Taken from the lyrics of the title song of Nigerian Hip Hop artist 2-Shotz's 2005 album *Nna-Men*, the lines "You no fit yarn *foné* pass American/so I choose to do am Naija style" represent a number of identity-related claims. First, it asserts both complementarity and optionality of "foné" and "Naija style" rapping in one and the same vein. But there is a sense in which the choice of Naija style results from a subtle admission or suggestion of American ownership of foné and a conscious decision to diverge and then settle for a Naija alternative. In the lexicon of Nigerian Pidgin, foné is the label for a prestigious Standard English variety often used to describe the highly educated or native-speaker-approximating performance of a nonnative speaker. In other words, native speakers are not described in this term. This is an interesting yet contradictory other-ascribed value considering that the language of much U.S. rap is described as a non-Standard variety of American English that lacks capital in Bourdieu's (1991) terms within the context of U.S. politics. On a hierarchy of languages (Blommaert, 1999, p. 431) and such hierarchies are more often than not managed by the ideological North, Nigerian Pidgin, a South language variety, would occupy a slightly lower stratum than AAVE based on the latter's sheer privilege of location in the North. One significant addition to make to this is the glaring postcolonial dimension entailed by varieties of English and the politics of that relationship and how that frames a discussion of Hip Hop and identity.

In line with the stated aim in Alim's introduction to this volume—to map "the intersections between issues of language, Hip Hop Culture, and globalization"—in this [reaading] I shall examine how African and Nigerian Hip Hop artists discursively carve out a recognizable creative patch and a legitimate nonsubordinate local identity whilst retaining membership in the global community. I shall examine the discursive strategies deployed by artists in an attempt to articulate Nigerian yet global identities. This will entail tracking evidence of the flow between the two cultural axes; local and global. My exploration will be based on data extracts from transcripts of a BBC 1 Extra audio interview of Daara J conducted by JJC,[2] Ice-T's (a.k.a Tracy Marrow) opening of the 2006 VH1 Hip Hop Honors Award ceremony in New York, commentaries by artists in media reports on Hip Hop websites (*Hip Hop World Magazine*), and song lyrics from the work of a selection of Nigerian artists including Lágbájá, Weird MC, P-Square, Ruggedman, D'banj, and 2-Shotz.

HIP HOP AS A SITE OF CONTESTED IDENTITIES

Intellectual exploration of Hip Hop as a site of contested identities with reference to Africa and more specifically to Nigeria is both new and complex. The latter is reflected in the claim by Afrolution Records (2006)[3] to the effect that:

> What has always held African Hip Hop back is a struggle for our own identity, our own sound—something that belongs to us and is not a second rate replication of the Western sound. Sure we all grew up on US Hip Hop, we acknowledge that and we are grateful for the opportunities it has created for us but one cannot deny that the true essence of Hip Hop is "keeping it real". Once we started to learn to do this we planted the fertile seeds that are now seeing our industry grow. If you're a label, an artist or an African Hip Hop disciple please get in touch and register so we can keep you in our loop. (http://www.afrolution.com/, accessed November 15, 2006)

The statement at once sets up "African Hip Hop" that is "our own" in contrast to a "second rate replication of the Western sound." In a sense, this represents a pitch for the local essence, even as it acknowledges that members of the African Hip Hop community "all grew up on US Hip Hop." Growing up on, I would argue, ascribes parental status through nurture if not nature to U.S. Hip Hop and therefore amounts to a subtle acquiescence to the mainstream narrative that assigns the birth of Hip Hop to the Bronx in New York City. In this [reading], I explore two contrasting theoretical constructs of Hip Hop and identity. One construct advocates multiple narratives of origin underlying the contemporary mutation of local and global in the formation of a new identity; a relationship of asymmetry and mutuality. The second, in contrast, constructs a single narrative of origin and one dominant source of dispersal of Hip Hop facilitated by globalization.

ALTERNATIVE NARRATIVE(S) OF ORIGIN AND IDENTITY

The claim of a single origin for Hip Hop that is located in the Bronx has fed claims that the versions found outside of the United States are mere imitation art. Toop (1984) credits the

Sugarhill Gang's chart hit *Rapper's Delight* in Harlem and the Bronx with the coming "to prominence in 1979" of Hip Hop. Afrolution Record's claim shows that African Hip Hop artists were struggling with the central Hip Hop mantra of "keepin it real" and are then challenged to create a Hip Hop that is more "African" than "American," something that they could claim as their own. This claim also is an indication that Hip Hop communities outside the United States construct themselves as "real" in their particular environments in order to narrate for themselves a history of participation in Hip Hop that privileges the local. The claim of a U.S. origin is pushed internally within the United States as well as without. The following extract from Ice-T's opening speech at the 2006 VH1 Hip Hop Honors Award ceremony is an instance of internal push:

> It's so cold, what's up pimpin'? Welcome to the 2006 VH1 Hip Hop Honors. Now you saw tha I'wa'n gon let somebody take my job tonight. Bloomberg may be the mayor of New York but I'm the original gangsta of hip-hop, you dig? This is our third time around and like Hip Hop itself we just get bigger and better every year. We're back to the home of hip-hop, New York City. Respec'. (my emphasis)

Best and Kellner (1992) in a similar vein to the above remarked that:

> Hip hop erupted from New York dance and party culture of the 1970s. Encompassing dance and performance, visual art, multimedia, fashion and attitude, hip hop is the music and style for the new millennium. A highly protean and assimilative cultural ethos, it is here to stay, as it absorbs new influences, is appropriated throughout myriad cultural forms and forces across the globe, and has become a major mode of the global popular. (Enculturation, 1999, p. 2)

Outsider Angus Batey made more or less the same claim in a London *Times* article titled "Home Grown—Profile—British Hip-Hop—Music" (2003) noting that:

> "UK rap" is a broad sonic church, encompassing anything made in Britain by musicians informed or inspired by hip-hop's possibilities, *whose music is a response to the same stimuli that gave birth to rap in New York* in the mid-Seventies. (my emphasis)

This view, until recently, was not regarded as contentious and has not been the subject of a critical challenge in the literature. However, in an attempt to unravel globalization and the processes of social change that are now associated with it, new worlds and interconnections hitherto either concealed or unobserved and therefore undocumented have been unveiled and with that an accompanying need to revisit existing narratives, theories, and methods that help us to get a clearer understanding of the ways in which the local relates to the global in the contemporary world. It is in this context that the claims above must now be placed side by side with emergent narratives, theories, and methods and reassessed.

The social practices which together make Hip Hop "a way of life" include mc-ing, rapping, freestyling, break/street dancing, graffiti, and overstanding (Toop, 1984). An important question to pose here is that if we take the position that Hip Hop's home is New York, can we regard its emergence in other "homes" around the world as creating a Hip Hop diaspora? It is almost impossible that the Hip Hop diaspora would be mirror replicas of U.S. Hip Hop if they interact with diverse sociocultural realities, a fact not taken on board by an *Imitation or Replica Hypothesis*. Replication invokes a relationship of asymmetry between the original and the replica. This is the framework in which Hip Hop of other parts of the world are represented as imitative (for example, Broder, 2006, p. 40 on Japanese rap). Bradley Winterton writing in the *Taipei Times* in an article titled "Japanese Hip-Hop, Imitation or Art?" (2006) queried:

> Does the spread of hip-hop to Japan mean that everything American, from Wal-Mart to McDonald's, is destined to cover the globe with a uniform and stultifying sameness, or does the exchange of cultural influence quickly mutate into local variations that blend the imported with the inherited and create valuable new cross-bred "species" in innumerable locations? (Japanese Hip-Hop, p. 18)

More recent studies have not only veered away from that position (Condry, 2006), they have also explored the nature of cultural exchange and mutation that globalization supports. An imitation model is simplistic in its assumption that Hip Hop anywhere else is a replica of a U.S. form without appreciating the cultural influences and genetic modification it undergoes in the new environment. Diversity is a firmly established feature of the Global Hip Hop Nation, so the more worthwhile undertaking is an exploration of diversity by looking at less known Hip Hop varieties such as Nigerian Hip Hop with a view to unraveling how such local phenomena respond to and fit into the global, especially against the background of postcolonial reality and "(un)fair trade" ideologies and practices. Alternative narratives of origin interrogate that relationship.

BOOMERANG HYPOTHESIS

Some of the component features of Hip Hop are now being identified as composite elements of the essential culture and identity of some West African societies. One such claim suggests that the genre is indeed part of a long-standing African oral tradition that was only transplanted to North America through the Middle Passage. I shall call this the *Boomerang Hypothesis* after the Senegalese Hip Hop group Daara J's 2005 album of that title (see also Pennycook and Mitchell, this volume) and the claim by group member

Faada Freddie in an interview with artist/broadcaster JJC which was broadcast as a four-part series on BBC 1 Extra between November 2 and 23, 2006:

> The ancestors of Hip Hop itself used to be incarnated by the griots. It was to report the history and the reality that the people were living in the Songhai Realm. The Songhai Realm was Senegal, Mali, Guinea, after came slavery. The culture, the African culture has been deported to America and had to grow in the plantations. Then after came the descendants of the slaves who brought out their modern oral tradition called hip-hop. Now rap music is back home, and that's the reason why we called the latest of the Daara J's album "Boomerang" saying that rap was born in Africa, grew in America but now rap is back home.

Earlier in 2003, Jayne Ifekwunigwe, anthropologist and cultural theorist had been quoted in a University of East London press report as noting that:

> Hip Hop is the single most powerful contemporary influence on music and youth culture world wide. It is an expressive and empowering form of musical resistance, and has been transformed and reborn in its journey through the African diasporas of the United States, Europe and Brazil. Moving full circle, rap and hip hop are now finding new forms of expression in Africa itself. (http://www.uel.ac.uk/news/press_releases/releases/hiphop.htm)

Paul Gilroy's (1993) critique of the quadrilateral transatlantic transactions that constituted the Black Atlantic provides anchorage for that line of argument. If we see the construction of alternative narratives as a strategy of postcolonial deconstruction, then it could be argued that what is described as freestyling in Hip Hop is a version of discursive practices such as *ewi*, a disciplined and tight Yoruba oral poetic form, and *orin ebu* or *orin owe*, the abuse songs and proverbial songs employed in "song-lashing" episodes (Omoniyi, 1995) among the Yoruba of southwestern Nigeria. Similarly, it may be argued that verbal dueling rhymes among Turkish adolescents (Dundes, Leach, & Özkök, 1972, p. 130) with, of course, the expansion of membership of its community of practice to include postteenage youths, is the alternative source of Turkish Hip Hop. Pangie Anno, who manages the oldest music studio in Ghana, claimed in an interview with BBC World Service's Masterpiece program that "The source of Hip Hop is an African tradition, an ancient African tradition of freestyling, which is spontaneous poetry to a rhythmic pattern." Similarly, the Nigerian artist Lágbájá (alter ego Bisade Ologunde) in the lyrics of his 2005 song "Afrocalypso" traces Black diaspora music forms to slave narratives and therefore to Africa:

> Africalypso, Africalypso
> Some four hundred years ago
> They took away my forefathers

From Africa to America
My forefathers took along their music
And some became jazz
Some became soul
Some became rhythm and blues
Swing, big band, bop, hip hop, funk, jazz, rap, reggae, ragga,
And some became calypso

But as with most myths of origin, it is to be expected that there would be variations and sometimes contradictions. For instance, in the BBC program cited above, Reggie Rockstone, described as a Ghanaian Hip Life star (blend of Hip Hop and High Life music), remarked that: "Everything that happened in the South Bronx with hip-hop is what's happening here, except we don't have any guns" thus conceding to the North American root of the genre narrative. Toop (1984) claims in the blurb that his book "takes Hip Hop culture as its central focus for the investigation of Afro-American rapping in all its forms. It begins with the music's African roots and ends in the electro-funk revolution." The reclamation of the origin of Hip Hop by some African artists has implications not only for the identity of the genre but also for the identities of those who (re)produce it.

These counternarratives prompted Omoniyi (2005, 2006a) to suggest that we may in fact be dealing with a case of reappropriation rather than an example of North American cultural imperialism spreading on the wings of globalization's structures. The current claim of reappropriation challenges the idea of an African appropriation of a U.S. form and suggests instead that the form which had been previously appropriated in the US is being reclaimed. The argument echoes Kadiatu Kanneh's (1998) in her exploration of Black American feminisms and women's narratives in which she argued that representations and imaginings of Africa in Black America cannot be anchored solely in histories of exile. In African American appropriations of Africa, she suggests, "memories of Africa and migration surge into the imaginary of Black America, creating representations of American nationality as a multi-layered and contested concept, challenged and redefined by urgent historical remembering" (p. 109). These different narratives of origin are artifacts enabling us to glean source information about the different elements from which contemporary global remixes are being constructed. Our focus ought to be on the determination of the nature of variation between the different forms of Hip Hop in its multiple homes and the identity implications of these variants. This is justification for the characterization I attempt later on in this [reading] by identifying the features of Nigerian Hip Hop. I wish to turn next to the agenda of Hip Hop inasmuch as it facilitates a clearer vision of the ideologies that inform it and how these serve identity constructions and negotiations. This agenda is conveyed in discourses of race, nation, class, and ethnicity.

HIP HOP, RACE, NATION, CLASS, AND ETHNICITY

A discussion of Hip Hop in relation to identity must address its association with race, nation, class, gender, and ethnicity as established variables in the sociolinguistics of identity (cf. Omoniyi & White, 2006). In Hip Hop's multiple locations around the world, these variables may or may not be equally relevant to a discussion of identity. The fact that Hip Hop became a formidable cultural phenomenon in the 1970s in the United States may be an indication of its purposeful evolution as a social and quasi-political movement and a replacement forum for postcivil rights articulation of Black resistance to persisting racial injustices in American society. Best and Kellner (1999) remark that

> Rap artists like Grandmaster Flash, Run DMC, Public Enemy, Ice-T, N.W.A., Ice Cube, Salt 'n' Pepa, Queen Latifah, Wu Tang Clan, Snoop Doggy Dogg, Tupac Shakur, the Fugees, and countless others produced a new musical genre that uniquely articulated the rage of the urban underclass and its sense of intense oppression and defiant rebellion. (p. 2)

This remark and others like it may therefore be seen to assert in part the ideological and political agenda that Hip Hop pursues in the North American context. The literature clearly shows that Hip Hop was extensively racialized in the United States, and justifiably so in the early days, in being predominantly associated with or identified as African American. One is not suggesting that this is no longer the case, but that there is additionally now a social class, nonracial dimension to it with the emergence of non-Black Hip Hop artists like the Beastie Boys (2006 VH1 Hip Hop Award Honorees) and Eminem (Marshall Mathers, III), allegedly the largest selling rap artist at the turn of the 20th century. The former and Vanilla Ice preceded Eminem as relatively successful White Hip Hop artists. The participation of the latter represents both ethnicity and class as legitimate identity variables. In a sense this claim is validated by the issues that underlie the narrative of the Hollywood blockbuster *8 Mile* (2002) which explores a rapper's (Eminem) struggle in coming to terms with his social circumstance and status in Detroit (cf. Kanye West's Fort Minor comment 2007).[4] In spite of belonging to different racial cohorts, all these artists still shared membership of an underclass in the political economy of the United States.

Considering that Hip Hop as a genre is now a global social practice and product, as the studies in this volume demonstrate, the issue arises as to whether or not race and class politics are on the agenda worldwide. Does Hip Hop convey the voice of a racial underclass around the world? If so, what is the nature and history of that underclass and how may it be identified? And if not, whose voice does it convey, and what purpose does it serve in a place like Nigeria? There cannot be one straight and simple answer to these questions considering on one hand the differences between the various contexts as we have already noted above. For instance, for MC Subliminal (Israeli Jew) and DAM

(Palestinian Arab-Israeli) Hip Hop presents a forum for engaging with the politics of nation, ethnicity, and religion within the state of Israel. However, in the wider context of Western versus Middle East politics, religion more than race and ethnicity could be applied to the Hip Hop produced by these two groups. On the other hand, the growing entwinement of global destinies so that all humanity is at once involved and implicated irrespective of location, as the debates on global warming and terrorism illustrate, introduce a completely different perspective to these questions.

Similarly, Hip Hop's contention with race in North America does not extend to Hip Hop communities in Africa, except perhaps in South Africa. It certainly is not the case in Nigeria where ethnicity rather than race is the relevant variable in the body-politik. The 30-month civil war of 1967 to 1970 had been ethnicity fueled. The complexity of the identity issue can be seen in the description of East African rapper Big Pin (Chrispin Mwangale) as the "King of Luo rap music," who was quoted as saying that "At the end of the day what matters is that I did my country proud" (http://www.AllHipHop.com, accessed April 16, 2006). The description of Chrispin Mwangale as the proclaimed "King of Luo rap music" invokes ethnicity as an identity variable for describing his art (Luo rap) while the artist himself drew attention to his national affiliation.

This is not to say that one excludes the other. They are copresent though not with the same degree of salience. They belong on different rungs on a *hierarchy of identities* (see Omoniyi, 2006b for an elaboration of this).

In contrast to the Mwangale example, Nigerian rapper, 2-Shotz, introduces an additional level of identification, a regional one, describing himself and Ruggedman, his collaborator, as "Ruggedman and I, Abia State's finest" in the lyrics of his song "Nna Men." Abia is one of the 36 states of the Nigerian federation; it is located in the southeast of the country. Ironically, in the same song 2-Shotz declares that he is "made in Alaba," a commercial suburb of sprawling Lagos City in the southwest, renowned mainly for trade in imported goods, hence its name, the Alaba International Market. Alaba is populated mainly by the Igbo settlers who are originally from the southeast. They are the third largest ethnic group in Nigeria, after the Hausa and Yoruba, with a population of about 18 million (*Ethnologue*, 2005 web edition). The declarative "made in Alaba," resonates with Ice-Cube's self-tagging remark that "My music is a product of who I am and where I came from. I'm made in America. I'm not from Mars or nowhere else" (cited Best & Kellner, 1999, p. 1). It is difficult to rule out the existence of a dialogue between the local and the global that enables 2-Shotz to appropriate and deploy intertextuality as a resource, considering the marking of Alaba as a commercial hub which itself signals certain ways of relating to the global *financescape* (à la Appadurai, 1996). There is also a complex social underclass in Nigeria that comprises youth from both middle- and working class-backgrounds. The economic downturn of the 1980s and extended periods of military dictatorship, World Bank and IMF-imposed structural adjustment programs destroyed the Nigerian middle class, part of the membership of which brain-drained and became global citizens. Still there were large numbers that couldn't leave. Large-scale unemployment (and some were unemployable) bred discontent and anger among young persons, some of whom channeled their frustration into creative enterprises including Hip Hop.

Postcolonial relations also need to be considered here. According to rapper AY (African Yoruba) "there is one painful truth: any form of hip-hop and R'n'B that isn't in English and is from outside of America is regarded as second class" (cited in http://www.bbc .co.uk/africabeyond/africaonyourstreet/hosts/jjc/18567.shtml; accessed April 18, 2008. A Hip Hop/postcolonial identity cross-analysis is as interesting as it is tricky considering that Hip Hop in colonizer nations like Britain and France has a subordinate status to U.S. Hip Hop through a narrative of origin and scale, implicit in which is a reflection of the relative statuses of two subgroups of the Black diaspora vis-à-vis the structure of the global political economy. The asymmetrical relationship between former colonizers (Britain and France) and their former colonies does not extend to Hip Hop Nation Language (HHNL) with the U.S. role-modeling globally. For instance, almost exclusively, rap artists and groups invited to participate in Hip Hop festivals in Africa, and Nigeria in particular, have been drawn from the United States. The official launch of MTV-Base Africa in April 2005 at which U.S. rappers Ludacris, and Will Smith together with DJ Jazzy Jeff performed alongside local artists in Abuja and Johannesburg respectively are an affirmation of this axis of influence. Factoring in the postcolonial experience introduces a further dimension to how we must look at HHNL in Africa and try to understand the intra- and interlanguage, intergenerational and intracultural variations that are discernible. Under a regime of oppositions, African Hip Hop artists can simultaneously be discursively other-constructed on the periphery of a global mainstream while they are self-constructing themselves as the essential core from which the dominant culture flow derived in their own versions of the narrative of origin. This ideological battling is carried on by deploying linguistic resources in constructing a series of propositions as we saw with claim-making in the narratives of origin discussion above. The processes entailed will become manifest in our discussion of language choice and identity in Nigerian Hip Hop.

NIGERIAN HIP HOP

There are convergences to and divergences from HHN-Global. The local is facilitated through divergences while the global norms are upheld through convergence by the various Hip Hop Nation Language constituencies. By HHNL I am referring to the totality of the codifying and signifying practices of the Hip Hop Nation that are indexical of the nation's identities. Consequently, HHN-Global is a multilingual, multiple, and multifarious codes community (cf. Alim, 2006; this volume). The naming practice is traditional

HHNL in most cases following the pattern MC This or MC That, or as we have in the data, Weird MC, 2-Shotz, P-Square. But while the adoption of aliases or street names constitutes a shared social practice of the HHNL-Global community, individual names may index local street realities at an interpretive level. There are postmodern tattoo parlors such as the Galleria on Victoria Island in Lagos, which are different in content from those associated with indigenous aesthetics. Another of the representations of Hip Hop culture is its association with affluence. The local dimension is in the size of the bling which is directly proportional to the size of the host economy. In other words, there are different economies of scale such that affluence in Naira may not necessarily translate into affluence in dollars.[5] Now let us look at the divergences in practice that set Hip Hop Nation-Nigeria apart from other varieties in Hip Hop Nation-Global.

Local Tenor

Hip Hop "a way of life" and "rap" one of its expressive modes seem to be synonymous with the focus on "Hip Hop language" in tracking the local tenor of the global. While it is undesirable to completely discountenance the importance of origin, whether myth or reality, in any consideration of Hip Hop identity, the more interesting task is to explore the ways in which members of various global Hip Hop communities furnish them-selves with a Hip Hop history and ideology that demarginalizes them and situates them squarely in the center. This pursuit of a local Hip Hop identity agenda is evident in this response to my e-mail enquiry by Vectortheviper (aka Lanre Ogunmefun) a Nigerian MC, winner of MNet's Channel O's "Storm the Mic" competition in 2006 and one half of the Badder Boyz:

Extract 1

> sorry bro,
> been really busy with school. yes there are battles in Nigeria, and vector has been undisputed in his battle ecapade [sic] for ever (ask channel O). Grafiti in Nigeria is crazy. check the walls of igbosere street close to city hall, lagos island. and in unilag there are tons of Mc's who do nothing but battle every friday. they range from your mama jokes to you yourself. Brutally, people kill each other here. we got game here in Nigeria nd i hope u'r proud of where ur from now. holla laters.

A number of interesting issues are raised here, including the writing convention adopted which is different from that learned in the formal school system but similar to established global forms in e-mailing and texting conventions. The manner in which these conventions index forms of identity is beginning to attract researchers' attention (see Blommaert & Omoniyi, 2006). We deduce from Vectortheviper's claim that in Nigeria Hip Hop entails more than simply rapping and includes other characteristic elements including graffiti and MC battles (freestyling). Interestingly, when I asked Vectortheviper why there was no graffiti on the University campus where there is evidence of other Hip Hop identity markers, he explains that "it is against the law." This conformity with the law and conventional norm seems to depart from the known stereotype of North American practice.

Couture

Even if one accedes to a theory of the spread of Hip Hop from the United States, still in sharp contrast to the U.S. context, the identities we discern in the HHNL community in Africa are not about "representing the streets" in the U.S. sense because Africa's streets for now have a different subcultural topography and belong to urchins also called *Area Boys* in Lagos. Rather, the HHNL community comprises politically conscious youths liberated by education and critical of the establishment. They display a different kind of angst; a disdain for maladministration, plundering of state resources, and a resultant harsh economic climate that have left them roughshod and battered. This informs MC Vectortheviper's deconstruction of some of Hip Hop's cultural symbols such as baggy jeans and baggy shirts in an interview. According to him, these items are derogated and perceived as either one-size-fits-all prison clothing (not cut to size) or "papa-dash-me" (hand-downs from father or older siblings). This critical view of fashion enables us to explore the moral and ideological concerns subsumed in its interpretation. Besides, the growth in indigenous popular youth fashion that incorporates local textile and design also instantiates divergence. Thus, in clothing styles, HHN–Nigeria contrasts with Robin D.G. Kelley's suggestion cited by Pennycook and Mitchell (this volume) that Hip Hop artists outside of the United States "mirror African American urban youth styles." The mirror is a euphemism for imitation. This difference in values and views on fashion further isolates rap as the shared practice at the core of Hip Hop identity.

Attitudes to Exogenous Standards

Attitude is a significant factor in our treatment and analysis of Hip Hop. Commenting on the nonpopularity of Hip Hop in Malawi, producer Mike Munthali (Dynamike/DJ Lick) remarked in an online article that "Hip Hop is a rejected art in the country mainly because the original proponents of the genre are associated with violence, drugs and crime. It is this stereotyped view that has mainly affected the growth of this music" (cited in http://www.bbc.co.uk/africabeyond/africaonyourstreet/hosts/jjc/18567.shtml; accessed April 18, 2008); youth are more critical of these; the myth of the native speaker and the redefinition of constituency—those we seem to have ratified by having changed between the generations.[6] 2-Shotz articulates his preference for Nigerian Pidgin in "Nna-Men" (featuring Ruggedman) when he says "He no fit yarn fòné pass American, so I decide to do am naija style." Fòné is a colloquial metaphor for prestigious standard native English varieties, especially American and British. Thus his claim may suggest that within the HHN Nigerian community, the latter are recognized as marking an external identity.

Positive attitude toward the local is also reflected in the choice of samples. Samples are the classics that MCs and DJs lay their poetry on. While the macrostructure is a global practice, localization is effected through the samples. In Nigeria, for instance the popular samples include Fela Anikulapo-Kuti, Orlando Owoh, I.K. Dairo, Ebenezer Obey, Haruna Ishola, Olisadebey, from music genres as diverse as Afrobeat, High Life, Fuji, and Apala. Afrobeat is now being sampled beyond the shores of Nigeria in London dance clubs.[7]

Language Choice

I return here to my earlier reference to linguistic resources. While multilingualism is widespread and growing as a result of global cultural flows, it seems that in some environments Hip Hop artists deploy linguistic convergence in performing in the dominant official language of the cosmopolis. This choice ensures optimum efficiency of delivery in terms of outreach and access to an educated community. However, divergence serves a more liberal purpose as demonstrated in Ngugi wa Thiong'o's switch from English to his native Gikuyu in order to reach the grassroots or indigenous peasantry and extensively undermine the political class as an act of subversion (Fox, 2003). Nigerian Afro-beat legend and social critic Fela Anikulapo-Kuti achieved this through Pidgin. Thus language choice can be a conscious act of political subversion and resistance (cf. Mitchell, 2000). Nigerian Hip Hop artists as social critics and activists explore language choice as a multilingual skill and in the process establish for themselves a creative patch and a legitimate nonsubordinate local identity within the global Hip Hop constituency. The multilingual Nigerian HHNL community facilitates this negotiation and construction of identity through language choice. The artists explore what Bucholtz (2003) referred to as strategic essentialism (see also Hall, 1996; Spivak, 1990), in other words, the manner of their use of ethnic languages departs from the traditional pattern of marking ethnolinguistic identity, and yet serves as a difference marking tool in relation to other constituencies around the world.

These artists flag up their membership of a new generation of Nigerians by rapping in multiple indigenous languages including those that are not necessarily their mother tongues, so that language crossing (Rampton, 1995; also Lee, 2006) facilitates the construction of a national/regional rather than an ethnolinguistic identity. In doing this they set up what may be construed as a pan-Nigerian identity that is an ideological departure from the kind of establishment identity we may associate with Nigeria's "English-as-official language" policy. All of the artists in the data perform multilingual rap with Nigerian Pidgin as the common denominator. The pervasive use of Nigerian Pidgin which is accessible to elite and nonelite alike and across ethnic groups undermines the description of English as the language of unity in early sociolinguistic research in Nigeria. The latter is often cited in justifying the official language policy.

Both Weird MC and D'Banj sing in English, Pidgin English, and Yoruba extensively. 2-Shotz, for instance, raps in Nigerian Pidgin and Igbo but predominantly in the former as we find in the lyrics of his song "Nna-Men"—ft. Ruggedman where he criticizes his peers who adopt an American accent of English. He remarks that: "He no fit rap *fòné* pass American, so I decide to do am naija style." The same criticism is echoed in a blog posting by AbaBoy on the http://www.naijajams.com site dated September 22, 2005, which subsequently attracted 52 responses:

> Listening to some of our hip-hop stars rapping in English (worst still—fake American twang) can sometimes turn into a very excruciating encounter. I am not trying to cut a critical remark just for its sake; the same will also apply to an American artist that decides to dive into the highlife scene. The artist will have to be very good to make it not sound like crap. To cut a long story short, Nigerian hip-hop stars should mc in either Pidgin English or their local language—cut the fake Yankee drawl. By doing this, some of them may perhaps achieve restricted crossover appeal, but more importantly they will essentially reduce the ability to make others cringe. Unfamiliar artists picking fights with world-renowned superstars on planes in Nigeria wouldnt really do the trick. And the Videos. ...[8]

In Africa where literacy rates are abysmally low according to World Bank statistics, Hip Hop has been deployed to articulate resistance to a dominant elite mainstream. But it is also difficult to describe it as the property of a social underclass when we consider that some of its contemporary exponents come from privileged, educated, and upwardly mobile socioeconomic backgrounds. The artists whose lyrics inform my discussion have a minimum of post-16 education. In other words, they have at least secondary school qualification and in some cases they have had tertiary education, that is, attended a polytechnic or university even though in some cases they may not necessarily have stayed on to graduate, having dropped out by choice in full realization that they wanted to pursue a career in entertainment.

Nigerian Hip Hop, as is the case with other African varieties, deploys a multilingual repertoire with the following discernible patterns:

1. Narrative in Language X and chorus in Language Y;
2. Call in Language X and Response in Language Y;
3. Narrative X and rap in Y;
4. Sample in X and remix in Y
5. Narrative in both Languages X and Y and chorus in X or Y or XY.

Such repertoires are both a property of urban multilingual performers as well as an indicator of groups that comprise individuals drawn from more than one ethnolinguistic community. In the song "If Life" by the multiethnic group Plantashun Boiz (2001), the song is rendered in English, the chorus is in Yoruba while the rap is in Pidgin (see extract below):

Extract 2

A: song extract
(i)
That is what I've got for you
Cos I need you in my life
All the way all the sky ???
I can see it in your eyes

(ii)
We'll be loving one on one
Till we see the morning sun
Girl it's you that I want

B: Chorus [in Yoruba]
Baby iwo ni mo nferan/Baby, it's you I like
Iwo gangan ni mo feran/It's you specifically I like
Iwo ni mo nfe o, girl,/It's you I desire
Iwo gangan ni mo feran 2x/It's you specifically I like

C: Rap extract [Pidgin]
After I check am na you be my desire/
I no dey tell you dis because I wan dey talk am/This is no empty talk
I dey tell you dis based on say na so I dey mean am/I say it because I mean it
And I mean am
So mek you try to understand my point of view/Make an effort
Day and night in fact *I just dey think of you/*
Na you I want and na you I get to have/It's you I want and you I've got to have
Na you dey make cry/You make me cry
Na you sef dey make me laugh ha ha/You also make me laugh
Remaining people na just to see/Others a mere vision
Just *maka* the simple fact say na you I need ["because" in Igbo]

Self-styled "revolutionary rapper" Ruggedman's (2006) "Ruggedy Baba" samples the rhythm of a traditional Edo folksong for his Yoruba chorus, while laying his rap in Pidgin and colloquial American English. Indeed he interrogates the presumed conflict between keepin' it real, language choice, and identity. Ruggedman asserts that:

Extract 3

From Nigeria the world only know Juju, Fuji and Afro beat
But we all know hip hop is running the streets

Wetin go make them know where your music come from [wetin = what will]
In the long run
Na the fussion of grammar, your slang and your mother tongue [na = is]

In the third verse he touches more directly on the subject of identity through an implicit binary opposition of Oyibo (European or White) and "your own people,"

Extract 4

Now let me address this issue of keeping it real
The one subject wey I go say dey make me vex still [that I'll say still vexes me]
Cos of how some emcees feel
About these three words whenever they open their mouths
Look my guy
I no fit shout [I can't shout]
I go only ask what's keeping it real? [I shall only ask]
Is it singing or rapping like Oyibo or doing what you and your own people can feel?
Some say I sell out because I do dance track they call me Baraje master
Forgetting it got me fame and money faster
Forget the latter I'll move to the next chapter faster
I'm just speaking my mind playing my controversial character
The way I've been known to do when I spit it straight out to you
You better recognize a real brother that's reaching out to you
Speaking pidjin and dance tracks no mean say I no keep am real
That's just me so how else I wan be to be real?
My rules are spit in whatever language but make sense
I did that and I've been hot ever since
(http://www.lyricsmode.com/lyrics/r/rugged_man/ruggedy_baba.html)

The same pattern is evident in Jazzman Olofin's "Angelina Remix" which is done in Pidgin, English, and Yoruba. Closely linked with the employment of multiple languages is the phenomenon of codeswitching which I shall discuss next.

Codeswitching
Codeswitching is an identity marker for the Nigerian brand within the global Hip Hop community. Following Alvarez-Cáccamo (2002), I have made the case elsewhere (Omoniyi, 2005) for a reconceptualization of codeswitching so that it accommodates an expanded category that includes not just language in the narrow sense of our understanding of communicative competence in sociolinguistics or discourse competence in sociopragmatics, but also modes of dressing, walking, and other patterns of social behavior. With particular reference to fusion music or remix, it is a relatively straightforward case to

make since the basic consideration still is language of the lyrics rendition. However, since Hip Hop is an entire "way of life" with definite and recognizable cultural paraphernalia, we need to examine the totality of its ways of encoding identity, including the talk, the walk, its entire fashion accoutrements including bling; that is, flashy jewelry of all kinds: neck chains, dental grills that adorn Hip Hop artists.

Trilingual codeswitching is a major feature of Nigeria's dialect of HHNL. All three artists have a sample of three languages in their songs. Weird MC has Yoruba, English, and Pidgin with Igbo borrowings. D'Banj has English, Pidgin, and Yoruba, and 2-Shotz has Pidgin and Igbo. The following excerpts taken from the lyrics of "Ijoya" and "Mr. Olopa" by Weird MC and D'Banj respectively illustrate this point:

Extract 5
From Weird MC's "Ijoya" [Yoruba: time to dance]

Yes, it's time to dance—dance	[American English accent] We own the
Awa la ni ijo	
Ah trust us, we OWN dis dance	
Awa la ni ijo	
Na we getam	[Pidgin: We own it]
Awa la ni *gini*	[Yoruba/*Igbo*: We own *what*?]
Awa la ni ijo	
Osigini	[Igbo: What did he say?]
Awa la ni ijo	

Extract 6
From D'Banj's "Mr Olopa"   [Yoruba: Mr. Policeman]

When we reached there stori don change [When we got there the story changed]
Dey even say I dey smoke high grade [They alleged that I smoked cannabis]
Said it's some cigarette
No na cigiweed [No it's cannabis in cigarette wrap]
Can I make a phonecall?
If I slap you, you go fall [If I slap you, you'll fall]
They charge me for robbery
Dey even charge Don Jazzy for accessory [They charged Don Jazzy as an accessory]
Before I know wetin dey happen [Before I realized what was happening]
All of dem wey dey there join hands again [They all joined in beating me up]

In the microanalysis of codeswitching, focus is on the structural pattern of the blend with a view to producing a descriptive grammar. However, with regard to codeswitching and identity in a macroanalytical framework, account is taken of the bi/multilingual repertoire and language choice patterns. In relation to Nigerian Hip Hop, codeswitching is both an identity construction tool, and a "language form." The social and political factors that determine the nature of collaboration between languages in codeswitching usage are significant. In other words, colonial history, current language planning, and policy issues and how these impact language practices and attitudes across contexts come into play. In the two extracts above collaboration is between Nigerian major languages: English, Yoruba, Pidgin, and Igbo. This language use practice is already extensively explored in Afrobeat music which Fela Anikulapo-Kuti deployed in over two decades of social commentary and political activism in Nigeria. Thus codeswitching in this mode is conceptually an ideological discursive tool rather than a mere combination of the resources of two languages. It serves Hip Hop's signifying and representing functions.

Working within a modified Three Circles paradigm (Kachru, 1990), one view is that oppositional and asymmetrical (native versus nonnative) relationships abound while an alternative view fueled by an ideology of resistance rejects the existence of unequal partnerships. HHNL is ideologically liberal hence the ease with which it is globalized. Competing myths of origin in the Bronx or precolonial Africa or contemporary urban inner-city all feed the oppositional viewpoint. However, this is only a productive line of inquiry to the extent that it can help our understanding of the complex processes of signifying offered by global rap and Hip Hop. The alternative framework I offer in relation to postcolonial contexts of signification is to conceive of Hip Hop identities as belonging to a global complex within which performers may move freely for whatever reasons they considered salient in the moments of identification in which they find and attempt to define themselves. For the sub-Sahara African HHNL community several frames of reference exist and these frames are interconnected in complex and interesting ways. Some of the more obvious ones include: Anglophone versus francophone, nationality, religion, ethnicity, home versus diasporic, global versus local connections, performing outside, collaborating with "global" or U.S. rappers, etc.

The function of codeswitching is to produce *appropriate* alignments and stances or positionings. These positionings and alignments would be in relation to any of the identity values listed above. Let us consider the following excerpt from Weird MC's interview with Naijajams.com (NJ):

Extract 7

NJ: You've been in the music business for some time now—how has the Nigerian music scene changed since you began performing?

WMC: It's evolved into something really exciting it's unbelievable all *eyes are on Nigeria* right now *we have to let the world know* what's up it's time to *put us on the map.* There's more quality than quantity, *artistes are* putting out great material.

The interviewer's question suggests identity options which the interviewee may or may not take up in her response. On this occasion she claims the offered positioning through an exploration of the pronominal system. "It," referring to "the Nigerian music scene" transposed from object to subject position reveals interviewee's acceptance. The moments within the stretch of utterance at which the italicized information were uttered constitute moments of identification in which Weird MC first isolates the Nigerian Hip Hop community as the object of global gaze, then by choosing the collective "we" and "us" she declares her membership of the community and assumes the role of spokesperson for the group. Weird MC's modest Ego as an objective commentator attributes "great material" to a plural third person, so that her inclusion in the category is only guaranteed if we return to the interviewer's initial ascription to her of a performer's identity. Let us attempt a similar analysis using an excerpt from Weird MC's "Ijoya" from the album *After da Storm*:

Extract 8
[Call and Response]

> Yes, it's time to dance—[American accent]
> We own the dance
> Awa la ni ijo   [Yoruba—"we own the dance"]
> *Ah trust us, we OWN dis dance*
> Awa la ni ijo
> Na we getam   [Igbo: What did he say?]
> Awa la ni *gini*   [Igbo word meaning *what*]
> Awa la ni ijo
> *Osigini*   [Igbo: He said what?]
> Awa la ni ijo
> Awa la ni jo o
> Awa la ni ijo
> *Yo*, take me home. [Yo: global trope]

The above refrain with which "Ijoya" ends flags up a coconstructed "We–Us" identity between Weird MC and her backup singers. It consists of claim assertions by Weird MC in the lead that are echoed and reinforced by the backup singers. From the line "Awa la ni gini?" to the end, traditional African "call and response" is utilized so that both the lead and backup singers ratify each other and by so doing imply their group solidarity. What is interesting here is that a claim is made to a specific dance—"this dance"—which within the wider system of genre form and brand marking may be regarded as an implicit reference to the local HHNL community. This claim is especially reinforced by the artist's use of Yoruba, English, Pidgin, and Igbo all within a space of 13 lines of refrain.

Another closely related and significant point to make is that the growing practice of using the indigenous languages including Pidgin in the HHNL Nigerian community raises the profile and status of languages that are otherwise subordinated through institutional language in education policies to ex-colonial languages; even more so considering that this is happening among a crucial and vibrant segment of the Nigerian populace, educated youths. 2-Shotz, whom I presented in my introduction, raps almost exclusively in Nigerian Pidgin (Naija style) and claims that he does so by choice for the functional purpose of ensuring that his fans understand him. It challenges the idea of a homogeneous HHNL community and reiterates the diversity within the community.

Further Evidence of Transcultural Flow
Omoniyi (2006a) identified cross-referencing as one of the discursive strategies employed in authenticating their reappropriations. This practice may also be seen as orchestrating a local–global dialogue, exchange, and interpenetration. These are facilitated by participation in transnational events such as the MOBO (Music of Black Origin) Awards, MTV Europe Awards which bring together artists from several countries sharing the same performance and discursive space (see also Pennycook, 2007). In addition to physical collaboration such as these, a borderless global media facilitates interpenetration so that referencing draws on not just the physical/material experience but also a virtual reality within which it is possible to conceptualize membership of a community, the Global Hip Hop Nation. The consequence is an expanded reality that includes local and global references. Nigerian rapper Mode 9 says in Elbow Room, "I'm hungry like snoop in the deep cover of death row" in clear reference to U.S. rapper, Snoop Dogg and Death Row Records. Perhaps the most obvious evidence of transnational culture flow lies in the impact that Nigerian popular culture, including Hip Hop has been having on language use around Africa instantiated especially by Nigerian English forms in Uganda.

Bridging
Bridging is a consequence of cross-referencing and it is achieved in a number of ways. The most obvious of these would be the practice of claiming or tracing links between established artists in one Hip Hop community and those in another community who may themselves not have declared the same publicly. This is often a periphery practice. In other words, within an existing global hierarchical structure that privileges the North, the South lays claims to North artists. The flip side of this coin is when North artists perform on a southern platform and declare that they had a very emotional experience and a sense of home-coming and connecting with Africa. The Africahit Music TV website ran a story on October 11, 2007 titled "The rapper Chamillionaire is Nigerian!" which traced the rapper Chamillonaire's (real name, Hakeem Seriki) roots to Oyo State, Nigeria.[9] Similarly, http://www.Nairaland.com an online forum, carried a discussion on the topic

"Is Nas Truly Nigerian?" for a whole year December 4, 2005 to December 20, 2006 in which 51 commentators participated.[10]

Another way that bridging is achieved is simply by allusions, analogies, and comparisons that incorporate values and referents from both local and global constituencies. For example, Hip Hop group P-Square (ft. Alaye) in the lyrics of their song "Temptation," say in Pidgin:

Extract 9

> All my friends dey call me number ten, [dey = habitual "be"]
> cos I dey play like Okocha,
> Dey score like Ronaldinho

Finally, bridging is institutionally achieved through the expansion of award categories to recognize, include, and validate forms of Hip Hop from the "periphery" in previously Western confined industry competitions. Such expansions and validations in turn also consolidate and change regional into global events thus raising their profile. The MOBO (Music of Black Origin) Awards and the MTV Europe Music Awards, both of which now have a Best African Act category, exemplify this. Nigerian Hip Hop artist, Tu Face/2 Face (Innocent Idibia) became the first African to win both these awards in 2005 and 2007 respectively. D'Banj was named the UN Youth Ambassador for Peace in 2007 and Best African Act at MTV EMA 2007. Such international forum appearances complement local events such as the Star Mega Jam organized by multinationals like Nigerian Breweries Plc. The This Day Independence Day Music Festival, also an annual event, takes international stars to Nigeria. Rapper Ruggedman notes in his bio:

Extract 10

> Now I run my own label in Nigeria "RUGGED RECORDS" Have performed alongside KC n Jojo, Guru, Sean Paul, Wyclef Jean, Akon, Wayne Wonder, Ja Rule, Kevin Little, Maxie Priest, Ruggedman's been performing all over Nigeria right now and is Nigeria's most wanted rap act. (http://www.ruggedmanonline.com/main.html)

The list includes some of the many U.S.-based artists that have performed on these bills and brought the global to the local.

CONCLUSION

That African Hip Hop or Nigerian Hip Hop is thriving or that U.S. Hip Hop has a trans-national pedigree which sets it on a pedestal may not be contentious judging by the pervasiveness of Americanisms in varieties of Hip Hop outside the United States. What is becoming contentious is the relationship between the varieties because this has direct implications for how we construct the global flow of Hip Hop culture and identity. In the foregoing sections I have taken a critical look at two contrasting accounts; one of a sole source of dispersal for Hip Hop and the other of the possibility of multiple origins both equally valid and varying by teller. I cited the evident diversity in form, content, and purpose to question claims that there are two Hip Hops: U.S. Hip Hop on one hand and its imitations on the other. I have suggested that there is a universal template to account for similarities while local cultural topographies create differences between the varieties. I presented discursive strategies and tools with which Nigerian Hip Hop artists construct their local identities while situating themselves within HHNL-Global. These include language choice, multilingual rap repertoires, codeswitching, fashion, social criticism, and ideology.

NOTES

1 I thank the editors for their comments on an earlier draft. Full transcript of interview conducted in September 2005 is available at: http://www.naijajams.com/weird-mc-interview

2 Abdulrazaq Bello aka JJC is a producer, broadcaster (BBC's "Africa on Your Street" program), and rapper with the award-winning Afropean/Nigerian Hip Hop group JJC & 419 Squad.

3 Afrolution Records is a London-based record producing and marketing company set up in 2006 to specifically to bring African Hip Hop to the world.

4 http://www.inthenews.co.uk/music/types-music/rap/kanye-attacks-white-adoption-HipHop-$15051097.htm

5 "The Infinity Jeep may not only have cruise control, a navigation system, keyless entry, trip/mileage computer and worth Millions of Naira, it must have a bug disperse censor as it simul-taneously caught Sunny Neji, Faze and even Blackface (assumed unfortunate of the outmoded Plantashun Boiz). They bought one of this 4 wheel drive each last week." Muma Gee's "N15 Million' Infinity Jeep –another point of reference." (http://www.hiphopworldmagazine.com/newsx.aspx?newsid=126)

6 http://hiphoparchive.org/thecircle/?p=495

7 http://www.npr.org/templates/story/story.php?storyId=1115091

8 AbaBoy is described on his website as "born in Manchester, brought up in Aba, living in London and still loving Nigeria' [http://www.naijajams.com/thoughts-on-the-nigerian-Hip

Hop-scene-part-1]. By "unfamiliar artistes picking fights …' AbaBoy is referring to Eedris Abdulkareem the Nigerian rapper who caused a fracas at the Lagos airport in December 2004 when he attempted to engage 50 Cent in a fight following which the latter broke off his engagement with Nigerian Breweries, organizers of Star Mega Jam and returned to the USA.

9 http://www.africahit.com/news/index.php?mod=article&cat=Nigeria&article=3288&page_order=1&act

10 http://www.nairaland.com/nigeria/topic-3541.0.html

DISCOGRAPHY

2-Shotz (2005). "Nna-Men" from the album *2-Shotz: Original Copy*, Umunnamu Music.

Daara J (2005). Boomerang. BMG, WRR, Wrasse, Pony Canyon.

D'Banj (n.d.). "Loke" from the *Run Down Funk U Up* album. Written and produced by D'Banj and Don Jazzy for Mo' Hits Records.

D'Banj (n.d.) "Mr Olopa" from the album *No Long Thing*. Mo' Hits Records.

Jazzman Olofin (2006). "Angelina remix" in *Mr. Funky*. Storm Records.

Lágbájá a.k.a. Bisade Ologunde (2005). "Afrocalypso" in *Africano...mother of groove*. Motherlan' Music.

Mode 9/Modenine (2005). "Elbow Room" Question Mark Entertainment.

Plantashun Boiz (2001). "If Life" in *The biginning BODY & SOUL*. Dove Entertainment.

P-Square (ft. Alaye) (2005). "Temptation" in *Get Squared*. Square Records.

Ruggedman (2006). "Ruggedy Baba," title track. Rugged Style Records.

Weird MC (2005). Ijoya from the album *After Da Storm*. 0907 Entertainment/Ahbu Ventures.

REFERENCES

Alim, S. A. (2006). *Roc the mic right: The language of hip hop culture*. London: Routledge.

Alvarez-Cáccamo, C. (2002, October 22–26). *Introduction: Class and ideology in code-switching research*. Paper presented at the International Symposium on Bilingualism, Vigo.

Appadurai, A. (1996). *Modernity at large: Cultural dimensions of globalization*. Minneapolis: University of Minnesota Press.

Batey, A. (2003, July 26). Home grown—profile—British hip-hop—music. *The Times*,. Retrieved April 18, 2008, from http://entertainment.timesonline.co.uk/tol/arts_and_entertainment/music/article845985.ece

Best, S., & Kellner, D. (1999). Rap, Black rage and racial difference. *Enculturation, 2*(2), 1–23. Retrieved April 18, 2008, from http://enculturation.gmu.edu/2_2/best-kellner.html

Blommaert, J. (1999). *Language ideological debates*. Berlin: Mouton de Gruyter.

Blommaert, J., & Omoniyi, T. (2006). Email fraud: Language, technology and the indexicals of globalization. *Social Semiotics,16*(4), 573–605.

Bourdieu, P. (1991). *Language and symbolic power*. Cambridge, UK: Polity Press

Broder, C. J. (2006). Hip hop and identity politics in Japanese popular culture. *Asia Pacific Perspectives: An Electronic Journal, 6*(2), 39–43.

Bucholtz, M. (2003). Sociolinguistic nostalgia and the authentication of identity. *Journal of Sociolinguistics, 7* (3), 398–416.

Condry, I. (2006). *Hip hop Japan*. Chapel Hill, NC: Duke University Press.

Dundes, A., Leach, J. W., & Özkök, B. (1972). The strategy of Turkish boys' verbal dueling rhymes. In J. J. Gumperz & D. Hymes (Eds.), *Directions in sociolinguistics: The ethnography of communication* (pp. 130–160). Oxford: Blackwell.

Fox, R. E. (2003). Engaging Ngugi. *Research in African Literatures, 34* (4), 115–128.

Gilroy, P. (1993). *The Black Atlantic*. Cambridge, MA: Harvard University Press.

Gordon, R. G., Jr. (Ed.). (2005). *Ethnologue: Languages of the world*, 5th ed.. Dallas, Tex.: SIL International. Online version: http://www.ethnologue.com/.

Hall, S. (1996). Cultural identity and diaspora. In J. Rutherford (Ed.), *Identity, community, Culture, difference* (pp. 222–237). London: Lawrence & Wishart.

Japanese Hip-Hop: Imitation or Art?, (2006, December 24). Features, 8. Retrieved April 18, 2008, from http://www.taipeitimes.com/News/feat/archives/2006/12/24/2003341835

Kachru, B. (1990). *The alchemy of English: The spread, functions, and models of non-native Englishes*. Urbana: University of Illinois Press.

Kanneh, K. (1998). *African identities: Race, nation and culture in ethnography, Pan-Africanism and Black literatures*. London: Routledge.

Lee, J. S. (2006). Crossing and crossers in East Asian pop music: Korea and Japan. *World Englishes, 25*(2), 235–250.

Mitchell, T. (2000, Fall). Doin' damage in my native language: The use of resistance vernaculars in hip hop in France, Italy and Aotearoa/New Zealand. *Popular Music and Society, 24*(3), 41–54.

Omoniyi, T. (1995). Song-lashing as a communicative strategy in Yoruba interpersonal conflicts. *Text, 15*(2), 299–315.

Omoniyi, T. (2005). Towards a retheorization of codeswitching. *TESOL Quarterly*, 729–734.

Omoniyi, T. (2006a). Hip hop through the world Englishes lens: A response to globalization. In J. S. Lee & Y. Kachru (Eds.), *World Englishes: Symposium on world Englishes in popular culture, 25*(2), 195–208.

Omoniyi, T. (2006b). Hierarchy of identities: A theoretical approach. In T. Omoniyi & G. White (Eds.), *The sociolinguistics of identity* (pp. 11–33). London: Continuum Press.

Omoniyi, T., & White, G. (Eds.). (2006). *The sociolinguistics of identity*. London: Continuum Books.

Pennycook, A. (2007). *Global Englishes and transcultural flows*. London: Routledge

Rampton, B. (1995). *Crossing: Language and ethnicity among adolescents*. London: Longman

Spivak, G. (1990). *The post-colonial critic: Interviews, strategies, dialogues*. New York: Routledge

Toop, D. (1984). *The rap attack: African jive to New York hip hop*. London: Pluto Press.

Winterton, B. (2006, December 2). Japanese hip hop, imitation or art. *Taipei Times*, p. 18. Retrieved April 18, 2008, from http://www.taipeitimes.com/News/feat/archives/2006/12/24/2003341835

"Respect for Da Chopstick Hip Hop"

The Politics, Poetics, and Pedagogy of Cantonese Verbal Art

in Hong Kong

By Angel Lin

> My message is to ask people to reflect, to use their brains to think and their
> hearts to feel—MC Yan.

INTRODUCTION: THE ARRIVAL OF HIP HOP ONTO THE MUSIC SCENE IN HONG KONG

The music scene in Hong Kong has been dominated by Cantopop (Cantonese pop songs) since the mid-1970s. The early prominent Cantopop lyricists and singers such as Sam Hui were legendary in laying the foundation of the genre and the tradition of the lyrical styles which appeal to the masses through the rise of local Cantonese cinema and television. With easy-listening melody and simple lyrics about ordinary working-class people's plight, Sam Hui's music and lyrical style marked the genesis of a new popular music form in Hong Kong, known as Cantopop (Erni, 2007). Cantopop has arisen as an indigenous music genre that the majority of Hong Kong people identity with. It has served as "a strategic cultural form to delineate a local identity, vis-à-vis the old British colonial and mainland Chinese identities" (McIntyre, Cheng, & Zhang, 2002, p. 217).

However, Cantopop since the 1990s has become increasingly monopolized by a few mega music companies in Hong Kong that focus on idol-making, mainly churning out songs about love affairs, and losing the early versatility that had existed in the themes of Cantopop lyrics (e.g., about working-class life, about friendship and family relationships, about life philosophy, etc.) (Chu, 2007).

It was against this background that Hip Hop as a music genre became visible in the mainstream music scene in Hong Kong in the mid-1990s, when the local underground band LMF (LazyMuthaFuckaz) suddenly emerged above ground and enjoyed a popular reception for some years with their angry lyrics about the everyday reality of work-ing-class youths in their debut song, "Uk-chyun-jai" (Housing Projects Boys) (Chan, 2003). However, LMF's music style was actually a fusion of rock and Hip Hop genres. Researching on the historical development of LMF, I interviewed Davy Chan, a former LMF member who composed and produced most of the music and songs for LMF in his studio—"a.room". According to Davy, who was also a founding member of the local indie rock band, Anodize, in the early 1990s, LMF was originally an ad hoc band loosely formed by members from different rock bands to jam music for fun at the end of major underground music events. It was Prodip, a rock guitarist and graphic designer, who turned the loosely organized LMF into a formally organized band by gathering members from several indie rock bands (e.g., Anodize, NT) and by managing negotiations with major music labels and sponsors. LMF gave the audience the impression of Hip Hop mainly due to the presence of DJ Tommy and MC Yan. Davy invited DJ Tommy to join LMF in the late 1990s for "they wanted to try something new, perhaps Hip Hop." MC Yan was a vocalist and rapper from the rock band, NT, in the early 1990s, and joined LMF with other NT members. Of the final 12 members of LMF in the early 2000s, only two members (MC Yan and DJ Tommy) had a Hip Hop music background.

LMF was disbanded in 2003. According to Davy, it was partly due to the loss of adver-tising sponsors along with increasingly negative coverage of LMF in the media, and partly because a managing executive of Warner-Brothers, who had signed LMF and had given them great creative autonomy, left the company. The constant touring, performing, and advertising jobs had also robbed them of the time and space for creating new songs. As artists who did not want to repeat themselves, they decided that it was time to disband.

The Hip Hop scene in Hong Kong has never been as animated since the disbanding of LMF. However, Fama, a two-emcee group was formed in 2000. In 2002 the two emcees came under the tutelage of DJ Tommy, and were signed by DJ Tommy's music production company. Fama has strived to keep local Hip Hop music alive in Hong Kong. Although still marginal to Cantopop in the mainstream music scene, it is popular among college and high school students and it is the only local Hip Hop group since LMF to enjoy some degree of commercial success.

Fama, however, has its own style, which they seem to want to distinguish clearly from the LMF style. LMF rocked the local music and media scene by being the first local popular band to put Cantonese *chou-hau* (vulgar speech) into their lyrics in publicly released albums and live performances, and by taking a strongly resistant, defiant, media-critical stance (see studies by Ma, 2001, 2002a, 2002b). LMF's lyrics were largely Cantonese, and when English was used, it was mainly English slang; for instance: "Do you know what the fuck I'm saying?! *Hahm-gaa-ling*!" (a Cantonese *chou-hau* expression literally meaning: "To hell with your whole family!"). LMF's sociolinguistic positioning can be said to be mostly that of the Hong Kong Cantonese working-class youth—the speaking style projects a powerful, defiant, angry, Cantonese, working-class, masculine image, with lots of "rage"—*fo* (fire) in Cantonese (more on this later).

Fama, however, from day one, seemed to want to rectify the popular notion in Hong Kong (largely due to LMF's influence) that Hip Hop music is related to Cantonese vulgar speech or the angry young man image. Li (2006), in her unpublished MPhil study of Hip Hop music in Hong Kong, pointed out that Fama seemed to want to rectify Hong Kong people's misconceptions about Hip Hop music. In a song by Fama called "F.A.M.A. Praise," Fama rapped explicitly in their lyrics about these misconceptions. They seemed to want to draw a line between themselves and the image of MC Yan, in particular, as a politically outspoken figure.

Fama thus seems to aim at dissociating themselves from the politically conscious image projected by MC Yan, who aligns himself with the Muslim cause and writes conscious raps that criticize the Bush government (e.g., in his song, "War Crime"). Fama also never uses Cantonese *chou-hau* in their lyrics. While LMF's lyrics were chiefly Cantonese (except for some vulgar English words), Fama readily uses English and crafts out Cantonese-English bilingual lyrics which sound more like middle-class bilingual college boys than LMF's Cantonese working-class men (Lin, 2007).

To date there has been only one published research project on alternative band culture in Hong Kong. Eric Ma's ethnographic studies on alternative bands in Hong Kong represent the first academic attempt to bring under lenses of cultural studies the emotional energies and cultural practices of alternative bands (Ma, 2002a, 2002b). After months of intensive ethnographic field work (e.g., hanging around with LMF band members in their recording studios, concerts, their everyday/night activities, interviewing band artists and their fans, observing the behavior of the audiences in the concerts, etc.), Ma published a series of research papers and photography books on the alternative band, LMF. Summarizing his analysis in an article, Ma (2002a) wrote:

> As illustrated in this case study, the emotional energies generated by Hong Kong alternative bands are polymorphous. They are partly fuelled by the rebellious spirit of independent music incorporated translocally...; they can be charged by personal frustrations in schools, families and the workplaces...; their production can be a tactic of differentiating a youth identity in contrast with the adult and the established world; they can be exploited by some privileged group members to serve as fashionable identity labels. ... Emotional energies can also be political. In the particular juncture of the post-1997 Hong Kong, subcultural energies have [been] articulated and channeled into popular anti-establishment discourses. There are obvious thematic parallels between alternative music and public sentiments on the widespread dissatisfaction with the tabloid media, the education system and the conservative polity. (p. 198)

While Ma seemed to be deeply sympathetic with the sentiments of the alternative band, his ethnographic analysis yielded less than optimistic findings about the progressive potential of the subcultural practices of the band members. Ma wrote critically about the lack of political critique of the band members he studied (Ma, 2002a).

It is at this point that we find Ma's ethnographic analysis, albeit rich and cogent in many aspects, lacking a sociolinguistic perspective. As a cultural studies researcher without any sociolinguistic background, Ma has not conducted any detailed linguistic analysis of the lyrics and might have thus drawn his conclusion a bit too hastily based mainly on the interview comments of some LMF members. The dearth of serious attention paid to the Cantonese *chou-hau* verbal art of Hip Hop lyrics by independent Hong Kong MCs might also explain the lack of understanding of how youthful (defiant) voices and agency are mediated first and foremost in *language* in their raps. I will turn to my attempt at such an analysis in the next section.

CANTONESE YOUTH VERBAL PLAY IN HONG KONG: CANTONESE CHOU-HAU AS A TRANSGRESSIVE ACT DEFYING MAINSTREAM MIDDLE-CLASS NORMS

Despite Hong Kong's international cosmopolitan appearance, over 90% of its population is ethnic Chinese; Cantonese is the mother tongue of the majority. The British were a minority that until July 1, 1997 had constituted the privileged class of the society. That was the date when Hong Kong's sovereignty was returned to China and Hong Kong became a Special Administrative Region (SAR) of China. The English-conversant bilingual Chinese middle classes have, however, remained the socioeconomically dominant group in Hong Kong, and English is still the most important language of social mobility even in the post-1997, post-British-rule era. English continues to be the medium of instruction in most universities and professional training programs in Hong Kong and English Medium Instruction (EMI) secondary schools are generally perceived by the public as "first class" while Chinese Medium Instruction (CMI) schools are generally perceived as "second rate."

As a local, taken-for-granted language, Cantonese is undervalued and invisible both in education and the "high" domains of society, yet it is a central, valuable medium in popular culture. However, for the majority of working-class children in Hong Kong, English remains something beyond their reach. Unlike their middle-class counterparts, they typically live in a lifeworld where few will (and can) speak or use English for any authentic communicative or sociocultural purposes. The English classroom often becomes a site for their local struggles and oppositional practices involving a great deal of creative work in the form of Cantonese verbal play. And this verbal play often capitalizes on the use of Cantonese *chou-hau* expressions to create a transgressive, subversive effect. For instance, in Lin's (2005) study of the Cantonese verbal play of Hong Kong working-class students in English lessons, a boy was seen to reply to the teacher's reading comprehension question using a euphemistic expression ("fell onto the street") to hint at the Cantonese *chou-hau* expression, *puk-gaai*. Literally, *puk* means "fall (onto)" and *gaai* means "street," but the illocutionary force of *puk-gaai* is similar to: "drop dead!" or "go to hell!". His fellow students' loud laughter upon hearing this seems to have arisen from this student's clever, implicit, transgressive rendering of a taboo Cantonese *chou-hau* expression as an answer to the teacher's formal question.

Cantonese *chou-hau* thus seems to be an unfailing linguistic marker of working classness in Hong Kong. The mere uttering of a Cantonese vulgar word or expression constitutes a highly marked, transgressive act, violating middle-class etiquette and sensibilities, often supposed to arouse unease and contempt from a mainstream middle-class audience. While swearing and cursing have constituted a legitimate research topic overseas and there has long existed a research literature on English slang and cursing (e.g., Hughes, 1991; Jay, 1992; Partridge, 1970), the research literature on Cantonese *chou-hau* is extremely limited. It must be pointed out that Cantonese *chou-hau* is much more socially taboo in Hong Kong than what the English word *slang*, suggests. While the word *slang* in English usually refers to colloquial expressions or jargon of specific social groups, Cantonese *chou-hau* is seen as highly "vulgar," conjuring up explicit sexual images, and is highly taboo in mainstream society in Hong Kong. It is perhaps due to the taboo nature of this topic that only two academic publications by two Western scholars can be found: Bolton and Hutton (1995, 2005). In the 1995 research paper, Bolton and Hutton studied triad language (the "triad society" is a criminal syndicate in Hong Kong) and related it to antilanguages and taboo language. The taboo nature of Cantonese vulgar speech and its connection to bad language, triad society, censored language, and law enforcement is made even clearer in the foreword written by Ip Pau-Fuk (a retired chief inspector of the Hong Kong Police Force) for Bolton and Hutton's *Dictionary of Cantonese Slang* (2005). In the foreword, Ip mentioned that the dictionary "will prove very useful to many people…,including legal personnel, social workers, teachers, and even law enforcement officers" (p. vii). Just as Bolton and Hutton (1995) pointed out, so far, serious official attention that has been paid to the study of Cantonese vulgar speech is mainly for social control and censorship purposes (e.g., legal enforcement, court witnesses). However, it seems that Bolton and Hutton themselves do not want to stereotype Cantonese vulgar speech; in their insightful words:

> All societies have taboos. … What makes a society modern in this context is therefore not the absence of linguistic taboos, but debate about those taboos in the context of debates about free speech and censorship. (Bolton & Hutton, 2005, p. 10)

In a sense, Hong Kong society might be seen as not having reached a modern level if judged by the above criteria: local studies of Cantonese *chou-hau* do not exist at all (i.e., none by local Chinese scholars). The only exception is a recent Chinese book by Pang Chi-Ming (a local cultural critic and newspaper columnist) musing about the origins and meanings of different Cantonese *chouhau* expressions (Pang, 2007). It, however, has to use a euphemism as the title of the book to escape censorship: *Siu gau laahn chaat haaih* (literally meaning: the puppy is too lazy to shine shoes; tone pattern: 2–2–5–3–4), which is actually a phonological recoding of five common Cantonese *chou-hau* words: *diu, gau, lan, chaht, hai*—all related to sexual organs/ acts (tone pattern: 2–1–2–6–1). This recoding is a prime example of clever Cantonese verbal play capitalizing on Cantonese tonal features: by changing one initial consonant (*diu → siu*), changing the tones of four of the taboo words, and lengthening two vowel sounds (*chaht→chaat; hai→haaih*), the recoded expression keeps almost all the rhymes of the original words intact (i.e., *iu, au, an, at, ai*), while changing the meaning to that of an innocuous, almost "cute" expression. However, phonologically the euphemism is highly suggestive of the original taboo words. The sharp contrast between the cute meaning of the euphemism and the taboo meaning of the original words creates a clever, playful, transgressive effect.

Similar to the observation made by Paul Willis of working-class youths in Britain, there seems to be "work ... in their play" (Willis, 1990, p. 2). Cantonese verbal play thus seems to be a kind of folk symbolic creative work and implicit ideological critique through mocking laughter and transgressive play (Bakhtin, 1981) to subvert mainstream linguistic taboos and social norms. While the government and mainstream middle classes in Hong Kong have made the everyday speech of the working classes taboo in the public spheres (e.g., TV, radio, newspapers, books), clever cultural critics and artists will always find a playful, mocking way to transgress these social, linguistic norms.

In MC Yan's words (more on him later), his use of Cantonese vulgar words is both deliberate and natural: "I want to test the boundary of free speech ... these are the most lively expressions ... this is the language of working-class people; this is the way we speak every day; we don't want to pretend to be those gentlepeople; this is who we are; we just want to be ourselves!" Using Cantonese vulgar words in his playful lyrics, MC Yan seems to be deliberately trying to shout out with a working-class voice about everyday working-class reality.

It is the aim of this [reading] to bring to the fore samples of the kind of Cantonese creative work that some independent Hip Hop MCs are displaying when they engage in Hip Hop music practices in Hong Kong. These independent (indie) artists seem to have found in this translocal music genre and subculture the powerful symbol- isms to express their defiant working-class voices to mainstream society. Through Cantonese-language rap, these artists express their sharp critique of society, of the education system, and of what they see as mainstream hypocritical practices and political injustice. Through using Cantonese vulgar speech in their artful and inventive rap lyrics, they construct alternative discursive spaces where their defiant voices and sharp social critiques can be heard when they perform their both poetic (aesthetic) and political raps.

In the next section, I shall draw on interviews conducted with a well-known first-generation Hip Hop artist in Hong Kong—MC Yan of the former Hong Kong alternative band LMF—and I shall analyze the Cantonese verbal art of his Hip Hop lyrics. In the concluding section, I shall connect the analysis to a discussion of the birth of Conscious Rap in Hong Kong.

CANTONESE SLANG AND VERBAL ART IN MC YAN'S HIP HOP LYRICS

Little attention has been paid to the Cantonese verbal art that is displayed in much of the lyrical work of Hong Kong MCs. A key element of Hip Hop is personal ownership of lyrics—you "rap your own shit"—the choice of language is very much part of an individual MC's lyrical style. MC Yan was the main rap vocalist in LMF, writing the hooks for many of the songs, while other songs were based on the heavy metal and rock styles inherited from the former underground rock bands before they came to form the LMF. In what follows, I want to draw mainly on MC Yan's works as he is by far the most respected and widely recognized first-generation Cantonese MC in indie Hip Hop circles in Hong Kong.

MC Yan has written and rapped many songs, and in his words, they were songs "with a message." His works (lyrics and rapping) appeared in songs such as: "Respect for Da Chopstick Hip Hop," "New Opium War," "Big City Night Life" (collected in the album by DJ Tommy—*Respect for Da Chopstick Hip Hop,* which has the same title as the song), "War," "Beautiful Skin," "Hong Kong Place" (collected in the album by Edison Chan—*Please Steal This Album*). The album, *Respect for Da Chopstick Hip Hop,* is worth noting, as it is a transregional collaboration among Japanese, Korean, and Hong Kong artists. MC Yan told the author that the album was meant to foster an alliance of Hip Hop artists from East Asia, especially from Japan, Korea, and Hong Kong. In all these three places, chopsticks are used, so they called their album *Respect for Da Chopstick Hip Hop.*

The album has only a niche audience (i.e., it's not part of the mainstream pop music scene). That is because independent or nonmainstream Hip Hop is still a marginal practice in Hong Kong and Asia; and although some mainstream commercial Cantopop songs have appropriated some Hip Hop rapping and musical styles, they are generally not regarded as "real" Hip Hop by independent or nonmainstream Hip Hop artists.

The latter album, *Please Steal This Album,* is often seen as part of the pop music scene mainly because Edison Chan is a Hong Kong Cantopop singer. The themes of the songs written by MC Yan usually convey some serious messages of social or political critique. Yan has written many songs on the theme of war. For instance, "War" conveys the theme of a war against the relentless tabloidization of mass media practices in Hong Kong. "Big City Night Life" offers a sharp observation and critique of the money-oriented lifestyles of many Hong Kong people. "New Opium War" offers a historical reminder of the British imperial invasion of China in the 19th century and reasserts a Chinese identity. The song, "Respect for Da Chopstick Hip Hop," expresses the message of respect for and solidarity of different cultures and music styles of East Asian Hip Hop artists. "Beautiful Skin" is a tribute to women: praising the contribution of wives and mothers to humanity, which is not a pervasive theme in Hip Hop songs whether Western or Eastern.

In this [reading] I shall focus on MC Yan's indie Hip Hop song, "War Crime" (*Jin-Jan Jeuih-Hahng*), because it is a song regarded by Yan himself as most representative of the recurrent themes in his songs.

MC Yan made the song "War Crime" in his home studio with DJ Frankie. He started circulating songs like "War Crime" on the Internet after launching his own website in 2002 (www.chinamantaggin.org). In the beginning it just consisted of beats, and then demos and the full song were released in 2003 on the Internet. MC Yan also sent it to his Hip Hop artist friends in the United States who were doing a compilation of anti-Gulf War songs at that time. MC Yan's anti-Gulf War song ("War Crime") was the only song from Asia in this compilation. The beats of "War Crime" were made by DJ Frankie, and the lyrics were created by MC Yan. He did the lyrics first and then chose the beats from Frankie's creations.

The idea of "War Crime" came from his anger about the Gulf War, as MC Yan described, "The song's lyrics were inspired by the current affairs." Both MC Yan and DJ Frankie thought that they should do something to voice their protest against the blatant injustice shown in the war. In Table 2.2.1, I first present my transcription of the Cantonese rap lyrics of "War Crime" using the Yale system (which is a well-established writing system for transcribing Cantonese in the linguistic literature), and then my English translation of the Cantonese rap lyrics.

"I started to bring in this style of writing lyrics since the 1990s," said MC Yan in an interview with the author. The "style" that MC Yan refers to is the style of Zack de la Rocha, a rapper, musician, poet, and activist in the United States. Zack is best known as the former lead vocalist and *lyricist* of the rock band, Rage Against the Machine (RATM), one of the most politically charged bands ever to receive extensive airplay from radio and television. Zack became one of the most visible champions of left-wing causes around the world. MC Yan said from day one both he and members of his former rock band (NT) were influenced by Zack. Yan first came into contact with Zack's music when he was studying visual art in France in the early 1990s. (Yan did not make it in the competitive

Hong Kong education system. After high school, he worked for a while and then went to France to study visual art because tuition fees were cheap in France.)In a rock concert in France he witnessed the power of Zack's music and was deeply impressed by his message. Since then, Yan has tried to infuse his lyrics with political messages by using word puns or words that signify political events.

TABLE 2.2.1 "War Crime" (lyrics written and rapped by MC Yan[1]) **Stanza 1**

1. 依家 終於知撚道
   yih-gaa jung-yu ji-lan-dou
2. 乜野叫做道理唔通講陰功, 公然當全世界 無到
   mat-yeh *giu-jouh* "douh-leih mh-tung gong yam-gung", gung-yihn dong chyuhn sai-gaai *mouh-dou*
3. 乜撚野叫做渣住雙重標準 黎做
   mat-lan-yeh *giu-jouh* jaa-jyuh seung-chuhng biu-jyun *laih jouh*
4. 乜野大恰細 乜撚野叫做 霸道
   mat-yeh daaih-hap-sai, mat-lan-yeh *giu-jouh baa-douh*
5. 人類 文明究竟去撚到邊撚度
   yahn-leuih mahn-mihng gau-ging heui-lan-dou bin-lan-douh

(There are 16 lines in Stanza 1 and 12 lines in Stanza 2, but due to limited space only the first 5 lines of Stanza 1 and the lines in the Hook are shown here.)

Hook (x 2 times) (::: indicates lengthening of the final syllable):

1. 唔撚::: 知呢乜撚野叫做戰爭罪行
   mh-lan:::-ji ne mat-yeh giu-jouh jin-jan jeui-hahng
2. 唔撚::: 想再相信新聞
   mh-lan:::-seung joi seung-seuin san-mahn
3. 淨係覺得你條撚樣呢 就目中無人
   jihng-haih gok-dak-neih tiuh lan-yeung ne, jauh muhk-jung-mouh-yahn
4. 淨係見撚到你嚮度恰尻人
   jihng-haih gin-lan-dou neih heung-douh hap-gau-yahn

English Translation of Cantonese Rap Lyrics: Stanza 1:

1. Now, I finally fucking know
2. What it means to say, "When (your action) is unreasonable, just say (you're) miserable". (The U.S is) publicly treating the (others in the) world as non-existent ...
3. What it fucking means to have double standards in one's actions.
4. What (it means to say) "Big boys bullying small ones", (and) what "hegemony" means.
5. Human civilization is heading towards which fucking direction?

Hook (rapped 2 times): (::: indicates lengthening of the final syllable)

1. *don't fucking::: know what is called War Crime.*
2. *don't fucking::: want to believe in TV news any more.*
3. *only feel that in your fucking eyes there are no others.*
4. *only fucking see that you are bloodily bullying others.*

---

1. Yale transcription of original Cantonese rap lyrics (line numbers added for easy reference).

Yan has also been under the influence of Western politically oriented, Conscious Rap artists such as Public Enemy. According to *All Music Guide* (www.allmusic.com, an authoritative source of information on music artists), Public Enemy was the most influential and controversial rap group of the late 1980s, pioneering a variation of hardcore rap that was musically and politically revolutionary. With his powerful, authoritative baritone, lead rapper Chuck D rhymed about all kinds of social problems, particularly those plaguing Black communities, often condoning revolutionary tactics and social activism. In the process, he directed Hip Hop toward an explicitly self-aware, pro-Black consciousness that became Hip Hop culture's signature throughout the next decade (Spady & Eure, 1991).

Another influence on Yan was the urban Hip Hop poet, Saul Williams, who started the Slam Poetry Movement in the United States. Yan frequently referred to the political messages of Saul in his urban poetry about different issues of racism and social and global injustice. We can see in the lyrics of "War Crime" that the message of anti-U.S.-military invasion is directly expressed. Although no explicit reference to Iraq is made, "George Bush Airport" in Line 11 (Stanza 1) refers to the Baghdad Airport in Iraq, which was renamed "George Bush Airport" after the U.S. military action. In Line 11 (Stanza 1) the rapper asks which national flag is now erected in the George Bush Airport. According to Yan, this line invokes double layers of meanings and images. The first layer signifies the invasion act of the United States by invoking the image of U.S. forces "erecting" the American national flag in the Baghdad Airport and changing the airport name to "George Bush Airport"—a blatant act of invasion and colonization of the territory of another sovereign country. The second layer invokes sexual connotations of "erection" of the male sexual organ in the act of penetration—the "rape" metaphor/image is invoked to refer to the military invasion of Iraq by the U.S. troops. In Cantonese slang usage, the phrase *che-keih* (*erecting a flag*), is often used to refer to the sexual act of penis erection (connotating the male sexual act and male sexual power).

The Cantonese vulgar word *lan*, is used in almost every line of the "War Crime" lyrics to express an angry voice in protest at and condemnation of the U.S. initiation of war on Iraq. In Cantonese vulgar speech, there are five monosyllabic, sex-related words frequently used to express anger or to intensify emotions: *diu* (to fuck), *gau* (penis), *lan* (penis), *chaht* (penis), *hai* (vagina). Although four of these five words are nouns in their literal meaning, their word class status often changes in different contexts. In the context of the "War Crime" lyrics, the noun *lan* (literally meaning "penis") is used not as a noun but as an emotion-intensifier in most instances. For instance, in Line 1 of Stanza 1, *ji-lan-dou* can be translated roughly as "fucking know." *Ji-dou* means "know" and inserting *lan* into the word (*ji-dou → ji-lan-dou*) does not change the basic meaning of the word but only adds a layer of strong emotional meaning—anger, frustration, condemnation, and so on (its meaning very much depends on the context). Almost every line of the "War Crime" lyrics is emotionally intensified by the insertion of *lan* into key compound words in each sentence. Table 2.2.2 shows some more examples of the emotion-intensifying usage of the vulgar word *lan* in the "War Crime" lyrics.

MC Yan said that the use of Cantonese *chou-hau* adds to the *fo* (fire) or "force" of the song. He said the frequent use of English slang in Western Hip Hop had encouraged him and made him bold enough to use Cantonese *chou-hau* in his songs—to be more lively, to speak in the real voice of *siu-shih-mahn* (literally: "little-city-people"; the expression refers to the underprivileged and powerless people in society). The liberal use of Cantonese vulgar words thus adds to the defiant tone and mood of the song, expressing the voice of the working classes and the marginalized.

Apart from conveying the attitude of the rapper, the insertion of the Cantonese vulgar word, *lan*, into bisyllabic/bimorphemic compound words to form trisyllabic/trimorphemic compound words (e.g., *jih-lan-dou, mat-lan-yeh, heuilan-dou, bin-lan-douh*) also serves poetic and musical functions. The resulting trisyllabic units synchronize well with the recurrent three-beat drum patterns of the music. This is a conscious poetic strategy

TABLE 2.2.2 Examples of the Use of the Cantonese Vulgar Word, "lan" (撚), as an emotion intensifier

Examples from Stanza 1:

知道 ji-dou (know) → 知撚道 ji-lan-dou (fucking know ...) (Line 1)
乜野 mat-yeh (what) → 乜撚野 mat-lan-yeh (what fucking ...) (Lines 3 & 4)
去到 heui-dou (go to) → 去撚到 heui-lan-dou (go fucking to) (Line 5)
邊度 bin-douh (where) → 邊撚度 bin-lan-douh (where fucking) (Line 5)
卑鄙 bei-pei (despicable) → 卑撚鄙 bei-lan-pei (fucking despicable) (Line10)
至大 ji-daaih (the biggest) → 至撚大 ji-lan-daaih (the fucking biggest) (Line 15)
自大 jih-daaih (self-important) → 自撚大 jih-lan-daaih (self-fucking-important) (Line 16)

Examples from the Hook:

唔知 mh-ji (don't know) → 唔撚:::知 mh-lan:::-ji (don't fucking know) (Line 1)
唔想 mh-seung (don't want) → 唔撚:::想 mh-lan:::-seung (don't fucking want) (Line 2)
見到 gin-dou (can see) → 見撚到 gin-lan-dou (can fucking see) (Line 4)

employed by MC Yan to tightly integrate the rapping with the music. Yan deliberately makes use of the special features of the Cantonese morpheme: every morpheme is realized phonologically as one syllable with one of the six different tones (i.e., six different pitches, which can form a melody; tones are meaning-differentiating in the Cantonese language). Yan said he consciously makes the different words (with different tones) function like the music beats made by an instrument such as the piano or the drum. For instance, when he spits out the words *ji-lan-douh*, the three-syllable unit fits well with the three-beat drum rhythm of the music.

We can see that in the first five lines of stanza one, there is a high density of such three-syllable units (see underlined in Table 2.2.1): jih-lan-dou, mat-lanyeh (twice), heui-lan-dou, bin-lan-douh. The Cantonese vulgar word *lan*, apart from serving as an emotion intensifier, also serves as a central rhyming pillar of the three-beat drum pattern; that is, X-lan-Y. This contributes to the overall assonance of the first five lines. This rhyme tactic is similar to that found in the lyrics of American rapper, Pharoahe Monch, as discussed by Alim (2003, p. 63); for example, "rhymes to spit," "dimes to git." Another example, in Yan's lyrics, of this pattern can be found in the phrase, *Diu-gau-neih, hap-gau-ngo*! (Fuck you! [You're] fucking bullying me!). The pattern is: X-gau-Y. Again, the vulgar word *gau* serves as a rhyming pillar in each of these three-beat units.

Adding "lan" in the hook also serves another musical function. The word *lan* in the first two lines of the hook are phonologically stressed and lengthened. This fits with the rhythmic pattern of the music for the hook. If "lan" is not inserted, the first word *mh* (don't), as a phonologically nonsalient syllabic nasal, cannot be stressed and lengthened. Inserting *lan* after *mh* to form *mh-lan*::: ("don't fucking:::") serves the need for a stressed/lengthened syllable in the second position of the line while also providing a repeated forceful phrase ("don't fucking:::") to start off the first two lines of the hook.

In this connection it is important to analyze the intertextuality between the "War Crime" lyrical text and other working-class media texts. For instance, the final line of the song, "Diu-gau-neih, hap-gau-ngo!" was actually a sampled conversation (Pennycook, 2007) from Anthony Wong, a popular Hong Kong movie star who plays a social underdog in a 1996 movie, *Yi-bo-laai Behng-Duhk* (The Ebola Syndrome, made by famous Hong Kong movie director, Herman Yau, in his early career). The dark movie was about an ex-prisoner and a social outcast, who perceived himself as being constantly bullied by others. In each instance of such perceived bullying, the male character responded by spitting defiantly the line: "Diu-gau-neih! Hap-gau-ngo!" MC Yan said this line is familiar to most working-class males in their 30s now in Hong Kong. In this short line of merely six monosyllabic words, two of the five powerful Cantonese vulgar words: *diu* (fuck) and *gau* (penis) appear three times. The emotional force of this utterance is very strong as its defiant tone is intensified by a high concentration of Cantonese vulgar words within a short utterance. By ending the "War Crime" song with the sampling of this utterance from Anthony Wong in the movie, it pushes the defiant *fo* (fire or force) of the song to the climax.

Apart from the use of Cantonese slang verbal art, lyrical euphony (i.e., harmony of sounds in the lyrics) in the song "War Crime" is achieved linguistically at several levels simultaneously: through phonetic, lexical, and syntactic units which are structurally parallel. In English-language Hip Hop a lot of rappers mobilize the strategies of homophony, metonymy, and both sentence internal and sentence final rhymes (Perry, 2004). For a comprehensive list, Geneva Smitherman's eight features of signification in rap lyrics are often cited in rap lyrics research: indirection, circumlocution, metaphorical-imagistic, humorous-ironic, rhythmic fluence and sound, teachy but not preachy, directed at person or persons usually present in the situational context, punning/play on words, introduction of the semantically or logically unexpected (cited in Perry, 2004, p. 62). Alim's (2003) fascinating analysis of the complex internal rhymes of Pharoahe Monch's *Internal Affairs* lyrics uncovers the highly sophisticated rhyme tactics that U.S. Hip Hop rhymers have mastered (e.g., compound internal rhymes and chain rhymes, back-to-back chain rhymes and mosaic rhymes).

In MC Yan's lyrics, we see another level of sound and word play that capitalizes on the special tonal and syllabic features of the Cantonese language. Cantonese is a monosyllabic, tonal language. Every character is pronounced as one syllable with a tone (i.e., each character has the following syllabic structure: (C) V (C) + pitch). Every character is usually also a morpheme that combines with other characters (morphemes) to form two-, three-, or four-syllable/character words. These multisyllabic/morphemic words or phrases have their own tonal patterns; for instance, "mh-lan-seung" ("don't fucking want") (tonal pattern: 4–2–2), which is identical in its tone pattern to: "tiuh-lan-yeung" ("that fucking asshole") (tonal pattern: 4–2–2) (both phrases appear closely together in the Hook lines, see Table 2.2.1). These two three-syllable phrasal units have the same tonal pattern (4–2–2), share the same central pillar ("lan"), and have the same rhymes in the last syllable ("eung"). MC Yan calls this "double rhyme" or "three-dimensional rhyme," meaning that several levels of phonetic parallelism can be drawn upon to create a multilevel rhyming aesthetic; for example, rappers can use words with same vowels (rhyming), same consonants (alliteration), same sounds (homonyms), same number of syllables, and same or similar syllable-pitch (tone) patterns for multisyllabic words. The aesthetic appeal in the song "War Crime" is partly constructed through different ways of creating a large number of two- or three-syllable words or phrasal units that have similar phonetic features (e.g., same or similar verbs, rhymes, and tonal patterns). This kind of multilevel rhyming is similar to what Alim (2003) calls "a multirhyme matrix" in US Hip Hop and the "moraic assonance" patterns (i.e., rhyming of the "moras"—syllable-like units) in Japanese rock (Tsujimura, Okamura, & Davis, 2007, p. 223). For instance, Pharoahe's multirhyming tactic is shown in a string of quadruple rhymes throughout the verse in Alim's analysis (2003, p. 62):

Feel	in	the	flow
Drill	in	the	hole
Kill	in	the	show
Grill	in	the	dough
Will	in	to	blow
Feelin	'em on	the	low

Similar quadruple but partial rhymes can also be found in MC Yan's "War Crime" lyrics, as shown in Table 2.2.3.

Apart from using different multisyllabic rhyming tactics, MC Yan also employs pairs of multisyllabic words which differ only in the tone value of one syllable and yet with totally different meanings to creative a contrastive effect. For instance, look at lines 15 and 16 in stanza 1:

15. 全世界至撚大 應該係聯合國
    cheuhn sai-gaai *ji-lan-daaih*, ying-goi haih lyuhn-hahp-gwok
16. 唔撚係你 自撚大 阿美利堅 合眾帝國
    mh-lan-haih neih *jih-lan-daaih* aa-meih-leih-gin hahp-jung-dai-gwok
    [15. In the whole world, *the fucking biggest* (organization) should be the
        United Nations.
    16. It's not you who are self-fucking-important—the American Imperialist Empire.]

By putting two similar trisyllable units that differ only in the tone of the first syllable in parallel syntactic positions in the two sentences, the meaning of the two words are put in sharp contrast: *ji-lan-daaih* (tones: 3–2–6; *the fucking biggest*) vs. *jih-lan-daaih* (tones:

TABLE 2.2.3 Partially Rhyming Four-Character Clausal, Phrasal, and Lexical Units with Similar Tonal Patterns

4-character clausal units	Tone Pattern	English translation
順你者昌 seuihn neih je cheung	6–5–2–1	... those who obey you will live
逆你者死 yihk neih je sei	6–5–2–2	... those who disobey you will die
4-character lexical units		
堂堂大國 tohng tohng daih gwok	4–4–6–3	... a big country...
合眾帝國 hahp jung dai gwok	6–3–3–3	... the imperialist empire
人道主義 yahn douh jyu yih	4–6–2–6	... humanism
帝國主義 dai gwok jyu yih	3–3–2–6	... imperialism
干預主義 gon yyuh jyu yih	1–6–2–6	... interference-ism

The six tones in Cantonese are marked by numerals: 1 = HL (High Level), 2 = HR (High Rising), 3 = ML (Mid Level), 4 = LF (Low Falling), 5 = LR (Low Rising), 6 = LL (Low Level).

6–2–6; *self-fucking-important*). In fact, this kind of contrastive lexical play is a characteristic of MC Yan's lyrical style; for example, dan *ngoh wah-neih-ji* (tones: 5–6–2–1; let *me tell you*), *ngoh wah-ji-neih!* (tones: 5–6–1–2; *I couldn't care less about you!*).

Apart from the above-mentioned verbal play, MC Yan also mobilizes metaphors, metonyms, and word puns to connote different levels of political meanings. For instance, as discussed earlier, the Cantonese metaphor of rape (*che-keih*—erecting the flag) is used to refer to the U.S. occupation of Iraq's territory. And in line 10 of stanza 2, "Sitting inside the planes and cannons (trucks), you depend on the fucking TV (screen)," the word *screen* has double references. On the literal level, it refers to the control screen of the military gear (e.g., inside the planes or cannon trucks). On another level, as MC Yan pointed out to the author, the "screen" refers to the screens of people's television sets at home. The whole notion of war, in contemporary times, is shaped and constructed by mass media practices through the "screen," and here MC Yan mentioned to the researcher that the screen (the media) has shaped and determined people's consciousness about the Gulf War—people's idea of the war has largely been shaped by mainstream media discourse ("the screen"). These are the double meanings that MC Yan wants to express through the lyrics in line 10 of stanza 2.

STARTING A CONSCIOUS RAP GROUP IN HONG KONG: THE YELLOW PERIL

While it seems that there is nothing new in saying that MC Yan has politically and socially conscious messages in his songs; this is, however, significant in the Hip Hop scene in Hong Kong for the mere fact that he is the only Hip Hop artist who has steadfastly done this all through his music career without any commercial support. Like the high school students who rejected progressive rap in the school project that Newman (2007) studied, most Hip Hop artists in Hong Kong have aspirations for commercial success and do not particularly care about politically or socially conscious messages. However, from the outset, Yan and members of his band, NT, have been under the influence of political activists such as Che Guevara and the Dalai Lama: Yan and his band members read Che and the Dalai Lama's books and wrote lyrics inspired by them. Later in the mid-1990s, NT was combined with other less politically oriented rock bands in HK to form the LMF. MC Yan told the author that he had been an odd man out in LMF, given his politically and socially conscious style, but he respected the collective works done with LMF members, for as a member of LMF he could not just have his own way. From the beginning, Yan wanted to do Conscious Rap. He defines his work as part of the translocal Conscious Rap movement, having been influenced by politically conscious artists in the U.S. such as Zack de la Rocha, Public Enemy, Tupac Shakur, Saul Williams, and Blackalicious. By "keeping it real" in the Hong Kong context—drawing on Cantonese *chou-hau* as a confrontational, transgressive lyrical style and defiant voice of the under-privileged—MC Yan can be said to have appropriated the spirit of many Conscious Hip Hop artists worldwide (who also do not shy away from using slang to voice the plight and everyday reality of the marginalized), and sown the seeds of Conscious Hip Hop in Hong Kong. While Yan's lyrics in the LMF days mainly centered on voicing the feelings of the underprivileged working-class youth in Hong Kong, in the song "War Crime" Yan has, in his words to the author, "evolved from talking about just social injustice in Hong Kong to talking about social injustice in the world." In a recent interview (conducted on October 10, 2007), MC Yan told the author that his lyrical style has evolved as he has read more books and learned more things about the world. "I want to self-educate and invite other Hong Kong people to self-educate, by learning about what's happening in the world, and we cannot just sit there and do nothing!"

MC Yan's "War Crime" will be included in a mixtape by a French street fashion web-zeen called *Black Rainbow* (http://www.bkrw.com/sommaire). It seems that he is much better received in some European Hip Hop circles than in Hong Kong. Yan wants to start a Conscious Rap movement in HK with his disciples, the three young rappers, ADV, Chef, and Double T in Yellow Peril (see Figure 2.2.1)—a Conscious Rap group which has recently started and performed their three debut songs ("Choice," "Yellow Peril," and "Unbri-dled") in recent gigs (e.g., on October 6, 2007, in Cizi—a live club; on October 26, 2007, in the Hong Kong Fringe Club). All of their songs are socially and politically conscious. Although MC Yan and Yellow Peril are rapping about global political issues (e.g., Bush's invasion of the Iraq), Yan's sentiments, I want to argue, are transposed from his previous LMF songs about the working-class youths in HK to the underclasses in the world. Yan

Figure 2.2.1 MC Yan (in cap) rapping with Yellow Peril and other indie rappers in a gig at the Hong Kong Fringe Club, October 26, 2007.

himself said he is above class and his music should be right for all classes for it is about the moral issues of social and global justice.

The choice of the name "Yellow Peril" symbolized Yan and his group's reflexivity in their ironic defiance of Western colonial discourse. "Yellow Peril," with its colonial image (Pennycook, 1998), was precisely what Yan wants to remind his group not to forget: how yellow people have been positioned in Western colonial discourse. For instance, when asked why they chose the name "Yellow Peril," Yan said that the word *Nigga* is historically a disparaging name that the Whites called the Blacks; however, his African American Hip Hop friends also call Yan *Nigga*, as an intimate term for "Brother." As many sociolinguistic researchers have pointed out (Low, 2007; Alim, 2006), "Nigga" has undergone semantic inversion to become a name for solidarity among those who are discriminated against by an outside group. In a similar way, Yan wants to infuse *Yellow Peril* with positive meanings, as a solidarity term for Asian people who have historically been under the Western colonialist gaze. "Yellow Peril," Yan said, "was a name given to us by Western colonialists, and we want to remind ourselves not to forget this...we want to be socially and politically conscious, to be self-reflective, so that we won't really become a danger and threat to the world. ... If the younger generations in China keep on copying the entertainment and consumption styles of the West, then Chinese people will really become a threat to the world ... we want ourselves to realize this first...we must self-educate ... not to become like the West. ..." The choice of "Yellow Peril" as the group's name can thus be seen as a deliberate postcolonial, symbolic act to defy the colonial discourse in the West.

In MC Yan and Yellow Peril's songs, we can witness the birth of Conscious Rap in Hong Kong. By doing their songs totally in colloquial Cantonese, without inserting any English (vs. Fama's Cantonese-English bilingual lyrical style), and by boldly using Cantonese *chou-hau*, which is taboo in mainstream Hong Kong society, MC Yan and his followers seem to be "keeping it real," and keeping it true to the translocal spirit of politically oriented Hip Hop artists such as Public Enemy, Tupac Shakur, and Saul Williams. In this connection, one has to remember that Cantonese *chou-hau* plays a symbolic role in asserting the voice of the working classes in Hong Kong. In defying the linguistic taboos of mainstream middle-class society, one can argue that MC Yan's Cantonese *chouhau* lyrics communicate his political message through transposing the Hong Kong working classes' defiant sentiments to the translocal underclasses' defiant sentiments.

While MC Yan is often seen as a "radical" even by other indie artists in Hong Kong, interestingly Yan told the author that his graffiti design has been invited to be part of a permanent collection in two museums in Britain, as part of their "China Design" collection. In a way, Yan has got some cultural capital (Bourdieu, 1984, p. 3) internationally, but strangely, not in HK. However, his strategy, as he told the author, is: after he has made a name overseas, he can do this in Hong Kong, "as Hong Kong people worship things overseas, especially those from the Western world." It is ironic that Yan's success in some progressive Hip Hop circles overseas relies precisely on his use of local taboo language that is rejected by the Hong Kong middle classes and inaccessible to the rest of the world.

Yan readily defines himself as a public intellectual and he says he will keep doing what he thinks is the right thing to do, although at present he has only a small audience in Hong Kong. It is, perhaps, by winning the recognition and respect of progressive Hip Hop artists and cultural critics in the West that Yan will eventually gain the cultural capital recognized by local Hong Kong middle-class people. Such an indirect route indicates how progressive cultural movements overseas (such as Conscious Hip Hop) can sometimes lend cultural capital to local artists, ironically, and precisely, because of the colonialist mentality of the local people ("who worship things overseas"). Ironically, the author finds herself employing a strategy similar to Yan's: by publishing in overseas progressive academic journals and books, the author's own research on a taboo topic in Hong Kong—vulgar lyrics in indie Hip Hop songs—might stand a chance of winning respect and recognition from local scholars and researchers.

In conclusion, it seems that there is a possibility of drawing on translocal Hip Hop culture and its artistic and linguistic creative practices as resources for a critical public pedagogy (Carrington & Luke, 1997) that reaches out to youth and people beyond the classroom and the school. There remains a lot of work to be done in this area to chart out what exactly such a pedagogy might look like and what effects that might have. A recent breakthrough for MC Yan is his Postcard Project hosted by *Ming Pao*, a well-respected middle-class newspaper in Hong Kong. Every Sunday, Yan gets a whole page to write and draw his message, and to invite the readers to send him a postcard in response to his message. He has received some interesting responses, as he told the author in an interview on October 10, 2007. MC Yan and Hip Hop artists like him in Hong Kong, albeit few as they are, seem to be the first street fighters in Hong Kong to set up good examples for us on how to figure out local tactics (de Certeau, 1984) when drawing on translocal Hip Hop graffiti art and Conscious Rap culture as resources for a possible public education project.

ACKNOWLEDGMENTS

The author is indebted to MC Yan for sharing his lyrics and his time in numerous research interviews over the past two years. Special thanks go to Francis Lee, Jaeyoung Yang, and Eric Ma for exchanging ideas with the author on this research and for their constant colleagial support. The author is also especially grateful to the editors for their critical and very useful comments on earlier drafts of the [reading].

REFERENCES

Alim, H. S. (2003). On some serious next millennium rap ishhh: Pharoahe Monch, hip hop poetics, and the internal rhymes of internal affairs. *Journal of English Linguistics, 31*(1), 60–84.

Alim, H. S. (2006). *Roc the mic right: The language of hip hop culture.* New York: Routledge.

Bakhtin, M. M. (1981). *The dialogic imagination: Four essays.* Austin: University of Texas Press.

Bolton, K., & Hutton, C. (1995). Bad and banned language: Triad secret societies, the censorship of the Cantonese vernacular, and colonial language policy in Hong Kong. *Language in Society, 24,* 159–186.

Bolton, K., & Hutton, C. (2005). *A dictionary of Cantonese slang.* Singapore: National University of Singapore Press.

Bourdieu, P. (1984). *Distinction: A social critique of the judgement of taste* (Trans. Richard Nice). London: Routledge & Kegan Paul.

Carrington, V., & A. Luke (1997). Literacy and Bourdieu's sociological theory: A reframing. *Language and Education, 11*(2), 96–112.

Chan, Ka Yan (2003, May 4–5). *Exploring youth subculture in Hong Kong: A case study on the local band LazyMuthaFucka (LMF),* MPhil Thesis. (Chinese)

Chu, Y. W. (2007). *Before and after the fall: Mapping Hong Kong Cantopop in the global era.* Paper presented at the International Conference on Inter-Asia Culture: Desire, Dialogue and Democracy, City University of Hong Kong.

De Certeau, M. (1984). *The practice of everyday life.* (S. Rendall, Trans.) Berkeley: University of California Press.

Erni, J. N. (2007). Gender and everyday evasions: Moving with Cantopop. *Inter-Asia Cultural Studies, 8*(1), 86–105.

Hughes, G. (1991). *Swearing: A social history of foul language, oaths and profanity in English.* Oxford: Blackwell.

Jay, T. (1992). *Cursing in America: A psycholinguistic study of dirty language in the courts, in the movies, in the schoolyards and on the streets.* Philadelphia: John Benjamins.

Li, W. C. (2006). *The emergence and development of Hong Kong Hip Hop and rap music since the 1980s.* Unpublished MPhil thesis, Department of Music, Chinese University of Hong Kong.

Lin, A. M. Y. (2005). Doing verbal play: Creative work of Cantonese working class schoolboys in Hong Kong. In A. Abbas, & J. Erni (Eds.), *Internationalizing cultural studies: An anthology* (pp. 317–329). Oxford: Blackwell.

Lin, A. M. Y. (2007, May 30–June2). *Crafting out a bilingual identity with bilingual hip hop lyrics in Hong Kong.* Paper presented at the International Symposium of Bilingualism, University of Hamburg, Germany.

Low, B. E. (2007). Hip hop, language, and difference: the N-word as a pedagogical limit-case. *Journal of Language, Identity, and Education, 6*(2), 147–160.

Ma, E. K. W. (2001). *Underground radicals.* Hong Kong: Ming Pao.

Ma, E. K. W. (2002a). Emotional energies and subcultural politics in post-97 Hong Kong. *Inter-Asia Cultural Studies, 3*(2), 187–190

Ma, E. K. W. (2002b). Translocal spatiality. *International Journal of Cultural Studies, 5*(2), 131–151.

McIntyre, B. T., Cheng, C. W. S., & Zhang, W. (2002). Cantopop: The voice of Hong Kong. *Journal of Asian Pacific Communication, 12*(2), 217–243.

Newman, M. (2007). "I don't want my ends to just meet; I want my ends overlappin": Personal aspiration and the rejection of progressive rap. *Journal of Language, Identity, and Education, 6*(2), 131–145.

Pang, C. M. (2007). *The puppy is too lazy to shine shoes.* Hong Kong: Subculture Hall. (in Chinese)

Partridge, E. (1970). *Slang: Today and yesterday.* London: Routledge.

Pennycook, A. (1998). *English and the discourses of colonialism.* London: Routledge.

Pennycook, A. (2007). Language, localization and the real: Hip hop and the global spread of authenticity. *Journal of Language, Identity, and Education, 6*(2), 101–115.

Perry, I. (2004). *Prophets of the hood: Politics and poetics in hip hop.* Durham, NC & London: Duke University Press.

Spady, J., & Eure, J. (Eds.). (1991). *Nation conscious rap: The hip hop vision.* Philadelphia: Black History Museum Press.

Tsujimura, N., Okamura, K., & Davis, S. (2007). Rock rhymes in Japanese hip hop rhymes. *Japanese/Korean Linguistics, 15*, 222–233.

Willis, P. (1990). *Common culture: Symbolic work at play in the everyday cultures of the young.* Buckingham: Open University Press.

Doin' Damage in My Native Language

The Use of "Resistance Vernaculars" in Hip Hop in France, Italy, and Aotearoa/New Zealand

By Tony Mitchell

In *Spectacular Vernaculars*, Russell A. Potter applies Deleuze and Guattari's comparison of Kafka's use of Prague German as a "minor language" with the use of English by African-Americans to what he regards as the heteroglossaic, marginal vernacular forms of African-American rap, which he sees as a de-territorialization of "standard" forms of English (66–68; cf. Deleuze and Guattari 16–17). Potter sees African-American rap as a form of "resistance vernacular" which takes the minor language's variation and re-definition of the major language a step further and "deform[s] and reposition[s] the rules of 'intelligibility' set up by the dominant language." He concludes that African-American rappers "have looked more towards the language and consciousness of the ghetto in search of a more authentically black identity" (69). But it is arguable that the ghetto vernacular practiced by many African-American rappers has become so atrophied and ossified in its relentless repetition of a severely limited range of expletives that any claims for "resistance" have long passed their use-by date. As Paul Gilroy noted in 1994: "Hip hop's marginality is as official, as routinized, as its overblown defiance; yet it is still represented as an outlaw form." He goes on to identify a need to interrogate "the revolutionary conservatism that constitutes [rap's] routine political focus but which is over-simplified or more usually ignored by its academic celebrants" (51). In this [reading] I examine the use of indigenous languages other than English in rap music in Zimbabwe, Switzerland, France, Italy, and Aotearoa/New Zealand as more appropriate examples of "resistance vernaculars" which re-territorialize not only major Anglophone rules of intelligibility but also those of other "standard" languages such as French and Italian. In the process, I also argue that rhizomic, diasporic flows of rap music outside the United States correspond to the formation of syncretic "glocal" subcultures, in Roland Robertson's sense of the term, involving local indigenizations of the global musical idiom of rap. The assertion of the local in hip hop cultures outside the United States also represents a form of contestation of the importance of the local and regional dialect as a "resistance vernacular" in opposition to a perceived U.S. cultural imperialism in rap and hip hop, and often corresponds to what Lily Kong has described, in reference to popular music in Singapore, as an expression of "inscribed moral geographies."

I start with an example from Zimbabwe that challenges the standard rhetoric about the Afrodiasporic and Afrocentric aspects of African-American rap and hip hop (e.g., Rose). In the title track of *Doin' Damage in My Native Language*, an EP produced in the United States in 1992, Zimbabwe Legit (brothers Dumisani and Akim Ndlouvu) provide English translations of key expressions employed in their Zimbabwe regional tribal dialect, Ndbele (Jones 111). These English expressions ("Power to the people"; "The ghettos of Soweto"; "You know where to find me—in Zimbabwe") serve for the Anglophone listener both to locate Zimbabwe Legit firmly in its county of origin, Zimbabwe, and to indicate the proximity of that country to South Africa. In addition, the brothers Ndlouvu prioritize their native dialect as the main source of their art of rhyming, which finds local equivalents for certain rhetorical attributes of African-American "nation conscious" rap. The back sleeve cover and the CD itself highlight and celebrate words in Ndbele as a form of "concrete poetry," but Zimbabwe Legit's raps also incorporate Shona, the more "standard" language of Zimbabwe. So the linguistic "damage" done by Zimbabwe Legit is directed not only against the English language of their colonizers—which Zimbabwe Legit needs to use in order to be accessible in the United States—but also against standard linguistic practices in Zimbabwe. This concern for linguistic authenticity is furthermore linked to broader notions of authenticity and Afrocentricity. In a track entitled "To Bead or Not to Bead," the brothers Ndlouvu criticize African-American rappers who assimilate African fashions such as hair beading. This track is entirely in English, and includes an apparent reference to the rhetorical embrace of the Italian-American Mafia by African-American gangsta rappers:

> Some MCs would rather be Italian / Now sportin' beads and a black medallion / Medallion on your chest, but do you feel it in your heart? / Jump off the bandwagon and pull the cart. (Qtd. in Jones 106)

Despite its inventiveness and its "authentic" African origins, Zimbabwe Legit was a distinctly minor voice in the chorus of African-American hip hop in 1992, and the group subsequently disappeared without a trace from the United States music industry. An entry about Zimbabwe Legit on the Rumba-kali African hip hop website describes it as the first African hip hop crew to break into the United States and European markets. When Zimbabwe Legit's Ndlouvu brothers were college students in the United States, they secured a record deal and an unreleased album produced by African-American hip hop producer, Mr. Lawng (for the Black Sheep label). Dumi Ndlouvu later went on to become part of the rap group called the Last 8th, and he now goes by the name Doom E. Right.

Another marginalized African rap group which shares Zimbabwe Legit's multilingual dexterity is Positive Black Soul, a duo from Senegal who rap in a combination of English, French, and their native Senegalese language, Wolof, thus managing to address two major global linguistic groups in the African diaspora as well as those in their own locality. In the track "Respect the Nubians," Positive Black Soul identifies itself in English in relation to African-American rap as "a brother man from another land known as the motherland." In "Djoko" (Unity), rapped in a mixture of Wolof and French, they address more local concerns, describing themselves as "a brand new (political) party ... we are underprivileged, but we want the good life." Their multi-lingual rhymes enable them to address their immediate constituency as well as audiences in the United States and the world at large (the album sleeve contains the lyrics to all their tracks in English translation). Unfortunately the United States and the world at large didn't seem to be listening, and the first album by this innovative group did very poor business in the English-speaking world.

Deleuze's notion of the "rhizome" is aptly applicable to hip hop culture and rap music, which has rapidly become globalized and transplanted into different cultures throughout the world. This rhizomic process is expressed directly in the work of another rap group, Silent Majority, which is based in Switzerland and raps in a mixture of English, Jamaican patois, French, Spanish, and Swahili. Referring to themselves as "funky multilinguals," Silent Majority's members foreground their collective linguistic dexterity in a track entitled "Dans une autre langue" (In another language). In it, guest Spanish rapper MC Carlos from the bilingual Lausanne-based group Sens Unik states:

> Ok! ok! el rap es americano / Pero, si el americano fuero amarillo / Mi musica saria una musica de chino /.... / La musica es contagiosa y al ritmo es una planta / Que cresce de Nueva York a Martignan

> [Ok! ok! rap is American / But if American was yellow my music would be Chinese music / .... / Music is contagious and rhythm is a plant / That grows from New York to Martignan]

This use of the trope of rap music as a "plant" neatly corresponds to Deleuze's "rhizome" and serves to emphasize the "glocalization" of rap, which, although a worldwide phenomenon, is, like African-American rap, still very much concerned with roots, family, locality and neighborhood. As Sens Unik's MC Rade puts it in the same track, in a mixture of French and English: "Our music is not a pale copy of the United States, Lausanne on the map, rhymin' is the art, part of a global thing." Perhaps one of the most peripheral examples of the global linguistic indigenisation of rap as a "resistance vernacular" is the Nuuk Posse from Greenland, which uses its distinctly minority language (Inuit) to rap about the domination of their country by the Danish language (Barnes 1997).

The variety of ethnic origins among French rappers, from the French Caribbean to the Arab populations of North Africa to other parts of Europe, is notable. The origins of French hip hop in the immigrant and working class housing projects of the *banlieues* (outer suburbs) of French cities, as displayed in Matthieu Kassovitz' 1995 film *La Haine* (Hate), are also notable. A broad variety of musical inflections ranging from hard-core rap to reggae and raggamuffin distinguish French rap from U.S. rap and give it features more in common with British and Italian hip hop. The "adaptation" period of French hip hop in the 1990s involved the growth of hard-core rap and Zuluism (based on Afrika Bambaataa's Zulu Nation), where African-American models were adapted directly to French realities, but other concepts, such as Afrocentrism, could not be translated wholesale into the French context. André Prévos shows how French rap crews like IAM attempted to circumvent the "return to Africa" ideology prevalent among some U.S. rappers in order to avoid playing into the hands of French right-wing anti-Arab movements like Le Pen's National Front ("Post-Colonial"). Consequently IAM constructed an elaborate "Pharaonic" ideology and mythology which boasts about Africa, but not black or Arabic Africa, rather adapting the Africa of Ancient Egypt into a religious symbology. They also mythologize their native Marseilles, a marginalized city with a high non-European immigrant population, as *"le côté oscur"* (the obscure side) of France, and rap in Marseilles dialect. As Steve Cannon has noted, there is in Afro-French rap "a closer physical and therefore less mythical relationship of (black) rappers in France to the *'pays d'origine'* [African homeland] than in the USA" (164). Cannon also notes that, despite the fact that only six percent of the population of France consists of non-European immigrants, rap and hip hop have become a vital form of anti-racist expression for ethnic minorities:

> studies of hip hop in France in the 1980s and 1990s suggest that not only is the most numerical participation in both production and consumption of hip hop "products" among people of minority ethnic origin, but also that hip hop in France is characterized to a great extent by its role as a cultural expression of resistance by young people of minority ethnic origin to the racism, oppression, and social marginalization they experience within France's *banlieues* and in its major towns and cities. (155)

Rap's rich impact on the French language was also illustrated by the publication in 1998 of a controversial dictionary of French urban slang partly derived from French rap, *Comment tu tchatches?* (How do you talk?) by a Sorbonne professor, Jean-Pierre Goudaillier. This charts the language of the French *banlieues*, known as *Cefron*, "a melting pot of expressions that reflect the ethnic make-up of the communities where it is used, borrowing words from regional dialects as well as Arab, Creole, Gipsy and Berber languages" (Bell). It also reveals that French rappers and North African immigrant youth are not, as the French mass media sometimes portrays them, an illiterate and uneducated subclass; rather, they are often talented linguists who speak French and *Cefron* as well as thier native "home" language. In "The Rapper's Tongue," Prévos suggests that the French rappers' use of the "reverse" slang languages *"verlan"* and *"veul,"* in which words are syllabically reversed, represents a hip hop vernacular which contests the rules of standard French. Combined with the use of borrowings from English, Arabic, Gypsy expressions, and words from African dialects, the vernacular of some North African immigrant French rappers displays a rich linguistic dexterity which constitutes another form of "resistance vernacular."

Like a number of other non-Anglophonic countries, the first compilation of rap music in Italy was almost entirely in English. Called *Italian Rap Attack* and released in 1992 by the Bologna-based dance label Irma, it included a brief sleeve note by radio DJ Luca De Gennaro declaring that "rap is a universal language, in whatever language and whatever part of the world it is performed." But in fact the only Italian-language track on the compilation was Frankie Hi NRG's "Fight da faida," with its half-English, half-Italian refrain urging resistance against Mafia blood feuds. This track deservedly became the most re-released and most famous Italian rap track of the 1990s. It was a courageous declaration of resistance against the Mafia, and, in marked contrast to the celebration of Martin Scorsese's Italian-American mafioso stereotypes in American gangsta rap, it became one of the dominant polemics of "nation conscious" Italian rap. Frankie Hi NRG's barrage of internal rhymes also illustrated the greater facility for rhyming that the Italian language had over English, while his use of a brief burst of a woman rapping in Sicilian dialect was also a first:

> *Padre contro figlio, fratello su fratello / Partoriti in un avello come carne da macello; / Uomini con anime / Sottili come lamine, / taglienti come il crimine / Rabbiosi oltre ogni limite, / Eroi senza terra / Che combattono una guerra / Tra la mafia e la comorra, Sodoma e Gomorra, / Napoli e Palermo, / Succursali dell'Inferno.*

> [Father against son, brother against brother, / Born in a grave like butcher's meat; / Men with minds / As sharp as blades, / Cutting like crime / Angry beyond limits, / Heroes without land / Fighting a war / Between the mafia and the camorra, Sodom and Gomorrah / Naples and Palermo / Regions of hell.]

Although there are Italian posses based in the major cities like Rome and Milan, a notable feature of Italian rap is a tendency to manifest itself in smaller and more marginal regional centers. If Turin and Naples became major localities for rap music, Sicily, Sardinia, Calabria, and Puglia were just as important. A nationwide network of *centri sociali* (social centers), which were often set up in occupied disused buildings, became the focal point for Italian hip hop culture. As Italian rappers began experimenting in their native language, they also Italianized U.S. hip hop expressions like *"rappare," "scratchare,"* and *"slenghare"* (to use slang) and began to rap in their regional dialects. Some rappers also revived the oppositional political rhetoric of the militant student groups of the 1970s, and in some cases began to excavate Mediterranean regional folk music roots which had been neglected since the Italian folk music revival of the late 1960s. A distinctive musical syncretism also emerged among the Italian rap groups that pushed out the parameters of hip hop and more often than not became fused with raggamuffin reggae ("ragga"), dance hall, and ska influences. This led to the coinage of the term "rappamuffin" in a 1992 Flying Records compilation of Italian rap and ragga entitled *Italian Posse: Rappamuffin d'Azione*. The Sud Sound System, based in Salento on the Southern Adriatic Coast, took this even further, referring to their hybridized music as "tarantamuffin," referring back to the dance tradition known as tarantella. The hybridizations of both Sud Sound System and the Marseilles-based Marsilia Sound System were studied by the French ethnomusicologist George Lapassade and his Italian collaborator Piero Fumarola, and as Felice Liperi has indicated, the use of dialect in Italian rap was partly a consequence of both technical considerations and the choice of polemical subject matter:

> Clearly the motivation was not only cultural, it was also technical. Italian DJs and musicians who chose the musical idiom of rap, which is based on the relation between words and rhymes, found dialect a more malleable language in which to combine rhythm and rhyme. But it is also true that once they found themselves talking about the domination of the mafia in the south and urban disintegration, a more coherent use of the language of these localities came spontaneously. Dialect is also the language of oral tradition, and this brings it closer to the oral culture of rap. (201)

This is particularly evident in the work of the Bari-based group Suoni Mudu, which superimposes a street map of Bari on its name and enacts a mock Mafia murder on the cover of its polemical 1996 mini-album, *Mica casuale sara* (Hardly by chance). The CD cover includes the lyrics to their track "Citt e camina (L'ambiente)" (City and hearth [where I live]) in both Barese dialect and "standard" Italian. This begins with an address to local Christian Democrat and neo-fascist politicians and then proceeds to mark out a criminal cartography of Bari:

> *[Ind'a Libbertà acchemmà] [nne l'omertà / Ind'a Sambasquàle acchemmà]*
>
> *[nne u criminale] / A Japigiè stene na Coop addò vennèvene la robba / A Carrassi uno scippo] [ogni due passi.*
>
> [A conspiracy of silence rules in Libertà / Organized crime rules in San Pasquale / There was a co-op in Japigia which sold drugs / In Carrassi a bag gets snatched every two meters.]

The track exposes a conspiracy between the government, the police, the Mafia and their Calabrian and Neapolitan equivalents (the *'Ndrangheta* and the *Camorra*), and expresses similar sentiments to those of "Fight da faida," but they are articulated very differently. The loping ragga beat gives the track a sense of grim resignation as well as denunciation, and the sung refrains—"*Poverannù*" (poor us) and "*Ste fatt'u sccèhe*" (the die is cast), which use a female voice—draw on local musical idioms to express a sense of grief. Barese dialect is also used for its musical attributes, as in the line "Ask me for two hits (of heroin), there, give him two hits," which in Barese is sing-song: "*Dì dù, da dà, de dù.*" As Goffredo Plastino has noted, "dialect is also used for its different musicality with regard to Italian, for the greater possibilities of rhythmic and musical organisation of phrases which it allows" (100). The use of local expressions, the perorations through the main precincts of Bari, and the roll call of politicians also give the track a specificity and sense of locality which "Fight da faida" lacks. Suoni Mudu provides a detailed and intimate cartography of the Bari criminal underworld which is fleshed out by its idiomatic use of the "minor language" of Barese dialect. "Fight da faida," on the other hand, like the Rome-based rappers Menti Criminali (Criminal Minds), addresses the whole of Italy by using standard Italian. As a member of Menti Criminali put it, "my rhymes are written in [Standard] Italian so that what I experience and feel is clear from Sicily to Milan." But this kind of clarity often involves sacrificing a sense of local identity which is vital to the regional diversity of Italian rap. In the case of the Sardinian group Sa Razza, rapping in Sardinian dialect serves as a means of defending local (and national) pride. As the group puts it in its track entitled "The Road": "We prefer Sardinian slang rap. You have to defend your pride in being Sardinian, brother. That's why we're rapping, here the only hope is for my people to survive. Survive on the road" (Qtd. in Pacoda 42). For the Sicilian group Nuovi Briganti, rapping in the dialect of Messina is a way of maintaining contact with the poor and dispossessed people of its locality, who have difficulty expressing themselves in "standard" Italian:

> We are based in one of the most devastated areas of the city, and the people in the neighbourhood have difficulty expressing themselves in [Standard] Italian. They've been used to speaking dialect since they were children. And they were our first reference point, the people who have followed us since we began. And rap is about communication. (Qtd. in Pacoda 42)

A more paradoxically polemical use of Italian dialect as "resistance vernacular" occurs in a track by the Calabrian group South Posse, which was based in Cosenza until it disbanded in 1995. In "Semplicemente immigrato" (Simply immigrated), Luigi Pecora, an Italian of Ethiopian origin, also known as Louis, uses the dialect of Cosenza as a way of expressing his adopted Calabrian "roots." As Plastino has stated, here "dialect serves the function of identifying the privileged interlocutors of a discussion, the people of Cosenza, and challenging them to a dialogue. At the same time ... it is a way of elaborating a personal style" (98). Influenced by the dialect ragga-rap of Sud Sound System,

Pecora wrote "Simply Immigrated" in dialect as a way of expressing his ability to belong to Cosenza, and to get closer to the inhabitants, who he addresses as "brothers":

> *Eppure molti dicono tutto il mondo è paese / Eppure troppi dicono vattene al tuo paese / Ma dicu ma moni tu chi cazzu vu l mia / Ca signu vinutu druacu a lavurà pe fatti mia ...*

> [Many people say all the world's your home town / Too many people say go back to where you came from / I'm telling you what the fuck do you want me to do / I came here to work and mind my own business.]

The simplicity of the language used here is abetted by musical repetitions of particular words, and there is a shift in the track from the direct address of "I" and "you" to "he" and then "we," indicating that the narrator identifies with both the immigrant and the native Italian. The use of dialect here is strategic, an act of defiance, and to emphasize this Pecora raps the first two lines in standard Italian before shifting into dialect in the second two.

As Plastino notes, this mixture of dialect and Italian corresponds to

> the way a young person from Cozsenza talks today, which is what Luigi Pecora wanted to identify himself with to communicate more clearly. ... The reference to "roots" is made to indicate the need to establish an exclusively linguistic relationship to one's region. (100)

But South Posse also uses dialect to rap about racism, in the context of both the discrimination against southern Italians by northern Italians and the exclusion of immigrants from Africa, who are often refered to as "extracomunitario," a euphemism used to describe non-Europeans.

In spite of the fact that Aotearoa/New Zealand is on the opposite side of the globe in relation to Italy, we find that there too indigenous language is used in rap as a form of "resistance vernacular." The native inhabitants of Aotearoa, the Maori, constitute about thirteen percent of the 3.36 million population of Aotearoa, but forty percent of Maori are in the lowest income group, and twenty-one percent are unemployed, compared with 5.4 percent for *pakeha* (persons of European origin). Seventy-five percent of the Maori population is under thirty years of age, but forty percent of Maori youth are out of work and four out of ten leave school without having graduated. Since the 1980s, steps have been taken by Maori towards a renewal of their cultural and social traditions, and to regenerate *te reo Maori* (the Maori language), which is only spoken by about eight percent of the inhabitants of Aotearoa. This establishes it as a "minor language," although it is the language of the indigenous inhabitants of Aotearoa, the *tangata whenua* (people of the land). The syncretization of aspects of traditional Maori *waiata* (song) and imported African-American musical forms is one which many Maori popular groups and performers have pursued in different ways and to varying degrees throughout the history of Maori popular music. Given the implausibility of entertaining strict notions of authenticity and purity in relation to Maori cultural traditions (or to any contemporary indigenous musical forms), the combination of traditional *waiata* (song) and popular musical forms from the United States is part of a cultural project of self-assertion and self-preservation which is linked with a global diaspora of musical expressions of indigenous ethnic minorities' social struggles.

Maori rappers were quick to adopt the trappings of hip hop culture and to explore its affinities with indigenous Maori musical and rhetorical forms. This is illustrated by the way concepts such as *patere* (rap), *whakarongo mai* (listen up) and *wainua* (attitude) are easily assimilated into hip hop discourse. The first Maori rapper to release a recording was Dean Hapeta (D Word), with his group Upper Hutt Posse. Hapeta was part of a "lost generation" of Maori youth who didn't have the benefits of learning the Maori language at school, as is now customary, and thus had to learn it himself. This informed the militancy with which he uses the Maori language in his raps. As Hapeta says, "Although I love and respect Hip-Hop, being Maori I only take from it what doesn't compromise my own culture. But in spite of this I have found them both very compatible" (Qtd. in Frizzell 48; cf. 50).

Hapeta and other Maori and Pacific Islander rappers and musicians have substituted Maori and Polynesian cultural expressions for the African-American rhetoric of hip hop, while borrowing freely from the musical styles of the genre (and it is an indication of the strong position traditionally held by women in Maori and Pacific Islander societies that the misogynist aspects of U.S. hardcore rap are totally absent from its Maori and Pacific Islander appropriations). The result is a further syncretization of an already syncretic form, but one which is capable of having strong musical, political, and cultural resonances in Aotearoa. In their 1996 album *Movement in Demand* (a title derived from Louis Farrakhan), Upper Hutt Posse combine the use of traditional Maori traditional instruments, militant *patere* and *karanga* (raps and calls to ancestors) and invocations of the spirits of the forest (*Tane Mohuta*) and the guardian of the sea (*Tangaroa*), and rhetoric borrowed from the Nation of Islam. The album also draws on the group's reggae and ragga inclinations, funk bass rhythms, blues guitar riffs, and hardcore gangsta-style rapping which switches from English to *te reo Maori*. One of the album's tracks, "Tangata Whenua" (The people of the land) is entirely in Maori, a choice which runs the risk of receiving virtually no radio or TV airplay, as the national media in New Zealand still regard the Maori language as a threat to its Anglophone hegemony. Nonetheless, Hapeta completed a powerful video for "Tangata Whenua," which was previewed on a Maori language television program. It tells the story of a polluted river, a consultation with a *kaumatua* (elder), traditional Maori gods destroying a factory, and an expression of Maori sovereignty:

Ko Papatuanuku toku Whaea, ko te whenua ia / Ko Ranginui toku Matua, kei runga ake ia / Whakarongo mai ki te mea nui rawa / He take o te Ao / He kaupapa o toku whakapapa /

Ko IO MATUA KORE, te matua tuatahi / E ora! koutou! toku Iwi, / Whaia te wairua o te ahi / Whakatikangia te kupu, te mahi, / Whakatahea nga hee o Tauiwi, / Kia rere ai nga hiahia, nga moemoeaa, / O te hinengaro / Kia toko ai hoki te whakaaro moohio / Taangata Whenua—Ko Te Pake—Whakapapa / Taangata Whenua—Ko Te Take Me Te Mana / Taangata Whenua—Ko Te Hana O Te Haa / Taangata Whenua—Te Ahi Kaa

[Papatuanuku is my mother, the earth / Ranginui is my father, he is above / Listen to the thing it's very important / A root of the world / A foundation level of my genealogy / It is Io-matua-kore, the first parent Live! you all! my people, / Pursue the spirit of the fire / Make correct the words, the work / Cause the wrongs of Tauiwi (the foreigner) to pass away / So the desires, dreams, can flow / Of the conscience / So wise thoughts can rise up also / People of the land—The durable lineage / People of the land—The root and the authority / People of the land—The glow of the breath / People of the land—The ever burning fire]

The track starts with a woman chanting a *karanga* (call to ancestors), and includes the sound of the *purerhua* (bull roarer), a traditional Maori instrument consisting of a piece of greenstone or wood rotated on a piece of string which makes a whir-ring noise associated with sounding the alarm. The track draws on key concepts in Maori philosophy, which are familiar to some *pakeha*, such as *whakapapa* (lineage), *mana* (authority), *tangata* (man), and *kaupapa* (strategy or theme of a speech). It also draws extensively on Maori oral traditions and rhetorical figures. The track is not translated into English on the lyric sheet of the album, which suggests that it is addressed to Maori only, although most New Zealanders know the meaning of the term "*tangata whenua*." To adapt Zimbabwe Legit's phrase, in "doin' damage in [*his*] native language," Dean Hapeta and the Upper Hutt Posse use the rhetoric, idioms, and declamatory styles of hip hop to express Maori resistance and sovereignty, and in so doing, they indigenize it. Rap becomes subservient to an expression of Maori philosophy and militant dreams, and is thus absorbed into the wider project of Maori sovereignty. On 1 January 2000, Hapeta released *Ko Te Matakahi Kupu* (The word that penetrates), a twenty track rap album entirely in Maori, under his Maori sobriquet, Te Kupu (D Word).

From our consideration of hip hop scenes in places like Zimbabwe, Italy, Greenland, and Aotearoa/New Zealand, we see that the the rhizomic globalization of rap is not a simple instance of the appropriation of a U.S./ African-American cultural form; rather; it is a linguistically, socially, and politically dynamic process which results in complex modes of indigenization and syncretisim. The global indigenization of rap and hip hop has involved appropriations of a musical idiom which has become a highly adaptable vehicle for the expression of indigenous resistance vernaculars, their local politics, and what Kong calls the "moral geographies" of different parts of the world. The "minor languages" of Maori and Italian dialects, together with the use of *verlan* and *veul* in French and the languages of other ethnic minorities within dominant languages such as French and English, however, pay a price for their status as "resistance vernaculars." While the use of these vernaculars can be regarded as constituitive of deliberate strategies to combat the hegemony of the English language in both the global popular music industry in general and in hip hop in particular (which, its African-American linguistic variants notwithstanding, still represents a dominant language), their limited accessibility in both linguistic and marketing terms largely condemns them to a heavily circumscribed local context of reception. In contrast, a hip hop group such as the Swedish crew Looptroop reflect the continuing dominance of the English language and American culture in the formation of global pop:

> We've all had English in school since we were 10 years old and there's a lot of sitcoms and films on TV that are English/American. The whole of Europe is becoming more and more like America basically. I guess we're fascinated with the language. But the way rap in Swedish sounds is a little bit corny and I think it's great that people as far away as Australia can understand us. I think that's the main reason why we rhyme in English. (Qtd in McDuie 31)

What Looptroop risks in their embrace of the Anglophonic and American homogenization of Europe, of course, is the erasure of any distinctively local or even national features in their rapping and breakbeats. In contrast, Maori rapper Danny Haimona of Dam Native sees the popularity of U.S. gangsta rap and R&B among young Maori and Pacific Islanders as the biggest threat to their appreciation of their own culture expressed in local indigenous hip hop:

> There's such an influx of American stuff, and we need to quell it, and we need to give these kids some knowledge on what's really up. ... Kids don't want to be preached to, so what I'm trying to do is put it on their level, and take all the good influences from hip hop, and bring it close to home. There is a good vibe out there for New Zealand hip hop, but it's being poisoned by the Americanisms—the Tupacs and the Snoop Doggy Doggs. You have to have a balance, and Dam Native are trying to help kids work out that they have their own culture, they don't have to adopt Americanisms. (Qtd. in Russell 18)

In this context, the choice of local indigenous "resistance vernaculars" is an act of cultural resistance and preservation of ethnic autonomy, and as such, it is a choice that overrides any global or commercial concerns.

NOTE

Throughout this [reading], translations from French, Italian, and Spanish are by Tony Mitchell; translations from Maori are by Dean Hapeta and Tony Mitchell.

WORKS CITED

Barnes, Jake. Review *Kaataq* (CD), by Nuuk Posse. *The Wire* 158 (April 1997): 65.

Bell, Susan. "Talk of Town Irks Academie." *The Australian* 20 Jan. 1999. (Rpt. from the London *Times*.)

Cannon, Steve. "Paname City Rapping: B-boys in the Banlieues and Beyond." *Post-Colonial Cultures in France*. Ed. Alec Hargreaves and Mark McKinney. London: Routledge, 1997. 150–66.

Deleuze, Gilles, and Félix Guattari. *Kafka: Toward a Minor Literature*. Tr. Dana Polan. Minneapolis: U of Minnesota P, 1986.

Frizzell, Otis. "Hip Hop Hype." *Pavement* (NZ) 8 (Dec. 1994): 44–50.

Gilroy, Paul. "'After the Love Has Gone': Bio-Politics and Etho-Poetics in the Black Public Sphere." *Public Culture* 7.1 (1994): 49–76.

Goudailler, Jean-Pierre. *Comment tu tchatches: dictionaire du français contemporain des cités*. Paris: Maisonnuveau et Larose, 1997.

Jones, K. Maurice. *The Story of Rap Music*. Brookfield: Millbrook P, 1994.

Kong, Lily. "The Politics of Music: From Moral Panics to Moral Guardians." International Association of Geographers' Conference, U of Sydney, 1999.

La Haine. Dir. Matthieu Kassovitz. Egg Pictures, 1995.

Liperi, Felice. "L'Italia s'è desta. Tecno-splatter e posse in rivolta." *Ragazzi senza tempo: immagini, musica, conflitti delle culture giovanili*. Ed. Massimo Canevacci et al. Genoa: Costa & Nolan, 1993. 163–208.

McDuie, Duncan. "A Looped Nordic Sample." *Revolver* (Sydney) 1 Nov. 1999: 31.

Pacoda, Pierfrancesco, ed. *Potere alla parola: Antologia del rap italiano*. Milan: Feltrinelli, 1996.

Plastino, Goffredo. *Mappa delle voci: rap, raggamuffin e tradizione in Italia*. Rome: Meltemi, 1996.

Potter, Russell A. *Spectacular Vernaculars*. New York: SUNY P, 1995.

Prévos, André. "Post-colonial Popular Music in France: Rap Music and hip hop culture in the 1980s and 1990s." *Global Noise: Rap and Hip Hop Outside the USA*. Ed.Tony Mitchell. Middletown, CT: Wesleyan UP, 2001 (forthcoming).

———. "The Rapper's Tongue: Linguistic Inventions and Innovations in French Rap Lyrics." American Anthropological Association Meeting, Philadelphia, 1998.

Robertson, Roland. "Glocalization: Time-Space and Homogeneity-Heterogeneity." *Global Modernities*. Ed. Mike Featherstone, Scott Lash, and Roland Robertson. London: Sage, 1995. 25–44.

Rose, Tricia. *Black Noise: Rap Music and Black Culture in Contemporary America*. Hanover, NH: Wesleyan UP, 1994.

Russell, John. 1997. "Rhymes and Real Grooves: Dam Native." *Rip It Up* (NZ) 240 (Aug. 1997): 18.

"Zimbabwe Legit." Rumba-kali African Hip Hop Website. rumba-kali.www.cistron.nl/zimbabwe. ht. 1999.

DISCOGRAPHY

Dam Native. *Kaupapa Driven Rhymes Uplifted*. BMG/Tangata Records, 1997.

Menti Criminali. *Provincia di piombo*. X Records, n.d.

Positive Black Soul. *Salaam*. Island Records, 1996.

Silent Majority. *La majorité silencieuse*. Unik Records, 1994.

South Posse. *1990–1994*. CSOA Forte Prenestino, n.d.

Suoni Mudu. *Mica casuale sarà*. Drum & Bass, 1996.

Te Kupu. *Ko Te Matakahi Kupu*. Universal/Kia Kaha, 2000.

Upper Hutt Posse. *Movement in Demand*. Tangata Records, 1996.

Various. *Italian Rap Attack*. Irma Records, 1992.

Zimbabwe Legit. *Zimbabwe Legit*. Hollywood Basic, 1992.

DISCUSSION QUESTIONS

1. Discuss imitation and cultural exchange. In what ways does the cultural exchange framework change how scholars analyze the work of global artists?

2. Compare and contrast how non-American hip hop artists have used the art as resistance.

3. Analyze the ways that Black American hip hop culture is co-opted by power, including state institutions and multinational entertainment corporations.

4. Identify and analyze the ways that hip hop culture has impacted public policy in different countries.

3 Performing Hip Hop Identity Against Inequality

By Anthony J. Stone Jr.

Born in the mid-1980s, I grew up during in an interesting time in music. I remember hearing upbeat pop tracks, over-the-top rock ballads, and big hair metal bands—all with unique sounds and flare. Although my mother played records by Patti LaBelle, Luther Vandross, Anita Baker, and Sade at home, in the neighborhood residents blared music by N.W.A., LL Cool J, and Salt-N-Pepa. Much of what I heard was background noise to me as a child. Hip-hop did not really catch my attention until I became an adolescent. Hip hop was more than music. It was the language we used at school. It was the clothes we wore. Although I lived in the Midwest, everyone was forced to choose a side when the East Coast–West Coast beef was on.

My mother did not have cable television so what I knew of hip-hop came from the radio and what my peers told me. In 1994 I began spending summers at my father's home in Columbia, Tennessee. With MTV, BET, and VH1 now at my disposal, I delved into the world that was music videos. I admired and was mesmerized by the artistry and visualization of the lyrics. I quickly became a more intense fan of the culture and, of course, particular artists. It was the shiny suits, braggadocio, and flaunting of excessive amounts of money by Bad Boy Records artists that sold me on the music and my allegiance to the East Coast.

Summer 1997 was full of anthems like "Mo Money Mo Problems" by The Notorious B.I.G., "Put Your Hands Where My Eyes Could See" by Busta Rhymes, "The Rain (Supa Dupa Fly)" by Missy "Misdemeanor" Elliott, and "I'll Be Missing You" by Puff Daddy. The swagger I was learning from artists like Jay-Z, 2Pac, and Ma$e came just in time for puberty and helped me navigate the "Changes" in my life as the world was also changing. The storytelling of hip hop let me know that the experiences of my family and friends were common and filled my head with dreams of what could be. The music and culture of hip hop offered motivation, leisure, and an escape. In 1998 I lost the most important woman in my life, my maternal grandmother. I often relished listening to "I'll Be Missing You." Even though it was a tribute by Puff Daddy to the late Notorious B.I.G., it helped me memorialize my grandma with words I could not muster myself.

Today, hip hop music fills my headphones when I work out, keeps me awake and "pumped" on long drives, and keeps me in touch with the ever-changing culture that I love. The swagger and confidence I borrowed from my favorite artists like Puff Daddy, the competitiveness from artists like DMX, and originality of artists like Eminem provided me with a way of "being" in a world that is not always welcoming for Black men. Yet, Black men are not alone. I am happy to see Black women are finally getting the recognition in hip hop they have always deserved. Although women have been a part of the supporting cast of hip hop since its beginnings in the Bronx, modern women of hip hop are leaving the margins and blazing a trail of accomplishments never before seen in the history of the art. Artists like Nicki Minaj, Cardi B, and Megan Thee Stallion are breaking records and stereotypes of what women in hip-hop are and are capable of. In this section, authors discuss how hip hop is influenced on the margins and how those on the margins influence hip-hop. Accordingly, the contributions of marginalized hip hop artists and enthusiasts who are women and members of the LGBTQ communities are centered here.

In "Imag[e]ining Hip-Hop Femininity: Contentions, Contradictions, and Contributions," Donyale R. Griffin Padgett, Cheryl D. Jenkins, and Dale Anderson delve into the relationship women have with hip-hop, and hip-hop with women. Griffin Padgett and colleagues lean on the works of Black feminists, womanists, and hip-hop scholars to theorize a new "hip-hop feminism." The authors contend that although hip-hop is rife with misogyny, certain female hip-hop artists engage with feminism in unique ways—posturing a hip-hop feminism that seeks to counter patriarchal misogyny. They argue that hip-hop must be examined using a feminist framework that offers an alternative method for hip-hop performers and scholars to understand and critique the art. The authors believe this allows for a counter to oppression and means to combat the negativity in the world that most, if not all, women experience. In their argument, Griffin Padgett and colleagues utilize a case study of female artists in Michigan to ascertain: what might be gained by theorizing hip-hop feminism? Do the ways Black women artists engage feminism in hip-hop offer a counter-discourse to misogyny? Does their engagement offer a deeper consciousness and critique of Black feminist identity?

They focus their case on two underground female emcees from Detroit, Bo$$ and Miz Korona. The authors discuss the identity performances used by Bo$$ and Korona and how their artistic expressions exist in a flow between resistance and acceptance of the masculine forms of performance within hip-hop—claiming that hip-hop allows women to accept and, simultaneously, reject marginalization. Griffin Padgett and colleagues compare the lyrics of Bo$$ and Korona to the writings of hip-hop scholars such as Tricia Rose and artists like Queen Latifah to demonstrate the nuance and fluidity that come with being a woman in an art dominated by men. The authors conclude that hip-hop feminists must utilize not only a counter discourse but also an alternative discourse to counter oppression.

In the tradition of archaeological anthropology, Oneka LaBennett makes visible the narratives of Bronx women's oral histories as they were produced through hip hop in "Histories and 'Her Stories' from the Bronx: Excavating Hidden Hip Hop Narratives." Specifically, LaBennett examines the Bronx African American History Project (BAAHP) and highlights the too-often-marginalized voices of women via hidden hip hop accountings that contrast what is usually debated in dominant discourses about who is hip hop and what hip hop is. LaBennett explores how these women use hip hop as a tool for education, activism, and conceptualizing a Diasporic Blackness. While LaBennett offers some foundational information on hip hop and a brief historical overview, she largely highlights the erasure of women in the creational narrative of hip hop where men are considered central characters. She focuses on the hidden female figures of the Bronx hip hop. Her purpose is to fill the gaps in the hip hop literature that ignore or minimize the role and placement of women while also increasing awareness of the notable contributions of women in the origin story of hip hop. This focus allows voices on the peripheries of hip hop, specifically women, to be heard, recognized and appreciated for their efforts. Importantly, LaBennett acknowledges that her narrative is influenced by her feminist insights on how she interviews as well as analyzes her subjects' oral histories that she refers to as "her stories." In each of the narratives covered, LaBennett points out that each woman takes a nontraditional path to hip hop and that collectively their voices build on and foster a feminist consciousness ignored in what is considered hip hop.

Jeffery Q. McCune Jr. presents (auto)ethnographic data from field excerpts, informal and formal interviews, and personal narratives to examine the ways Black men navigate their queerness while on the "down-low" (DL). In "'Out' in the Club: The Down Low, Hip-Hop, and the Architexture of Black Masculinity," McCune examines how hip-hop music, culture, and fashion shape the narrative of down-low Black men as they negotiate between "masculine bravado and Black queer culture." From data collected at "The Gate," a club in Chicago with a Friday-night queer party, McCune shows how "DL brothas" perform a heterosexual identity while also working to secure their discreet, queer sexual desires. McCune presents evidence from the narratives of his interlocutors Shawn and Tavares—using Shawn to "illuminate, complicate, and outline some of the contradictions and complexities" of going out as a DL man—and using Tavares to story a DL man's introduction to queer desire. These men attend The Gate on Friday night while adorned in loose sagging jeans, oversized shirts, and "baggy wear." Their motive is to maintain not only a level of coolness in their dress and actions but also "straightness." Moreover, the men McCune observes utilize what scholars Majors and Billson (1992) refer to as the "cool pose," or an enactment of coolness and hyper masculinity that acts as a survival mechanism for Black men. This posture, seemingly, allows them the flexibility to physically define their presence in ways that may be acceptable within spaces that are not necessarily tolerable of members of the LGBTQ communities.

McCune refers to the nuance and layers of this performed identity as made up by *architexture,* a term well-suited to describe the relationship between the internal manifestations of masculinity within queer Black men and queered places, as well as the external constraints or freedoms of those spaces. These architextures, McCune tells us, help describe both the structure and feeling of the spaces and people that make up the sites of queer production. Notably, hip hop and queerness have both traditionally disrupted normativity, making their union unique. McCune argues that postmodern Black queers are likely to express their identities in intersectional ways: having sexual identity as one part of the self, and participant in traditional Black cultures such as hip-hop as an example of another self. McCune writes, "Hip-hop at the Gate provides a unique experience for Black queer subjects to embrace such desires while maintaining an allegiance to macro-cultural forms of expressions." He informs us that at the Gate, Black queer men are not "comin' out," but "comin' in" to a space where their queer desires are available, but they do not have to claim membership in one identity. For DL Brothas, at the Gate, there is a separation of the queer world and their everyday performances of a heteronormative identity.

Collectively, the studies in this section provide a more holistic understanding of the participation of women and members of the LGBTQ communities in hip hop. It is hoped that a robust examination of these often-ignored experiences will lead to a broader critique of the art form that results in the mainstreaming of historically excluded voices.

▌ REFERENCE

Majors, Richard, and Janet M. Billson. (1992). *Cool pose: The dilemmas of Black manhood in America.* New York, NY: Touchstone.

Imag[e]ining Hip-Hop Femininity

Contentions, Contradictions, and Contributions

By Donyale R. Griffin Padgett, Cheryl D. Jenkins, and Dale Anderson

Are we still perplexed by this new hip-hop generation?

Rising, shouting, resisting

the degeneration of an entire nation

    and generation XY

Zzzzzzzzzzzzzz

Wake up sisters (and brothers)

    Take back the mike

        And take back the night

    And take back the right

        To rhyme ...

—Janell Hobson, "Hip-Hop Hegemony"

MIC CHECK

Hip-hop is undoubtedly a pop culture phenomenon. Born in the basement of a housing complex to a man by the name of Clive "Kool Herc" Campbell, hip-hop ultimately ventured away from the streets of New York City and has been influential throughout the globe. In fact, from music and fashion, to literature and language, the impact of hip-hop has gone from being a microcosm of New York's African American, Afro-Caribbean, and Hispanic communities to a mass-mediated cultural phenomenon that transcends race, class, and geographical boundaries. Torn between consciousness-raising rhetoric and capitalistic gain, hip-hop is becoming one of the most controversial sociocultural movements of the twenty-first century.

While historically, hip-hop's sociopolitical significance is undeniable, this genre is often relegated to "booty music," which dilutes the organic messages that have challenged the status quo and served as a part of hip-hop's history since its inception in the late 1960s / early 1970s. Today, rap music leads as the primary defining element of hip-hop culture and drives its marketability. In fact, the term *hip-hop* is often used synonymously with "rap music" (Bennett, 2000; Dyson, 2003, 2007). This is problematic, particularly when we consider that the music that emerges from this genre with the most commercial appeal is widely negligent, misogynistic toward Black women, and void of cultural accountability.

The contradiction is that hip-hop provides one of the only avenues that expresses social, cultural, and economic inequities, while, at the same time embracing the capitalistic structures that are implicated in the disenfranchisement [of traditionally marginalized groups]" (Weheliye, 2001, p. 294). Therefore, while hip-hop is praised for being artistically expressive, the music is riddled with degrading images of Black men and women that ultimately challenge Black cultural identity formation.

In her work *Black Noise*, Tricia Rose (1994) attempted to rein in hip-hop culture by defining it. She writes: "Hip-hop is a cultural form that attempts to negotiate the experiences of marginalization, brutality, truncated opportunity, and oppression within the cultural imperatives of African American and Caribbean history, identity, and community" (p. 21). She further states, "Rap music and hip-hop culture are cultural, political, and commercial forms, and for many young people they are the primary cultural, sonic, and linguistic windows on the world" (p. 19).

It was Rose who told us that hip-hop was a platform from which voices from the margins could "spit at" the social, economic, and political imbalances that had long plagued urban communities. Furthering the notion of hip-hop's role in providing a voice for the marginalized, Peoples (2008) states that from its inception, "hip-hop has represented resistance to social marginalization, and later resistance to and commentary on the political and economic oppression that makes social marginalization possible" (p. 23).

A source of much contention within and outside of the hip-hop community is the movement away from the social consciousness and political and social commentary that helped to put rap music and hip-hop culture on the charts. The "organic" message of traditional rap music has been diluted and tainted with the ink of the dollar bill. This phenomenon has placed capitalistic gain above raising the world's consciousness with more emphasis on pimped-out rides, bling, ride-or-die chicks, and a gangster lean than was evident when KRS-One of the group BDP first made us *think*, with the hit single "My Philosophy."

After first laying a foundation for Black feminist thought, feminist scholars like Collins (1991) and Guy-Sheftall (1995), along with feminist writer Morgan (1995), helped us to understand the contention that has been the source of much anguish in the Black community relative to rap music and hip-hop culture—misogyny toward Black women. Parallel to that work, scholars like Davis (1995) and Byrd (2004) have pushed our theorizing further, using the term *hip-hop feminism* to signify the link between women, feminism, and hip-hop. Since that time, a new generation of scholars has contributed to this discussion of hip-hop feminism, which characterizes "women [who] have been influenced by both the feminist movement and by hip-hop culture (Peoples, 2008, p. 26). Pough (2007) further defines hip-hop feminists as "women and men who step up and speak out against gender exploitation in hip-hop" (p. 80).

Upon answering the obvious question of what misogyny is from a conceptual standpoint, this [reading] examines its pervasiveness in hip-hop culture and rap music and the unique ways in which female hip-hop artists engage feminism. We localize this discussion by highlighting the bourgeoning hip-hop culture in Michigan, with a discussion of local artists and their contributions to this dialogue. We ask, what are the opportunities and contradictions of theorizing hip-hop feminism? Do the ways in which Black women artists engage feminism within hip-hop offer an alternative discourse in response to misogyny or opportunities for a deeper consciousness and critique of Black feminist identity?

IMAG[E]INING THE BLACK FEMALE BODY IN HIP-HOP

The degradation of Black women is not a modern phenomenon. Notwithstanding, the assault on African American women perpetuated by the system of slavery in the United States normalized their oppression (Adams & Fuller, 2006; Dyson, 2007).

> From the beginning of slavery, black women have been viewed as deviant sexual beings possessed of insatiable carnal urges. Black women were viewed as oversexed because they had to meet the erotic demands of their sexually feared black men. Until the second half of the twentieth century, black women were seen as incapable of being raped; their alleged exceptional sexual capacity meant that no white man would have to take what they would freely offer. (Dyson, 2007, p. 128)

This point is key to the argument that misogyny "is a part of a larger social, cultural, and economic system that sustains and perpetuates ... blatant stereotypical characterizations and defamations" of Black women (Adams & Fuller, 2006, p. 941). Moreover, how do we conceptualize misogyny? According to Adams and Fuller (2006), misogyny is "the hatred or disdain of women. It is an ideology that reduces women to objects for men's ownership, use, or abuse" (p. 939).

Nowhere is the misogyny toward Black women more evident and debated than in rap music. Adams and Fuller claim further that the ways in which Black women are characterized in rap music "ultimately support, justify, instill, and perpetuate ideas, values, beliefs, and stereotypes that debase [them]" (p. 940). While Adams and Fuller (2006) and Dyson (2007) attempt to contextualize the misogyny dilemma within a U.S. capitalistic patriarchal system, Hobson and Bartlow (2008) articulate a broader characterization of this milieu. They assert that "women in varying cultures have been portrayed either as decorative, fetishistic, manipulative, fragile, or in need of rescuing (or submission) in contemporary popular music lyrics, and music videos" (Hobson & Bartlow, 2008, pp. 2–3). What these scholars are ultimately saying is that misogyny exists across geographic lines and functions at multiple levels of society.

Why are misogynistic lyrics so mainstream? As Gilkes (1983) notes, "Black women emerged from slavery firmly enshrined in the consciousness of white America as 'Mammy' and the 'bad black woman'" (p. 294). According to Adams and Fuller (2006), "misogynistic rap has been accepted and allowed to flourish, generating wealth for some of the artists and the music industry as a whole" (p. 940). They juxtapose images of the Sapphire (Bitch) with the Jezebel (Ho) to illustrate how Black women have been demonized in American society. Clearly, as Collins articulates in her book *Black Feminist Thought*, Black women's oppression reflects an intersection between "race, class, gender, and sexuality [that] could not continue without powerful ideological justifications for their existence" (Collins, 2000, p. 69). Collins goes on to say that portraying Black women as mammies, matriarchs, welfare recipients, and hot mammas helps to justify their oppression (p. 69). In her book, she deals with the image of the Jezebel, which, she says, "represents a deviant Black female sexuality" (p. 81). Adams and Fuller (2006) describe the Jezebel (referred to in rap as the "ho" or "whore") as a "loose, sexually aggressive woman … who wants and accepts sexual activity in any form from men, and she often uses sex as a means to get what she wants from men" (p. 945). In Ludacris's song "Ho," he says:

> *You gotta run in your pantyhose*
> *Even your Daddy knows*
> *That you sucking down chocolate like Daddy-o's.*

That last line clearly refers to a woman performing a sex act on a man. In this song, he lists characteristics of a ho, from "hos never close they open like hallways" to "can't turn a ho into a housewife ['cause] hos don't act right." Even though further down in the song he says, "Niggas is hos too," it is clear here that this is a woman of little value. In another song, "Money Maker," Ludacris says:

> *Shake, shake, shake your moneymaker*
> *Like you were shaking it for some paper*
> *It took your momma 9 months to make ya*

Might as well shake what your momma gave ya

This song makes the clear connection between women exchanging sexual favors for payment, a key feature of the "hoochie" image, of women who "attract men with money for a one-night stand" in hopes that it will land them pregnant (hence the phrase "hoochie mama") and in a "long-term relationship with a man with money" (Collins, 2000, p. 82). While these images are widespread and damaging, female hip-hop artists create alternative dialogues through their own engagement with hip-hop feminism. For instance, with her song "How Do I Love Thee," Queen Latifah defied the White patriarchal myth of the "Black Jezebel" by presenting an image of Black female sexuality that was not based on promiscuity (Collins, 2000).

As Adams and Fuller (2006) note, in contrast to the Jezebel, the image of the Sapphire grew out of the mammy figure, "generally depicted as an overweight, dark-skinned woman who appears to be asexual" (p. 944). Although by some accounts, the mammy was an asexual figure, the Sapphire is not (Morton, 1991, p. 7). They describe the Sapphire (referred to in rap as "the bitch") as a "socially aggressive woman who tries through manipulation to control her man. She is filled with attitude, has a fiery tongue, and she squashes the aspirations of her man or men in general" (p. 945). Keyes (2002) asserts that "some women of rap take a middle road" view to the term "bitch," saying that it depends on the context within which the word is used. For instance, in her interview with Queen Latifah, the rapper says:

> I don't really mind the term. I play around with it. I use it with my homegirls like, "Bitch are you crazy? Bitch is a fierce girl." Or "That bitch is so crazy, girl." Now, that is not harmful. But "This stupid bitch just came down here talking ...," now that is meant in a harmful way. So it's the meaning behind the word that to me describes whether I should turn it off or listen to it. (p. 200)

Addressing the counterdiscourse of Black female hip-hop artists, Keyes (2002) presents results of interviews with Black women performers and audience members. More specifically, Keyes draws from the work of Hazel Carby (1985) to explore how their discourse articulates a struggle over the objectification of female sexuality in order to reclaim their bodies and present images of themselves that mirror "the lifestyles of African American women in contemporary urban society" (p. 189). The images Keyes outlines include Queen Mother, Fly Girl, Sista with Attitude, and the Lesbian. According to Keyes, Queen Mother is reminiscent of "African-centered icons" like the Asiatic Black Women and Nubian Queens that reflect "sistas droppin' knowledge to the people" (p. 189). Queen Latifah's *All Hail the Queen* album (1989) is an example of this image. One of the most popular groups of their decade, Salt-N-Pepa, represented the Fly Girl, described as a woman with "voluptuous curves, but contrary to other 'mainstream' images of sexy, acquiescent women, ... speaks what's on her mind" (p. 194). Keyes's next category, the Sista with Attitude, "comprises female MCs who value attitude as a means of empowerment and present themselves accordingly" (p. 200). MC Lyte and Eve are examples of this image. Her final category, the Lesbian, presents another response to White patriarchal power and sexual objectification by male rappers. Keyes chronicles the work of Queen Pen, recognized as "the first female MC to openly discuss lesbian culture" (p. 206).

There is much debate over where the misogyny toward Black women actually originated. At issue is whether rap music (as the leading element of hip-hop culture) creates and projects these negative images or whether it is merely reflective of a dominant social discourse that renders Black women inferior and without voice. In fact, in his article on Don Imus's gross misstep on the airwaves in which he referred to Black women on the Rutgers University basketball team as "nappy-headed hos," James Peterson wrote, "Hip hop is blamed for the racist assault on young Black women by a powerful, arrogant sixty-six-year-old white man who probably couldn't tell you the difference between Black Thought and Ja Rule" (p. 130). Peterson draws from an interview in which Imus defended his choice of words using the justification that hip-hop's own artists demean Black women. In his comments, Imus said:

> "I may be a white man, but I know that ... young black women all through that society are demeaned and disparaged and disrespected ... by their own black men and that they are called that name." In the interview, Imus said black rappers "call them worse names than I ever did." (p. 130)

Cultural critic Michael Eric Dyson weighed in on this debate in his book *Know What I Mean: Reflections on Hip-hop*. He argues critics of hip-hop have "got the line of detrimental influence backwards." Hip-hop has not helped mainstream misogyny that its artists invented; it is that the "ancient vitriol" toward women has been amplified in the mouths of some young Black males (Dyson, 2007, p. 135). Dyson adds further:

> White culture venomously attacked black women long before the birth of hip-hop. In fact, hip-hop has made the assault on black women stylish and perhaps more acceptable by supplying linguistic updates (like the word "ho") to deeply entrenched bigotry. (p. 135)

For Dyson, there are moral contradictions in society (i.e., young Black men who praise their mommas, but slam their baby mammas) that exist outside hip-hop culture and serve as a backdrop for hip-hop's misogyny. For him, these stereotypical images need to be discussed in a way that is both critical of the music and the sociopolitical space in which it exists (Dyson, 2007).

Dyson's argument adds a dichotomous contradiction not commonly addressed in discussions about the often degrading lyrics in rap music that specifically target Black women. The fact that the contradiction exists inside and outside of the realm of rap music leads to the necessity to fill a gaping hole in the research on misogyny within this music. In retrospect, the Imus controversy along with other high-profile instances of the use of racial and insensitive language in popular culture (i.e., comedians Michael Richards and Andy Dick's use of the "N" word) have done more to advance this discussion of the use of offensive language guised as entertainment than the analyses of the hip-hop culture and its use of similar offensive expressions. *Washington Post* writer Nekesa Mumbi Moody (2007) states in her article "Rappers Cleaning Up Lyrics Post-Imus" that the Imus controversy may be the catalyst that brings focus to offensive language in rap music. She notes months after the controversy, some artists' publicly abandoned offensive language and even some corporations began dropping rap acts from sponsorships due to explicit language.

With such highly charged debates about the "language of hip-hop," one would assume that the frequent targets of such language would stand unified and vocal about the toxic influence that misogynistic lyrics can have on the culture. Here lies the stark contradiction. What is characterized by many scholars as a perpetual influence of "Black-on-Black" hate on masses of young people who embrace and are part of the hip-hop culture, is seen by others as a hypocritical double standard when it comes to characterizing the use and meaning of some of the most degrading language in rap music. However, it is debatable whether hip-hop fosters internalized hostility toward African American females or engenders a form of feminism in its own right that positively heightens gender identity among Black women (Henry, 2010; Henry, West, & Jackson, 2010). Feminist scholars Patricia Hill Collins and Joan Morgan see this double consciousness as a congruent fixture in the sometimes turbulent nature of African American male and female relationships.

Despite the fact that hip-hop culture, particularly rap music, is heavily male-dominated, "a number of strong female voices have emerged from within the hip-hop industry, using rap music forms and other subgenres of hip hop music like neo soul to assert their own identities and to critique the limited identifications offered for women within the genre" (Bost, 2001). "Women are achieving major strides in rap music by continuing to chisel away at stereotypes ... by (re) defining women's culture and identity from a black feminist perspective" (Keyes, 2002, p. 208). Keyes goes on to argue that while women in this male-dominated industry "face overt racism," these MCs "move beyond the shadows of male rappers in diverse ways" (p. 208).

These "alternative voices" in hip-hop music are often integral in negating the perpetual influence of misogynistic and demeaning language found in much of rap and hip-hip music today. The influence of positive or conscious female hip-hop music has successfully taken root across the globe. In their article "Oppositional Consciousness within an Oppositional Realm," Phillips, Reddick-Morgan, and Stephens (2005) state that many historical accounts and critical analyses of the hip-hop phenomenon have tended to downplay the contributions of women. They state further that "women have played pivotal roles as artists, writers, performers, producers, and industry executives. Women have influenced rap style and techniques, ultimately shaping aesthetic standards and technological practices by both men and women" (p. 254). To localize this discussion, we focus on hip-hop's art in Detroit, Michigan.

THE DETROIT CONNECT

All the elements of hip-hop (deejaying, emceeing, b-boy or girling, and tagging or graffiti) are well represented in Detroit, Michigan. The hip-hop scene in Detroit has blazed a similar path as what has been seen around the world since the inception of this unique culture. The misogyny of the male-dominated music genre and the counterinfluence lead by positive female hip-hop artists have both coexisted in Detroit's rich hip-hop culture. Although women are underrepresented on the local scene, a few female artists have managed to make their mark. Two underground female emcees have emerged from the men's club of rap in Detroit. Bo$$, a gangster rapper from Michigan, has worked with DJ Quik and was signed to Def Jam West. Miz Korona has had a successful local career and made an appearance in the movie *8 Mile*. In the movie, Korona played the role of a female battle rapper during the scene at the automotive plant's lunch truck.

Unfortunately, just like female artists on the national scene, the women on Michigan's hip-hop scene experience pressure to masculinize their identities and images for the sake of marketing. Rose (2004) argues that for critics of hip-hop "it is far easier to re-gender women rappers than to revise their own gender-coded analysis of rap music" (p. 292). Hip-hop simultaneously marginalizes women and stripes them of the gender identity while providing a space for a feminist perspective. Roberts (1991) points out that rappers like Queen Latifah, MC Lyte, and Roxanne Shante have successfully linked discourses of racial oppression with antimisogynistic lyrical content. This is an interesting phenomenon in a musical form largely considered misogynistic. To understand gender in the Detroit hip-hop scene, an analysis female performers from Michigan is essential.

Despite the disproportionate representation, Tricia Rose (2004) acknowledges that women have contributed to the narrative of resistance in hip-hop. This is true of Detroit native Bo$$. She operated as an early female voice in gangsta rap. Bo$$'s image as a rapper was "posing with automatic weapons and spitting malevolent rhymes about cop killing, liquor swilling, street hustling and being the 'b—that's legit" (Smith, 2004). She joins the long tradition of hip-hop artists that provide a voice of resistance to marginalizing and oppressive structures. This resistance is in simultaneously pushes back against racist structures, while reinforcing misogynistic behavior. The use of the word "b—" can obviously be construed as oppressive, but it is the two words ("that's legit") that followed it that sent the marginalized message. These three words together imply that a woman that is authentic is an anomaly in hip-hop or street culture, thus prioritizing masculine identity traits over feminine identity traits.

According to Gan, Zillmann, and Mitrook (1997), Black female rappers match their male counterparts when it comes to sexually degrading content about other women. This can be seen in the song "Mai Sista Izza Bitch" Bo$$ has AMG, a male guest emcee, lyrically objectifying women with the line "Cause she's on some new improved shit / Cause this ho is a ('Bitch!') that ho is a ('Bitch!') / So my sista is a motherfuckin ('Bitch!')." These misogynistic lyrics occur alongside Bo$$ distancing herself from the women AMG is talking about. "[B]e creepin and freakin, ho after ho every weekend / But see I'm out to get a grip, a sista like myself / I'll grab the gat and get hazardous to a n—'s health." With this line, Bo$$ is sending the message that she is not like these other women, but the comments made by AMG are never condemned. In fact, she refers to herself using the same terminology. Bo$$ participates as "one of the guys" in "Mai Sista Izza Bitch." This gender imagery does not fit into Collins's (2000) framework of the typical depictions of Black women in popular culture—mammies, matriarchs, welfare recipients, and hot mammas. Similar to rapper Da Brat, Bo$$'s image as "one of the guys" does very little to resist oppressive structures. As Bost (2001) argues, to retain their positions, rappers like Da Brat "must present an image that appears superficially consistent with hip-hop stereotypes."

Bo$$'s identity construction calls for an additional lens to analyze the Black female imagery in hip-hop. Womanism allows for the exploration of Collins's (1991) concept of the dialectic of identity between race, gender, and class that Black women must reconcile. Hip-hop has long provided a platform to discuss racial oppression and social class imbalances. However, hip-hop still lacks a sizable space for the discussion of gender oppression. Female artists like Queen Latifah suggest an area for the unique marginalization faced by African American women in the songs. In her song "Ladies First," she says, "A woman can bear you, break you, take you / now it's time to rhyme, can you relate to / A sister dope enough to make you holler and scream." Through the lens of womanism, we see congruence between Queen Latifah's empowering message and the Bo$$'s discourse of resistance to hip-hop's limited possibilities for Black women.

In contrast, Miz Korona represents a place where lyrical ability is the most important trait. Somewhere between the male-appropriated traits of Bo$$ and the empowerment message of New York's Queen Latifah, Miz Korona is "a lioness in a lion's den." This statement supports the man's club mentality of hip-hop and describes Korona as a resister to this phenomenon. The space carved by Korona for herself in this male-dominated sport is much like Bo$$ through appropriating masculine behaviors. This is evident in her song "Rock Out." "It ain't coming / I'm gunnin' for all you bastards / ... see if it's a game when I send your ass to ER." She uses violence to claim her place as the "lioness," not creating a new identity but using the accepted hip-hop aesthetic. Both Korona and Bo$$'s hip-hop identities support Tricia Rose's (2004) claim that "women rappers employ many of the aesthetic and culturally specific elements present in male rap lyrics." Both of these female Detroit rappers are adhering to the masculine themes of sex, power, and violence; however, Korona's songs are less oppressive to women.

Some might argue that using violent imagery, Miz Korona and Bo$$ regender themselves for the purpose of success in the rap music industry. Crossing that line of criticism of those who sexually objectify women is Bo$$'s song entitled "Recipe of a Hoe." While it is important to note that the male/female relationships in rap lyrics are complex, this complexity is reflected in Bo$$'s use of the words "bitch" and "ho," while at the same time questioning the conquest of males. "Claimin' they getting' it, / but on the real they really ain't getting shit / Steadily stressin' you knockin' the boots." Bo$$'s complicated identity proves that hip-hop is a form of discourse that allows space for confronting power (Morgan, 2005). Sexism remains apparent in rap music, but because of the resistant nature of the culture, women can simultaneously accept and reject marginalization.

Herein lays one of the major contradictions within hip-hop culture: Do lyrics that are consistent with hip-hop's stereotypes aid in the uplift and empowerment of Black women? Is it enough that women like Bo$$ and Miz Karona create a counterdiscourse to their male counterparts, or should we advocate an alternative discourse that allows for new possibilities for Black women to "represent" images that analyze the status quo? While these women comment on male references to women as hos and bitches, much like Da Brat, they make any feminist content difficult to decipher (Bost, 2001).

CONTRADICTIONS AND CONTRIBUTIONS: THE ROAD TO AN ALTERNATIVE DISCOURSE

Issues of race confound issues of gender. This is never more evident than when hip-hop magazine *The Source* revealed a tape made by a teenage Eminem disrespecting Black woman (Reid, 2003). In this "lost tape" Detroit emcee Eminem rhymes "Black girls only want your money cuz they dumb chicks," and "never date Black girls, because they only want your money / and that shit ain't funny." The fact that Eminem is a White male points to a troubling aspect of depictions of Black women in rap lyrics. Eminem credits these lyrics to a bad break-up; if this is the case or not cannot be confirmed. It does call into question how these messages about African American women in rap music affect the perception of Euro American male listeners of the music. According to Bakari Kitwana (2005), 70 percent of rap music is purchased by Euro American youths.

Emerson (2002) and Adams and Fuller (2006) illustrate how hip-hop presents distorted interpretations of Black women's sexuality. Use of words like "bitch" and "ho" about women, particularly Black women, undoubtedly has a negative effect on the receivers of this message. For Whites, this is exacerbated by the fact that they are likely to have less exposure to alternative depictions Black women. For example, a suburb just a few miles from the city of Detroit, Livonia is the "whitest" city in the United States with over

100,000 people, while Detroit has the highest majority of Black persons among cities over 100,000 accounting for 82.7% of residents in 2010 (French, 2002, 2012; U.S. Census Bureau, 2013). This provides limited opportunity to have interracial interactions. Providing a space for a communal discussion of the distorted characterizations of Black women in rap lyrics/videos, which may be the only representations White male youths experience, is essential to countering these images.

The work of Dyson (2007), Collins (2000, 2006), Morgan (1995) and others have shown how hip-hop music and culture has contributed to oppressive images of Black women. When analyzing the lyrics of Eminem and Ludacris, it is undeniable hip-hop music can further marginalize women. Even when the music is performed by female artists, as seen in the case of Bo$$, the marginalization female identity can be seen. In the case of Eminem's lost tape, some come from Euro American males. It is important to note that while these lyrics do not reflect the totality of hip-hop is, it definitely reflects the music that mainstreams.

One.Be.Lo from Pontiac, Michigan, on his song "E.T.," expresses the relationship between a man and women in a much different way than AMG in the Bo$$ track. "Communication is the key, unlock / We put our heads together like a Mt. Rushmore / I found what I was / lookin for, plus more / Now with you I wanna spend the rest of days / Cause you shine in an extraterrestrial way." Los talks of relationships as mental not purely physical, as a union, not oppositional, and describes the woman with the word "shine" not "ho."

The image presented by One.Be.Lo is counter to Adams and Fuller's (2006) Sapphire and Jezebel. It even provides an alternative depiction for those provided by Collins (2000) of Black women as mammies, matriarchs, welfare recipients, and hot mammas. His lyrics present an intellectual attractiveness—a move away from the body-confining identity presented in the words of Ludacris discussed in this [reading].

Why a feminist analysis? The real benefit of a feminist analysis of this phenomenon is the opportunity it provides for moving beyond mere images and representations of Black women in hip-hop lyrics, toward a concrete discussion of how Black women artists engage feminism within this cultural framework. In other words, how do they carve out a space to express their feminist dialogue within the art form? Peoples (2008) contends that as we engage hip-hop feminism in terms of how it operates in the sociopolitical space we call hip-hop, we can begin to better understand the nature of resistance it represents (p. 21). For many women artists, hip-hop not only lends a space for them to critique hegemony and racism, but also to articulate a counterdiscourse of liberation from the hypersexed, money-driven female hustler depictions that have plagued them in and out of this culture.

As we continue to engage hip-hop feminists' contributions to the debate on misogyny, we must abandon the notion of hip-hop feminism as merely a *counter*-discourse that perpetuates hatred and disdain between Black men and women and embrace the notion of an *alternative* discourse where hip-hop feminists (men and women) can seek to counter oppression that is ever present and foster coping strategies to combat the negativity that has become normalized in everyday life. We must also pursue the transformative space that is created when Black female rappers use hip-hop as a platform for their own feminist discourse because it is this discourse that makes the alternative possible. Jamila (2002) urges that "as women of the hip-hop generation we need a feminist consciousness that allows us to examine how representations and images can be simultaneously empowering and problematic" (p. 392).

As Hobson and Bartlow (2008) point out, artists like "MC Lyte, Queen Latifah, Yo-Yo, Da Brat, Sistah Souljah, and Eve, have all evolved from simply 'talking back' to sexist scripts produced by men to articulating their own perspectives on sexual, racial and class politics in their music" (p 4). In addition to this list of female artists, Erykah Badu, Lauryn Hill, and Jill Scott are members of the larger realm of hip-hop culture, which encompasses a broader scope of the genre and adds positive social and political messages to the hip-hop culture. While these women have contributed to the dialogue on the imaging of Black women in hip-hop, there are other artists whose work presents a barrage of contradictions. For instance, Lil' Kim and Foxy Brown and Trina "have largely embodied tropes of black female hypersexuality" not only by conforming to the notion of being a sexual object, but by flaunting that sexuality as a false sense of power in the further commodification and objectification of the female body (Hobson & Bartlow, 2008, p. 4). Often in relating to power (that Foucault says is always present), we become complicit in the very power we struggle against. While some, like Queen Latifah, have broken away from the oversexualized images perpetuated in much of rap's music, artists like Da Brat, the Bo$$, and Miz Karona uphold more traditional stereotypical images of Black women. It seems that what makes Latifah and the rest "feminist" is their resistance to the dominant discourse (Hobson & Bartlow, 2008). Bost (2001) argues that the ways in which rappers like Latifah, MC Lyte, and Yo-Yo enacted their critique of rap music's misogyny "distanced them from dominant media images of hip-hop gender roles and thus limited their audiences."

Tricia Rose and Patricia Hill Collins help to make the argument that a continued evaluation of Black women artists *only* in relation to their male counterparts and *only* in relation to the misogynistic lyrics that help to keep them subjugated prevents a deeper exploration of the broader goal of hip-hop feminists, which is to examine the contradictions and contributions that lie at the intersection of the feminist movement and hip-hop culture.

For Collins and Morgan, the struggles within the hip-hop community mirror the struggles within the Black community—reflecting a need to repair the damaged relationship between Black men and women that is central to the survival of the Black family and ultimately the Black community. In fact, as Collins (2006) articulates, Morgan is one of the leaders in the discussion of Black hip-hop feminism being an intersection of Black women's relationships with "their personal and political histories," with themselves and with Black men (p. 192). As for the nexus between racial and gender identity with hip-hop, Collins notes the historical significance of having a collective identity, which can only be preserved through "community work" activities in the African American community as a means of understanding the dialectical relationship between Black men and women.

Collins (2006) describes "community work" in the African American community as a form of reproductive labor to (1) ensure the physical survival of African American children; (2) build Black identities that would protect African Americans from White supremacy; (3) uphold viable African American families, organizations, and other institutions, of Black civil society; and (4) transform schools, job settings, government agencies, and other important social institutions to ensure fair and equal Black participation. How does hip-hop affect this discussion of community and empowerment? Collins's research provides opportunities to open the dialogue on the use of hip-hop as a social force to reclaim sociopolitical power in the Black community. There is much discussion about the potential of hip-hop to provide liberation and "progressive political practice" (Peoples, 2008, p. 20). For this to happen, however, we must overcome the contradictions and take a reflective look at how hip-hop culture and the music it produces is merely a reflection of the limited "sociopolitical space" that has historically existed for African Americans as a part of mainstream culture.

In her article "Fly Girls, Bitches, and Hoes" (1995), Morgan states that rap music is essential to the struggle against sexism "because it takes us straight to the battlefield" (p. 153).

> My decision to expose myself to the sexism of Dr. Dre, Ice Cube, Snoop Doggy Dog, or the Notorious BIG is really my plea to my brothers to tell me why they are who they are. I need to know why they are so angry at me. Why is disrespecting me one of the few things that will make them feel like men? What are they going through on the daily that's got them acting so fucked up. (p. 153)

Although the notions of community work and a collective struggle for community have had historical significance in explaining the relationship between Black men and women, today's social ills and oppression have tainted these ideological notions of a Black community. In fact, Collins asserts that gendered structures of power continue to impede the Black community and that notions of Black feminist empowerment have not had much effect on African American women and girls. This lack of empowerment, Collins notes, explains to some degree why there is sustained support for Black rap artists whose work is "riddled with misogyny, the cavalier use of terms such as 'bitches' and 'hos' to refer to black women in everyday speech" (2006, p. 136).

In her analysis of Julia Cooper's work at the turn of the twentieth century, Carby (1985) characterizes the plight of Negro women in that day in a way that we can similarly embrace. She said for Cooper, "to be a woman of the Negro race in America" was to be able to "grasp the deep significance of the possibilities of the crisis ... [it is] to have a heritage ... that is unique in the ages" (p. 265). According to Carby, Cooper saw the responsibility of the Black woman as reshaping the society "to stamp weal or woe on the coming history of this people" (p. 265). Young women like Moya Bailey from Spelman College signify the possibilities and contributions that can be created through this kind of role modeling. When she led a protest of rapper Nelly and his appearance on Spelman's campus for a charitable event because of his misogynistic lyrics in controversial songs like "Tip Drill." There are many other examples of this kind of blueprint for raising the consciousness of rap music and hip-hop culture, including *Essence* magazine's "Take Back the Music" campaign (2005) and the Rock the Vote and Vote or Die campaigns to increase participation of urban youth in the voting process.

Clearly, there is liberating potential in both rap music and hip-hop culture. The real test will be women and men who are not afraid to engage the misogynistic discourse in ways that create space for the role, positionality, and image of women on a local and global level that counter the patriarchal abuse of Black women's sexuality (Carby, 1985; Hobson & Bartlow, 2008). According to Keyes (2002), "black women rappers are in dialogue with one another, black men, black women, and dominant American culture as they struggle to define themselves ... and to refute, deconstruct and reconstruct alternative visions of their identity" (p. 209). Hip-hop's historical roots provide an opportunity from which we can understand the potential and problematic of Black male/female relationships, the multiple and sometimes muted voices of female artists, and the myriad ways that these women manifest resistance to oppression within and outside of their own communities.

REFERENCES

Adams, T.M., & Fuller, D.B. (2006). The words have changed but the ideology remains the same: Misogynistic lyrics in rap music. *Journal of Black Studies, 39,* 938–957.

Bennett, A. (2000). *Popular music and youth culture: music, identity and place.* New York: Palgrave Macmillan.

Bost, S. (2001). Be deceived if ya wanna be foolish: (Re) constructing body, genre, and gender in feminist rap. *Postmodern Culture, 12*(1). Retrieved via ProQuest from http://muse.jhu.edu.proxy.lib.wayne.edu/journals/pmc/v012/12.1bost.html.

Byrd, A. (2004). Claiming Jezebel: Black female subjectivity and sexual expression in hip-hop. In V. Labaton & D.L. Martin (Eds.), *The fire this time: Young activists and the new feminism* (pp. 3–18). New York: Anchor Books.

Carby, H.V. (1985). On the threshold of woman's era: Lynching, empire, and sexuality in Black feminist theory. *Critical Inquiry, 12*(1), 262–277.

Collins, P.H. (1991). *Black feminist thought: Knowledge, consciousness, and the politics of empowerment.* New York: Routledge.

Collins, P.H. (2000). *Black feminist thought: Knowledge, consciousness, and the politics of empowerment.* 2nd ed. New York: Routledge.

Collins, P.H. (2006). *From Black power to hip hop: Racism, nationalism, and feminism.* Philadelphia: Temple University Press.

Davis, A.Y. (1995). Afterword. In R. Walker (Ed.), *To be real: Telling the truth and changing the face of feminism* (pp. 279–284). New York: Anchor Books.

Dyson, M.E. (2003). *Open mike: Reflections on philosophy, race, sex, culture and religion.* New York: Basic Civitas Books.

Dyson, M.E. (2007). *Know what I mean? Reflections on hip-hop.* Philadelphia: Perseus Books.

Emerson, R.A. (2002). "Where my girls at?" Negotiating Black womanhood in music videos. *Gender and Society, 12*(1), 115–135.

French, R. (2002). *New segregation: Race accepts divide.* Retrieved from http://www.detnews.com/specialreports/2002/segregation/a01-389727.htm.

French, R. (2012). Wayne State University: In a Black-majority city, but one of the worst at graduating African-Americans. Retrieved from http://www.mlive.com/news/detroit/index.ssf/2012/02/at_wayne_st_easy_to_get_in_dif.html.

Gen, S., Zillmann, D., & Mitrook, M. (1997). Stereotyping effect of Black women's sexual rap on White audiences. *Basic and Applied Social Psychology, 19*(3), 381–399.

Gilkes, C.T. (1983). From slavery to social welfare: Racism and the control of Black women. In A. Swerdlow and H. Lessinger (Eds.), *Class, race, and sex: Dynamics of control* (pp. 288–300). Boston: G. K. Hall.

Guy-Sheftall, B. (Ed.). (1995). *Words of fire: An anthology of African-American feminist thought.* New York: W.W. Norton & Company.

Henry, W.J. (2010). Hip-hop feminism: A standpoint to enhance the positive self-identity of Black college women. *Journal of Student Affairs Research and Practice, 47*(2). Retrieved from http://journals.naspa.org/jsarp/vol47/iss2/art1/?sending=11039.

Henry, W.J., West, N.M., & Jackson, A. (2010). Hip-hop's influence on the identity development of Black female college students: A literature review. *Journal of College Student Development, 51*(3), 237–251.

Hobson, J., & Bartlow, R.D. (2008). "Representin': Women, hip-hop, and popular music. *Meridians: Feminism, Race, and Transnationalism, 8*(1), 1–14.

Jamila, S. (2002). "Can I get a witness? Testimony from a hip-hop feminist." In D. Hernandez and B. Rehman (Eds.), *Colonize this! Young women of color on today's feminism* (pp. 382–394). New York: Seal Press.

Keyes, C.L. (2002). *Rap music and street consciousness.* Urbana: University of Illinois Press.

Kitwana, B. (2005). *The cotton club: Black-conscious hip-hop deals with an overwhelmingly white live audience.* Retrieved from http://www.villagevoice.com/2005-06-21/music/the-cotton-club/.

Moody, N.M. (2007). Rappers cleaning up lyrics post-Imus. *The Washington Post*. Retrieved from http://www.washingtonpost.com/wp-dyn/content/article/2007/08/02/AR2007080201607.html.

Morgan, J. (1995). Fly-Girls, bitches, and hoes: Notes of a hip hop feminist. *Social Text, 45*, 151–157.

Morgan, M. (2005). Hip-hop women shredding the veil: Race and class in popular feminist identity. *South Atlantic Quarterly, 104*(3), 425–444.

Morton, P. (1991). *Disfigured images: The historical assault on Afro-American women*. Westport, CT: Praeger.

Peoples, W.A. (2008). "Under construction": Identifying foundations of hip-hop feminism and exploring bridges between Black second-wave and hip-hop feminisms. *Meridians: Feminism, Race, Tran nationalism, 8*(1), 19–52.

Phillips, L., Reddick-Morgan, K., & Stephens, D.P. (2005). Oppositional consciousness within an oppositional realm: The case of feminism and womanism in rap and hip hop, 1976–2004. *Journal of African American History, 90*(3), 253–277.

Pough, G.D. (2007). "What it do, Shorty?" Women, hip-hop, and a feminist agenda. *Black Women, Gender, and Families, 1*(2), 78–99.

Reid, S. (2003). *The Source digs up tape of Eminem using racial slur*. MTV Online. Retrieved from http://www.mtv.com/news/articles/1480512/20031118/eminem.jhtml.

Roberts, R. (1991). Music videos, performance, and resistance: Feminist rappers. *Journal of Popular Culture, 25*(2), 141–152.

Rose, T. (1994). *Black noise: Rap music and Black culture in contemporary America*. Rose, T. (2004). Never trust a big butt and a smile. In M. Forman and M.A.

Neal (Eds.), *That's the joint! The hip-hop studies reader* (pp. 291–306). New York: Routledge.

Smith B. (2004). *Same as the old Boss*. Metro Times Online. Retrieved from http://www.metrotimes.com/editorial/story.asp?id=6344.

Turner, K.K. (2002). *Sun Messenger*. Metro Times Online. Retrieved from http://metrotimes.com/editorial/story.asp?id=3013.

U.S. Census Bureau (2013). *State and county quick facts: Detroit (city) Michigan*.

Retrieved from http://quickfacts.census.gov/qfd/states/26/2622000.html. Weheliye, A. (2001). Keepin' it (un) real: Perusing the boundaries of hip-hop culture. *New Centennial Review, 1*(2), 291–310.

Histories and "Her Stories" from the Bronx

Excavating Hidden Hip Hop Narratives

By Oneka LaBennett

Popular and academic understandings of the cultural production of hip hop tend to focus on the music as a site of misogyny, aggressive masculinity and rampant consumerism. Historical accounts of hip hop have privileged male narratives, stifling women's stories and their valuable contributions to hip hop music and culture. This [reading] utilizes oral history interviews from the Bronx African-American History Project (BAAHP) to shed light on hidden hip hop narratives constructed by female Bronx-based artists who reside at the margins of the music industry and are peripheral to the dominant discourses surrounding hip hop music. Utilizing an anthropological approach to oral history research, I explore the unexpected, complex and often contradictory ways in which women's "creation narratives" figure into their use of hip hop as an educational tool, as a mechanism for political activism and as a springboard for articulating feminist ideologies. I argue that for contemporary Bronx female artists, hip-hop represents a means for demonstrating a feminist consciousness and for claiming racialized belonging. I further assert that women's hip hop narratives generate critical understandings of how Diasporic Blackness is (re) conceptualized in relation to local and global racializations (Thomas and Clarke 2006).

My title "Histories and 'Her Stories' from the Bronx: Excavating Hidden Hip hop Narratives," borrows from a long-standing tradition in feminist oral history research and is inspired by a collaboration between the pioneering feminist oral historian, Sherna Gluck (whose work began in the 1970s) and her students. That paper was entitled, "Whose Feminism, Whose History? Reflections on Excavating the History of (the) U.S. Women's Movement(s)" (Gluck et al.: 1998). The notion of "hidden narratives" is related to James Scott's concept of "hidden transcripts" which he characterizes as "discourse that takes place ... beyond the observation of power holders" (Scott 1990: 4). In his framework, "the hidden transcript is produced for a different authence and under different constraints of power than the public transcript" (Scott 1990: 5). Scott sees such hidden transcripts as "representations] of power spoken behind the back of the dominant" (Scott 1990: xii). I aim to illustrate how Bronx women's oral histories reveal hidden narratives surrounding women's critical oral traditions and their ways of defying social norms that de-legitimize women's role in hip hop. In this [reading], I wish to uncover or excavate what is valuable about women's narratives—narratives that often remain obscured from the public realm but which are vital contestations of how women are represented in mainstream hip hop. In turn, I will also emphasize the usefulness of oral history research for uncovering a second, related hidden narrative—the ways in which Puerto Rican and Dominican women use hip hop to claim local and global notions of African Diasporic belonging.

THE HISTORY AND "HER" STORY OF HIP HOP

> So get ready to learn the truth about your hip-hop heritage. The Mercedes Ladies may not have reaped the monetary benefits or the glitz that "the game" soon delivered. But one thing we do have is the title of being the first all-female DJ and MC crew from the Bronx. Nobody can ever take that away from us. We will forever be a part of history. Wait a minute—let me rephrase that. Not just "His" story. That is "Her" story. Our story—Sheri Sher, *Mercedes Ladies: A Novel*

Before turning to the three women whose oral histories inspired this [reading], I must say a bit about the larger research project and the history of Bronx hip hop. I began working on a hip hop history initiative for the BAAHP in September of 2007. Although a number of the Project's now 200 plus interviews had centered on hip hop even before I formally began this initiative, much of the Project's early work focused on recording oral histories of Bronx residents who grew up in the borough in the 1940s and 1950s. Much of this work was based around interviewing individuals who played prominent roles in the Bronx's other vibrant musical traditions—jazz, Doo Wop and salsa, to name a few. With hip hop poised to enter its fifth decade of existence-it made sense to launch an initiative centered on its early history.

The common understanding is that hip hop originated in the South Bronx in the early 1970s. However, scholars of and participants in hip hop culture acknowledge the African diasporic origins of the musical form, which borrows from African, American and Caribbean traditions. Paul Gilroy explores these cultural currents in *The Black Atlantic*, writing, "hip hop culture grew out of the cross-fertilisation of African American vernacular cultures with their Caribbean equivalents rather than springing fully formed from the entrails of the blues" (Gilroy 1993: 163). As in all recuperative representations, there is, however, a hidden component in the historical understanding of the origins of hip hop. I found, in my larger research on popular youth cultures, gender and the African

Diaspora, that much of what is written on hip hop focuses on male artists and on what I call the "creation narrative of hip hop." Researchers from Gilroy to Jeff Chang rely on a creation narrative that represents hip hop as springing forth almost entirely from men. Gilroy posits, "The immediate catalyst for [hip hop's] development was the relocation of Clive "Kool DJ Here" Campbell from Kingston to 168th Street in the Bronx" (Gilroy 1993: 103). Indeed, Clive Campbell, popularly known as DJ Kool Here, is widely credited with pioneering hip hop soon after he migrated from Jamaica to the Bronx in 1967 and started spinning records at house parties held in the recreation room of 1520 Sedgwick Avenue in the early 1970s. In a chapter entitled, "Making a Name: How DJ Kool Here Lost His Accent and Started Hip Hop," journalist and hip hop historian Jeff Chang writes,

> It has become myth, a creation myth, this West Bronx party at the end of the summer of 1973. Not for its guests—a hundred kids and kin from around the way, nor for the setting—a modest recreation room in a new apartment complex; not even for its location—two miles north of Yankee Stadium, near where the Cross-Bronx Expressway spills into Manhattan. Time remembers it for the night DJ Kool Here made his name" (Chang 2005: 67).

While Chang refers to this as a "creation myth" I prefer to focus on the creation *narrative* created by Chang, by Kool Here himself and by other hip hop scholars ~ most of whom rely on this account in tracing the origins of hip hop. Chang goes on to note that the party known for starting hip hop was actually the brainchild of Here's sister, Cindy Campbell, who, motivated by a desire to earn money for a new back-toschool wardrobe, obtained the space, purchased the refreshments and advertised the party. Still, Chang does not position Cindy Campbell as central to the creation of hip hop. Drawing on interviews with Kool Here and Cindy Campbell, Chang focuses instead on how Here's father, Keith Campbell a record collector and owner of a Shure P.A. system played a vital role in these parties. The elder Campbell provided the sound system with which Here went on to spin records first inside 1520 Sedgwick and later at now famous outdoor block parties in surrounding neighborhoods. Here would go on to print "Father and Son," business cards acknowledging his father's central role. However, I suggest refocusing this creation narrative around the ways in which Cindy Campbell was both instrumental and largely overlooked. Chang is to be credited for even mentioning Cindy Campbell; she is completely absent from Gilroy's account. Even versions of hip hop's creation narrative which include the role played by Cindy Campbell, recount the story with male protagonists. Cindy Campbell not only promoted Here's first party, but many of the other early parties that made him famous and that cultivated the critical dance and fashion elements of hip hop. I am arguing, therefore, that hip hop's "creation story" is one that marginalizes the role of women like Cindy, instead presenting men as miraculously giving birth to the hip hop infant with little help from women. Gwendolyn D. Pough's book, *Check it While I Wreck It: Black Womanhood, Hip-Hop Culture, and the Public Sphere* offers an academic response to the male-centered hip hop creation narrative. Pough writes, "Women's contribution to Hip-Hop culture has been lost, or rather, erased. To hear some self-proclaimed Hip-Hop historians tell it, there were no significant women in Hip-Hop's history" (Pough 2004: 8). My present endeavor builds on Pough's project, yet charts a distinct course in that while she emphasizes the contributions of commercially successful and/or popularly known artists such as Roxanne Shante, Queen Latifah, Missy Elliott and Lil' Kim, I am more concerned with female hip hop artists whose narratives have remained largely hidden from the mainstream, mass-marketed hip hop industry. In so doing, my analysis is in debt to the work done by Pough and by a number of other scholars who have offered critical theorizations on the gender politics of hip hop (Rose 1994, 2004, Guevara 1996, Gaunt 1997, Morgan 1999, Keyes 2004, Perry 2004).

Sharon Jackson (also known as "Sha Rock"), a Bronx-based emcee who, in 1976 became the first female member of the seminal hip hop group, The Funky Four, is one of a few women recognized for contributing to hip hop's early development. In her 2008 novel, *Mercedes Ladies*, Sheri Sher presents an important revisionist history. Based on Sher's real experience as a member of the first all-female hip hop emcee and DJ crew, *Mercedes Ladies* reveals the ways in which women's work as early promoters, emcees, DJs, graffiti artists and break-dancers remain largely invisible. Yet, Gilroy and Pough's academic cachet and Jeff Chang's journalistic credentials position their accounts as more legitimate than Sheri Sher's novel. The cover of Chang's book, *Can't Stop Won't Stop: A History of the Hip-Hop Generation* boasts "Introduction by DJ Kool Here". While Chang's cover flaunts collaboration with a "true" hip hop pioneer, Sheri Sher's book employs both the actual names of early hip hop actors (such as Sha Rock) and fictionalized names, with monikers such as "Shelli Shel" (instead of Sheri Sher) replacing "real" historical actors. If one considers the risks women in hip hop culture have faced when they dare to speak out on a number of issues, especially domestic violence, we can understand that the strategy of utilizing pseudonyms is often times a necessary protection when one is recounting hidden narratives.[1] *Mercedes Ladies* details the physical abuse, sexual

---

1   Violence against women within the social space of hip hop culture figured prominently in a roundtable discussion 1 organized under the auspices of the BAAHP's Bronx is Building Lecture Series on January 22, 2009. The discussion, entitled, "Women in Bronx Hip Hop" featured three panelists: Sheri Sher, emcee/ actress Patty Dukes and journalist Elizabeth Méndez Berry. Berry who has written for such mainstream popular hip hop magazines as The Source and Vibe, recounted how she struggled to find a publisher for her investigative report on domestic violence in the hip hop industry entitled, "Love Hurts: Rap's Black Eye." Berry also related how many of the women she interviewed, including some commercially successful female artists, only participated under the condition that they would remain anonymous. Both Berry and Sheri Sher emphasize that hip hop women who report abuse face a real threat of further violence. Liza Rios, the widow of the platinum-selling, Bronx-based, Puerto Rican rapper, Christopher Rios ("Big Pun") is a noted exception; Liza spoke with Berry on the record, describing the physical abuse she suffered at the hands of her late husband and chronicling it

harassment and tooth and nail struggles the group encountered as they transitioned from a crew of teenage girls whose hard-edged style and presence at all the right parties won them popularity and references on tracks by accomplished DJs, into the first, bona fide all-female emcee and DJ hip hop act. Not an academic treatment, Sheri Sher's work belongs in the genre known as "street lit" or street literature. There is, of course, a long tradition of incorporating elements of fiction in women's cultural writings, most notably perhaps with the work of Zora Neale Hurston and Ella Deloria and continuing with contemporary female ethnographers such as Karen McCarthy Brown. Regarding Hurston, Kamala Visweswaran writes, "there is not a clear-cut demarcation of her work into novelistic, autobiographical, or ethnographic genres, or even a clear sense that she worked for a time only in one form to begin with another (Visweswaran 1994: 3–4). Still, although feminist writers such as Visweswaran have acknowledged that all ethnographies (and histories, for that matter) are stories and that literature has influenced ethnographic writing in valuable ways, accounts such as Sheri Sher's, while holding street credibility, have arguably less status than the more formal accounts which often position men at the center.

With women's roles erased and women's narratives stifled, one might listen to the "official" creation story of hip hop and think that it is therefore no wonder that hip hop developed into an overtly masculine cultural form. Even if we think beyond rap music and incorporate the other elements of hip hop; dance, graffiti art and fashion, a cursory glance at mainstream hip hop confirms the notion that this is an aggressively masculine cultural product. In her book entitled, *Pimps Up, Ho's Down: Hip Hop's Hold on Young Black Women*, T. Denean Sharpley-Whiting argues that hyper-sexualized and derogatory images of Black women are a crucial element of contemporary hip hop music and culture (Sharpely-Whiting 2007). Sharpley-Whiting is referring to the basic formula for most hip hop videos; numerous, scantily clad young Black and Latino women, whose rear-ends and breasts fill almost every frame, and who appear to have no other desire than to give sexual pleasure to the male rap star. Scholars and cultural critics such as Sharpley-Whiting, Tricia Rose and Nelson George, who have addressed misogynous lyrics in hip hop, have noted that from about the mid-1980s to today, many rap lyrics have centered not on the verbal dexterity of the artists, but rather on "bitches," "ho's" and on explicit slang for female genitalia (Sharpley-Whiting 2007, Rose 1994, George 1998). Yet, the actual experiences of the marginalized people, artists and consumers who grew up with hip hop and who continue to use it in meaningful ways, are glaringly absent from this dialogue.

---

in a 2002 documentary. The silencing of women's narratives as they relate to violence in hip hop culture is apparent not only in abuse survivors' reluctance to speak but also in the industry resistance Berry faced as she attempted to get her article published.

AN ANTHROPOLOGICAL APPROACH TO ORAL HISTORY INTERVIEWING

I saw a hip hop history initiative focused in particular on Bronx women's experiences as a way to fill this gap. This [reading] draws most heavily on a BAAHP oral history interview with an artist named La Bruja (Caridad de la Luz) and incorporates two additional oral histories, one with Patty Dukes (Patricia Marte) and another with Lah Tere (Teresita Ayala) from the musical group Rebel Diaz. I conducted all three interviews in the fall of 2007.[2] The three women are Bronx-based performers who utilize hip hop in unexpected ways in their musical performances, in their personal lives and in their work as activists.

Like the majority of the BAAHP' s interviews, these three oral histories were recorded in the Department of African and African American Studies conference room at Fordham University. Lasting between one and two hours long, the interviews were audio and video recorded and were based around open-ended questions. As an anthropologist, however, I strove to contextualize the three interviews beyond the confines of what was "performed" in our conference room. I did this by interacting with the artists at numerous performances and events, by communicating with them via email and by listening to their recorded music. These three women know each other and are part of a close-knit community of artists/activists. Therefore, for example, I saw Patty Dukes perform at an event organized by Lah Tere. I knew a good deal about La Bruja (the Spanish word for "witch") even before recording her oral history because I had viewed a documentary film made by Bronx filmmaker Felix Rodriguez entitled, "La Bruja: A Witch from the Bronx." I interviewed Rodriguez first, recording his life story but also asking him questions about Caridad. Even before she came to our office for an interview, La Bruja's mixtape CD "Brujalicious" became the informal soundtrack of Fordham's Dealy Hall for several weeks. In the fall of 2008, almost a year after first recording their oral histories, I invited Rodriguez and La Bruja to present a screening of the aforementioned film at Fordham, followed by a question-answer period in which I learned even more about La Bruja's life and work. Along similar lines, on January 22, 2009, the BAAHP's "Bronx is Building" lecture series featured a panel discussion entitled "Women in Bronx Hip Hop" in which both Patty Dukes and the aforementioned Sheri Sher participated.

Before I turn to La Bruja's life story I want to briefly reflect on the life history genre as it has been utilized in anthropology. Lila Abu-Lughod, following Geyla Frank, Vincent

---

2   The La Bruja oral history was conducted on October 23, 2007, 1 interviewed Lah Tere and Patty Dukes on December 1 1, 2007 and December 14, 2007 respectively. BAAHP Affiliated Scholar, Dr. Natasha Lightfoot, acted as a secondary interviewer on the Patty Dukes Interview. Patty Dukes' emcee partner, Rephstar was interviewed simultaneously. BAAHP Principal Investigator, Mark Naison, acted as a co-interviewer on the Rebel Diaz oral history.

Crapanzano and Ruth Behar reminds us "we need to recognize that life histories are actually stories that people tell about themselves, texts requiring attention to the conventions of storytelling and the context of the elicitation" (Frank 1979, Crapanzano 1980, Behar 1990, Abu-Lughod 1993: 30). As Delia Pollock has noted, "... the telling of stories is inherently performative: an interviewee puts on a show, creates an identity, within the context of talking to the interviewer" (Pollock 2005: xi). Scholars such as Abu-Lughod, Gluck and Marjorie Shostak caution us to always be aware of the anthropologist's positionality and how this affects what the narrator tells and how she tells it. Along these lines, my own positionality as a feminist researcher creeps in later when I interpret La Bruja's approach to gaining recognition from her male peers. In terms of thinking about La Bruja/Caridad's narrative as a *performance* or a *story she told me about herself*, I will say this: La Bruja is both a talented emcee/poet and an impressive story teller. In fact, I would argue that those two things always go hand in hand. So I was not surprised when she deftly drew my undergraduate assistant, our videographer and me into the story of her life.

LA BRUJA: A KITCHEN POET'S HEIR

La Bruja is a Bronx-born Puerto Rican hip hop emcee, performance artist and spoken word poet who gained some national recognition after appearing on Russell Simmon's "Def Poetry Jam." She is also the mother of two young children who recently separated from her husband and lives one block away from her parents in the South Bronx. A community activist who routinely volunteers to teach Bronx children at various schools and centers, La Bruja was born in 1973 and is the oldest of the three women I interviewed.

When I asked La Bruja what first influenced her to become a spoken word poet and later a hip hop emcee, she told me that it was her maternal great grandmother, a talented poet who lived with her family in the Bronx. Caridad spent her early childhood memorizing the old woman's poems.

> OL: Did your great grandmother write the poems or did she recite them to you and then you memorized them?

> LB: She recited them. She didn't know how to read or write, and she had a memory of gold. She had eleven children ... she never did poetry as a mother. Once she was older and wasn't in the kitchen anymore she said, that's when her memory, it clicked and she started sharing all these poems. She started sharing and my grandmother was like, we never heard you do this! So, it came to her later on and it was great ... She died when I was ten. That's when I started writing, because I couldn't remember her chorus, and

... I felt crushed ... I was like, "Oh my god, she's gone and I don't remember!" So I think that I've been trying to recite, or reword what she taught me. Her messages- because a lot of my poems, especially the ones that really made me popular, were about my grandmother or about my house, the Latino experience, the Puerto Rican experience. ...

La Bruja presents a female-centered creation narrative. Her birth as an artist sprung from her great grandmother's unexpected creative talents. Significantly, Caridad's great grandmother was not able to cultivate her own poetic abilities until after raising her children. In *Krik? Krak!* a collection of short stories inspired by Haitian women's oral traditions, Edwidge Danticat defines what she calls "kitchen poets."

And writing? Writing was forbidden as dark rouge on the cheeks or a first date before eighteen. It was an act of indolence, something to be done in a corner when you could have been cooking. Are there women who cook and write? Kitchen poets, they call them. They slip phrases into their stew and wrap meaning around their pork before frying it. They make narrative dumplings and stuff their daughters mouths so they say nothing more (Danticat 1996: 219–220).

Caridad's great grandmother was a true "kitchen poet" in Danticat's sense because her poetry was an oral tradition, confined to the private realm and imparted to her female heir. She shared her "hidden narratives" only after fulfilling her socially prescribed role of being a mother. Later, Caridad revealed that although her own Spanish was "not very good" she often felt like she was channeling her great grandmother when she recited poetry in Spanish. In this way, La Bruja's identity as a hip hop witch is predicated on notions of possession common in creolized Caribbean religions such as Santería and Vodou. In fact, santería and possession figure prominently in La Bruja's one-woman show, "Boogie Rican Blvd." in which she explicitly connects her pseudonym to her African ancestry and to creolized African religions. La Bruja's identity as an emcee also developed around Caridad's role as a teacher. I asked La Bruja how she transitioned from being Caridad, the poet to La Bruja, the hip hop emcee.

LB: I would do writing workshops in the community for youth, if I said, "Work on your poetry," they looked at me like, "Ugh, this is torture." "Okay," I changed it up, I was like, "Who listens to hip hop? I'm going to teach you how to write rhymes." And in the end, I was teaching them the same thing with a different title, and they were like "yeah!" you know? And then, I too was like, "Well, their language is in rhyme, it's flow, so I have to develop my flow," so I knew that I was a poet, I knew that I was pretty good at it— at the spoken word—and I was like, now I got other things developing, and I can do it with them. ...

OL: Where was this that you were teaching?

LB: At the East Harlem Tutorial Program, it was on 106th and 2nd, and I worked there for a bunch of years and did stuff at The Point Community Center [located in the South Bronx]. So, from the beginning of being La Bruja in '96 I would do hooks for people they would be like, "Yo we need a girl to sing this, this is what the song is about," so I would go. I would write a rhyme, 1 would drop the lyric ... drop the verse. Eight bars or whatever, and I kept doing that for this person and that person, "You want a hook, you need a hook? Okay, I'll write a hook, I'll sing the hook." I wouldn't get paid, but I would build a relationship, I would build a connection, and get to hone my own skills. So by the time "Brujalicious" came on, it was like ten years into, or nine years after doing that, I felt like all those dudes that I paid, that "Brujalicious was the fruit ofthat labor. Because then I was able to get big names with me ...

OL: What was it like negotiating yourself in that new role; I mean by doing those hooks for other people, you know, relating to men in the industry, what was that like?

LB: I would have to defend myself. There were certain things I would tell them I'm not going to do. If it's a gang song I'm not going to do it ... I'm not going to do no guns, no this, no that. Actually, on "Brujalicious" it's a great story because the "Olvídate" song that has all those guys on it and I'm just singing the last verse. When I first went in there, they were all talking about pigs and shooting and I was like, "Hmmm, none of y 'all live like that so don't even try," [laughter] ... I was like, "Please what is it that you're selling?" ... So, in the end of it, Don Dinero was like, "Why don't you just rep you, say what you have to say, just do it your way, let us do it our way ..." So, I wrote about, "I'm here to celebrate, to dance, I didn't come here to fight, and I'm gonna make you forget about fighting." So that's what the whole "Olvídate, was, forget about that." The whole premise of "That's not what I'm here for, I'm living my grandma ..." That's really what it was about, it was like trying to school these guys at the end of it.

Here, La Bruja brings her feminine creation narrative to bear on the contemporary problems surrounding hip hop's reliance on violence. She connects the nascency of her album, "Brujalicious," with her work as a teacher in urban youth centers. For La Bruja, poetry, teaching youth to write and hip hop are inter-related. The idea that hip hop is predicated on violence or misogyny is not part of her artistic process. However, I steered the discussion from her early years singing hooks, a traditionally feminine role in hip hop, to her interactions with male artists. Here, La Bruja reveals that she used her great grandmother's wisdom to "school these guys." After she finished this explanation I said:

> **OL:** What you just said made me think of this in an entirely different way than I've ever thought of it before, because it sounds like when you went into that particular recording session where you said, "I'm not going to sing about that," because you were female, you had the freedom to sing about something else, where they felt they had to present their masculine identities. But because you're female, you had a little bit more freedom, which is interesting to think about.

> **LB:** It is. The others think they're soft. I'm a writer woman, I can be soft ... I can be whatever I want to be. Then I've heard girls fall into the same thing and they're ... talking hard. Don't be hard. Look at Remy Ma. Remy, she's got children ... I read something in an interview about [her] just you know, "I'm keeping it real"? What? ... I long for some, some substance and I feel ... that Remy got caught up in that too. That they have to be hard to get respect from the dudes.

The above exchange is significant in terms of excavating a hidden narrative that goes against the grain of popular hip hop representations. It is also an important moment in which I injected my own interpretation into the oral history process, interpreting La Bruja's experience from my perspective as a feminist researcher. I brought this perspective into the narrative itself and La Bruja corroborated my interpretation but also offered that being female does not always release an artist from the pressures of "keeping it real." Gluck warns that "questioning our interpretations [the researcher's that is]" of the storyteller's narrative "is a critical part of reflecting on women's oral histories" (Gluck 1998: 75). Gluck goes on to suggest, in a statement than can be applied to my example, "...This was exploration of meaning and a discussion of interpretive authority but at the same time it put[s] meat on the query with the use of narrative excerpts to illustrate the kinds of activities in which the women engaged and the ways in which they seem to express a feminist consciousness" (Gluck 1998: 75). It is significant that La Bruja described herself as a "writer woman" rather than as a "woman writer." The awkward phrasing that she chose, "writer woman" puts writing first and emphasizes her role as a writer before identifying her gender. Moreover, La Bruja expresses a feminist consciousness in Gluck' s sense because for her, "writer" and "woman" are inseparable.

In the telling of her own life story, in her recorded music, in her live performances and in her work as an activist, La Bruja routinely expresses a feminist consciousness. Here I am using Abu-Lughod's minimal definition of "feminist," that is, showing "a concern with women's conditions and with the political, economic, social, and cultural implications of systems of gender for them" (Abu-Lughod 1993: 4). La Bruja is not the only Bronx hip hop artist expressing such a consciousness. She, Patty Dukes and Lah Tere are all part of an artistic community of Bronx artists who use hip hop to create feminist spaces both figuratively through their music and literally through workshops and public events.

LAH TERE: "THIS IS NOT JUST RAPPING YOU KNOW"

"Momma's Hip Hop Kitchen: The Soup Kitchen for the Hip Hop Soul" was one such event. Organized by Lah Tere and a Fordham undergraduate named Kathleen Adams, "Momma's Hip Hop Kitchen" took place on February 16, 2008. Lah Tere described her vision for the event when I interviewed her along with the other members of the group Rebel Diaz (Rod Starz, a.k.a. Rodrigo Venegas and G-1, a.k.a. Gonzalo Venegas).

> **LT:** It is hip hop for the soul, right. And it's specifically for women of color who are going to be reporting back about their organizing in HIV/AIDS and their organizing in reproductive rights. So it's a space where women are free to express themselves with whatever art form they feel, whether it be graffiti, just regular painting, emceeing ... There are going to be female DJs. Every element that you can think of in hip hop is going to be there, and it's going to be women doing it. So it's not only for women, but it's a women's event.

I attended Momma's Hip Hop Kitchen (where Patty Dukes performed) and interpreted it as a gathering of "kitchen poets" who demanded that their art, struggles and experiences be heard in the public sphere. Born in Chicago on September 24th, 1979, Lah Tere is the daughter of two teachers who migrated from Puerto Rico to Humboldt Park, a largely Puerto Rican community located on Chicago's northwest side. Lah Tere attended Jose Riego grammar school in Chicago, a public school with a political tradition. Many of Lah Tere's teachers were Puerto Rican and she attributes her early engagement in political activism to the education she received at Jose Riego. Like La Bruja and many other women who become hip hop emcees, Lah Tere began as a singer rather than as a rapper. She joined what she described as a "politically resistant salsa band" while in high school. Making frequent trips to Puerto Rico during her adolescence, she also incorporated the Afro-Puerto Rican musical tradition known as *bomba y plena* into her singing style. However, Lah Tere recounted how, during her high school years, hip hop became as important a musical element as more distinctly Puerto Rican genres.

> **LT:** [Starting from] my freshman year ... I liked music. Wherever there's a beat, it sounded to me like bomba and salsa. It's the same thing, the sounds are the same, the beats are the same ... I would put the free-styling, the free-style singing into the freestyle cipher. That's pretty much where I fit into the whole category.

Lah Tere was lured to the Bronx when Gonzalo Venegas arranged for a job interview for her with the social justice organization, Mothers on the Move (MOM), located in the South Bronx. MOM hired Lah Tere and she joined them in organizing Bronx residents on educational, housing, and environmental injustice issues. Lah Tere's job at MOM coincided with the birth of the group Rebel Diaz on April 10, 2006. The group sees their organizing work and their production of hip hop music as related parts of what Lah Tere described as a "spiritual calling." "The work that we do is front-line work," she said. "This is not just rapping, you know?" When I asked Lah Tere if the close, sibling-like relationship she has with her band mates, the Venegas brothers helped her negotiate her identity as a female hip hop artist, she said:

> I have these awesome brothers, as a woman, as a queen, I feel like a queen everyday ... Even when we're fighting there's a level of respect where I feel safe, I feel protected. It's a real community, a real unit.

When I asked Lah Tere if she felt that as a female she had to play a different role than the male members of Rebel Diaz, she responded:

> I feel like its up to you to do what you feel like you have to do in [hip hop] culture. Who cares if this girl is popping her ass over there, doing her thing ... I am a completely different person, and I have a whole other purpose. I can't sit here and worry about everything that's happened in the hip hop culture in regards to women and use that as a way to help me mold my thoughts in this movement. I don't have time for that! ... I'm sorry that that is what has happened in hip hop. And we can talk about it, but right now I have this work that I have to do. I have to speak for the immigrants. I have to speak for the women of color with AIDS and HIV. I have to talk about reproductive rights. If I focus on the negative there's no way I'll be able to move.

Here, Lah Tere echoes La Bruja's choice to chart her own course as a female emcee, one that diverges from the dominant representations of women in hip hop. Much like La Bruja, Lah Tere infuses these ideas into her rhymes and uses her talents to teach and organize. When they discussed their roles as female hip hop artists, similar currents of agency and determination rang through all three women's oral histories.

Notions of African diasporic belonging were another common thread throughout the three interviews. While the Bronx African American History Project is ostensibly aimed at recording the oral histories of Bronx residents of African descent, the project has interviewed individuals from many ethnic and racial backgrounds in order to reflect not only the diversity of the Bronx, but also to document how cross-cultural exchanges between several different ethnic and immigrant groups inform the history of the Bronx's Black residents. Negotiations between Latina and Black identities were central to each of the three life stories I conducted, with each woman revealing how identifying with African ancestry became a critical element in her work as a hip hop artist. These themes were especially prevalent in Patty Dukes' oral history.

PATTY DUKES: "PUT A MICROPHONE IN FRONT OF A LITTLE GIRL AS OPPPOSED TO A BABY"

Patty Dukes, née Patricia Marte, was born on November 13, 1979. Marte got her stage name when the well-established spoken word poet, Lemon, jokingly punched her in the arm. The blow was hard and Patty retaliated by sneaking up on Lemon and punching him in the back of his head. In front of a rather large group of on-looking friends, Lemon was shocked that Patty had "put up her dukes" and he responded, "Who do you think you are, Patty Dukes?!?!" The name suited Marte and it stuck.

Patty's family is from Puerto Rico but relocated to the Dominican Republic where she was born. The family moved once again to the Bronx when Patricia was around five-years-old, soon settling at 167th St. and Jerome Avenue. Patricia's father, who had been in the military in Puerto Rico, began working as a building superintendent and her mother stayed home to care for the couple's three children. Patty recounted how she attributes the unconventionally feminine persona she cultivated as a little girl both to her father's influence and to her identification with hip hop.

> It was really interesting, I think because of my father's influence. I mean my mother was ... [a] homemaker and really just a girly girly type. And my father was really ... a man's man ... he would wake us up at six in the morning on a Saturday to go jogging, military style. And I used to hate it but in some way or another, I was such a tomboy. I was always in sports and my brother- every time he would pick something, I wanted to do whatever he was doing ... whether it was basketball, and at that time music started coming out as far as like the Wu-Tang and all this other harder and aggressive stuff. While my mom and sister were listening to more bachata and meringue, the stuff like from the country, I was more into Mary J. Blige. So culturally I was completely different than my family. Even though we were all Dominican and Puerto Rican, I was definitely more of the New York kid. The hip hop kid. My sister is still that Dominican girl that listens to Spanish music, she doesn't really listen to hip hop. I'm the hip hop type, you know what I mean? So it was interesting though, I'm also the darkest one, I must say that had to do with it as far as skin color because my mother is really light ... And my dad is really, really dark.

Significantly, Patty connects her "tomboy" persona to her affinity for hip hop and her darker skin. In the above narrative she positions Dominican musical genres such as bachata and meringue as more feminine while situating hip hop as "harder and aggressive." The hip hop artists Patty mentions as early influences, Wu-Tang Clan (a hardcore all-male rap group who came to prominence in the early 1990s) and Mary J. Blige (a Bronx-born, R&B/hip hop singer known as "the queen of hip hop soul") are both New York-based acts known as much for their commercial success as for their street credibility. Patty revealed that her family equated her darker skin with her love of hip hop and that she was often explicitly told she was "the ugly one."

> Yes, so there is also a lot of resentment ... I love my family and now I'm able to have conversations with my mom and she is able to understand what that did... [when I was young] we had conversations where they would be like, you know you're the dark one, you know the ugly one. I was made fun of because of my lips, because they were too big and then if I listened to Mary J. Blige, "you're trying to be Black."

Patty's family's admonitions that her darker skin and fuller lips were "ugly" reflect the Latin American and Caribbean discourse of *blanqueamiento* (whitening), which renders Blackness as in-authentically Puerto Rican or Dominican and seeks to erase African heritage (Stinchcomb 2004, Godreau 2006, Godreau et al. 2008). "What is considered attractive, *de buena apariencia*, are a number of traits that Europeans are believed to have: thin lips, straight hair, and lightercolored skin. The phenotypes opposite those traits—thick lips, kinky and/or curly hair, and darker-colored skin—are described as *ordinarios* (ordinary), *malos* (bad) ..." (Stinchcomb 2004:5). As a girl Patty was explicitly discouraged from playing with Black dolls. She related her aunt's reaction when she chose a brown-skinned Cabbage Patch Kid doll.

> My aunt comes, "Why you want this ugly thing for?" Snatched it out of my hand, threw it to the back of the pile and picked up this little white boy, with frizzy hair, with perfect teeth and said, "Here!" And any little Barbie, my sister had all the Barbie collections and all this stuff. I hated it ... I hated all the typically girly stuff my sister would play [with] ... Now she has two kids. You become those things that you set out to be also when you're little. And people don't see that. Put a microphone in front of a little girl as opposed to a baby.

In the above narrations, Patty equates her family's hegemonic gender and beauty ideals with a conventional femininity that does not suit her. She distances herself from traditional femininity and advocates putting "a microphone in front of a little girl as opposed to a baby." Patty claims Blackness as a legitimate part of her identity and, by suggesting that a microphone is a more valuable plaything than a doll, she positions hip hop as an a crucial antidote to conventional femininity. In this way Patty uses hip hop to simultaneously subvert the discourses of *blanqueamiento* and traditional femininity.

Patty defied her parents by having African American friends and became even more of an outsider when she sacrificed weekend outings with her father and sister to attend acting classes. To her family's surprise she remained dedicated to acting, writing and emceeing beyond her teenage years. She continues to travel, to perform widely and stars in an podcast hip hop program called, "The Patty Dukes Show." Significantly, Patty has co-opted the 1960s predominantly white sitcom, "The Patty Duke Show," re-articulating it as a counter-hegemonic element within the realm of hip hop culture. Like La Bruja and Lah Tere, Patty only came to think of herself as an emcee after pursuing other artistic mediums. She began writing plays at an early age and only started rapping after meeting her emcee partner, Rephstar (Almicar Alfaro).

> I didn't feel like I had permission to do that (write rhymes) until later on. I used to always listen to Method Man or other rappers and I would transcribe their rhymes and then repeat them back. Just to get their flow and their rhythm and their cadence-to go over the beats. So I would constantly memorize and recite it. I didn't know necessarily how to organize a rhyme, it's very different from organizing a poem or anything else. I sort of had to learn everything else before I could write a rhyme, which I'm more grateful for because I understand how to write in general. I started writing plays at sixteen. I wrote my first play, got it produced at the theater, was in it, got my friends in it, then I started writing poetry, which was more condensed ... rhythmically there was more rules than rhyming. ..That's where I starting meeting Rephstar, is when I started to write rhymes and get it out there. And he sort of encouraged me to ... go do it and start in ciphers. I was terrified of cipher. There were no girls doing it.

While La Bruja channeled her great grandmother as an entryway into writing rhymes, Patty Dukes transcribed the lyrics of established hardcore male rappers such as Method Man. Both women initially felt that writing hip hop rhymes was not typically female behavior but both felt compelled to act unconventionally in order to express their creative talents in the realm of hip hop. The cipher, a circular formation where rappers compete by taking turns improvising rhymes until an individual is stumped, is a traditionally masculine space in hip hop. One of Patty Dukes' first experiences in a cipher was when she free-styled at a workshop in a youth detention center in California. The inmates had never seen a female emcee and the experience empowered Patty. "So right there they showed me I had the power to do this ... the fact that I may be able to show them a female that can do this." Patty and Rephstar started an organization designed to encourage young girls to write hip hop rhymes. She now sees her role as that of a "teaching artist."

I still see young people today, right now in the Bronx. I've been to schools in
the Bronx, I've been to schools in Brooklyn~I've traveled. They tell me that
they have not seen a female emcee, in front of them rap. And it's shocking,
and that's why ... it motivates me ... I got to keep going, I've got to keep on,
people need to know that there are [female emcees]. It's not even for me. It's
for the sake of the movement.

Like Lah Tere and La Bruja, Patty Dukes sees hip hop culture as a potentially transformative social movement. Significantly, while these women are aware of how mainstream
hip hop is interpreted as a site of violence and misogyny, they view hip hop music and
culture as a positive political tool for women and girls.

CONCLUSIONS

In this [reading] I have argued that the public history of hip hop, which prioritizes male
narratives, bolsters a contemporary cultural form that on the surface, presents itself
as a male space. Bronx women's creation narratives, as they relate to hip hop's early
incarnations, have remained largely hidden and their roles in developing hip hop culture
in the contemporary context have been marginalized. All three women took indirect
routes to becoming hip hop emcees because emceeing is not a traditionally feminine
role. Patty Dukes echoes a sentiment articulated by the two other women and suggests
that social norms initially discouraged her from writing rhymes when she says, "I didn't
feel like I had permission to do that."

I want to emphasize that Bronx women's hidden hip hop narratives speak as much to
social constructions of Blackness as they do to feminine subjectivities. For Patty Dukes,
identifying with hip hop, a cultural form her family equated with Blackness and with
non-traditional femininity, was a rebellious act. Lah Tere's experience was markedly
different since her parents always encouraged her appreciation for *bomba y plena*, a
musical tradition associated with Afro-Puerto Rican heritage. From an early age, Lah
Tere's family taught her to be proud of her African heritage: "I didn't have a choice. It
was from inception. My parents, my mom has always been a proud Puerto Rican woman
... And my father is Black ... so he made us conscious ..." It is significant, however, that
in this quote Lah Tere describes her light-skinned mother as "Puerto Rican" and her
dark-skinned father as "Black" although both parents are from Puerto Rico. This subtle
distinction perhaps speaks to the findings of scholars such as Isar Godreau, who argues
that Puerto Ricans associate authentic, national Puerto Rican identity with modernity and
with lighter colored skin, while equating Blackness with an inauthentic, antiquated past
(Godreau 2006). The three women's stories also reveal "the ways people understand,
perform, or subvert racial identities by mobilizing knowledges gleaned both from the
particularities of their local circumstances and from the range of ideas and practices

that circulate within their public spheres, showing that racial subjectivities are always 'coalitional, contingent, and performative'" (Thomas and Clarke 2006: 4, Visweswaran 1998: 77). All three women's racial subjectivities were contingent on African diasporic racializations (stemming from either Puerto Rico or the Dominican Republic), on local notions of racialized belonging (based on life in the Bronx) and on performative identity constructions (derived from and articulated within the cultural production of hip hop). Their subjectivities are also coalitional in the sense that they build upon and foster a feminist consciousness.

La Bruja, a fair-skinned Puerto Rican woman, did not question why her life story was being recorded as part of the Bronx African American History Project. Her reliance on Santería, a creolized Caribbean religious practice in claiming the name, La Bruja, and on hip hop as her chosen genre both acknowledge a debt to African Diasporic cultural forms. Yet, her self-identification as Black did not come up until the very last moments of telling her story, when La Bruja pulled a printed page from her purse and began to read a poem she had composed. I want to conclude this [reading] with the poem La Bruja read—which underscores the utility of oral history for illustrating how feminine, African diasporic identities are socially constructed. This final, unexpected recitation La Bruja offered is indicative of the improvisational and inherently performative nature oral history and hip hop share. It reveals how, "The stories told, often deeply expressive of history's burdens, lay claim on us for retelling so that history may be known, shared, perhaps overcome" (Pollock 2005: xi). We had been sitting and listening to La Bruja's life history for almost two hours, with the air conditioner in the BAAHP's small conference room buzzing and gurgling loudly as it seemed to struggle to keep the room cool. And, due to the humidity, La Bruja's straightened hair had, at this point, begun to curl up, with small beads of sweat appearing on her forehead as she clutched the printed page. She began in the same even-toned voice she had been using throughout the interview but then, as she started reciting the poem, she gestured triumphantly with her hands and her rising voice defeated the noisy air conditioner.

LB: I was inspired by Längston Hughes ... because of his poem, "I, Too Sing America," and how they talk of "You can't eat here because you're black, and you can't be here because you're black." (Reading poetry):

Although you may find me fair
With medium brown eyes and not too curly hair
Of mixed heritage too many to name
One thing was the same,
We've all shared despair
Believe it or not, in fact,
I too am black.

I have been stabbed in the back for being too much of this
And not enough of that
Have been compared to what exists
And been told how much I lack.
You may not know it now,
But it's a fact,
I too am black.

Color lines run deep in my veins
Behind covered mouths I've been called many names
Instead of hope they taught me shame,
But I chose to play another game.
With ears I hear but heart unchained,
You can keep it or take it all back.
You have eyes but are blind to the fact
That I too am black.

Black, like the Ebony tree
The deeper you carve into me
You can easily see the beauty,
The strength,
Shape me,
Shine me,

In the finest homes you'll find me
While strange fruit still hangs inside me,
With all the love I can muster,
My face glows with luster
It took more than the slave trade to make us cry,
But let me break it to you with truth and tact.
I am proud of the fact
That I too am black!

REFERENCES

Abu-Lughod, Lila. 1993. Writing Women's Worlds: Bedouin Stories. Berkeley, Los Angeles, Oxford: University of California Press.

Armitage, Susan H. and Shema Berger Gluck. 2006. "Reflections on Women's Oral History: An Exchange." In The Oral History Reader: Second Edition, Robert Perks and Alistair Thomson (eds.), London and New York: Routledge, pp. 73–83.

Behar, Ruth. 1990. "Rage and Redemption: Reading the Life Story of a Mexican Marketing Woman." Feminist Studies 16:223–58.

Berry, Elizabeth Méndez. 2005. "Love Hurts: Rap's Black Eye," in Vibe, March, 162–68.

Chang, Jeff. 2005. Can't Stop Won't Stop: A History of the Hip-Hop Generation. New York: St. Martin's Press.

Crapanzano, Vincent. 1980. Tuhami: Portrait of a Moroccan. Chicago: University of Chicago Press.

Danticat, Edwidge. 1996. Krik? Krak! New York: Vintage Books.

Frank, Geyla. 1979. "Finding the Common Denominator: A Phenomeno logical Critique of Life History Method." Ethos 7:68–94.

George, Nelson. 1998. Hip Hop America. New York: Penguin Books.

Gilroy, Paul. 1993. The Black Atlantic: Modernity and Double Consciousnes. Cambridge: Harvard University Press.

Gluck, Sherna Berger in collaboration with Maylei Blackwell, Sharon Cotrell, and Karen S. Harper, 1998. "Whose Feminism, Whose History? Reflections on Excavating the History of (the) U.S. Women's Movement(s)." In Community Activism and Feminist Politics: Organizing Across Race, Class, and Gender, Nancy A. Naples (ed.), New York: Routledge, pp. 31–56.

Godreau, Isar P. 2006. "Folkloric 'Others': Blanqueamiento and the Celebration of Blackness as an Exception in Puerto Rico," in Kamari Clarke and Deborah A. Thomas, eds., Globalization and Race: Transformations in the Cultural Production of Blackness. Durham and London: Duke University Press.

Godreau, Isar P., Mariolga Reye Cruz, Mariluz Franco Ortiz and Sherry Cuarado. 2008. "The Lessons of Slavery: Discourses of Slavery, Mestizaje and Blanqueamiento in an Elementary School in Puerto Rico," in American Ethnologist, February, Vol. 35, Issue 1, pp. 115–135.

Guevara, Nancy. 1996. "Women Writin', Rappin', Breakin'," in William Erick Perkins, ed., Droppin' Science: Critical Essays on Rap Music and Hip Hop Culture. Philadelphia: Temple University Press.

Keyes, Cheryl L. 2004. "Empowering Self, Making Choices, Creating Spaces: Black Female Identity via Rap Music Performance," in Mark Anthony Neal and Murray Forman, eds., That's the Joint!: The Hip-Hop Studies Reader. New York and Oxford: Routledge.

Morgan, Joan. 1999. When Chickenheads Come Home to Roost: My Life as a Hip-Hop Feminist. New York: Simon and Schuster.

Perry, Imani. 2004. Prophets of the Hood: Politics and Poetics in Hip Hop. Durham and London: Duke University Press.

Pollock, Della. 2005. "Introduction: Remembering," in Della Pollock, ed., Remembering: Oral History Performance. New York: Palgrave Macmillan.

Pough, Gwendolyn D. 2004. Check it While I Wreck It: Black Womanhood, Hip-Hop Culture and the Public Sphere. University Press of New England: Northeastern University Press.

Rose, Tricia. 1994. Black Noise: Rap Music and Black Culture in Contemporary America. Middletown, Connecticut: Wesleyan University Press.

--- 2004. "Never Trust a Big But and a Smile," in Mark Anthony Neal and Murray Forman, eds., That's the Joint!: The Hip-Hop Studies Reader. New York and Oxford: Routledge.

Scott, James C. 1990. Domination and the Arts of Resistance: Hidden Transcripts. New Haven, CT: Yale University Press.

Sharpley- Whiting, T. Denean. 2007. Pimps Up, Ho's Down: Hip Hop's Hold on Young Black Women. New York and London: New York University Press.

Sher, Sheri. 2008. Mercedes Ladies: A Novel. New York: Vibe Street Lit.

Shostak, Maijorie. 2006. "'What the Wind Won't Take Away': The Genesis of Nisa—The Life and Words of a !Kung Woman." In The Oral History Reader: Second Edition, Robert Perks and Alistair Thomson (eds.), London and New York: Routledge, pp. 382–392.

Stinchcomb, Dawn F. 2004. The Development of Literary Blackness in the Dominican Republic. Gainesville: University of Florida Press.

Thomas, Deborah A. and Kamari Clarke. 2006. "Introduction: Globalization and the Transformations of Race," in Kamari Clarke and Deborah A. Thomas, eds., Globalization and Race: Transformations in the Cultural Production of Blackness. Durham and London: Duke University Press.

Visweswaran, Kamala. 1994. Fictions of Feminist Ethnography. Minneapolis and London: University of Minnesota Press.

--- 1998. "Race and the Culture of Anthropology." American Anthropologist 100 (1): 70–83.

"Out" in the Club

The Down Low, Hip-Hop, and the Architexture
of Black Masculinity

By Jeffrey Q. McCune Jr.

For whom is outness a historically available and affordable option? Is there an unmarked class character to the demand for universal "outness"? Who is represented by which use of the term, and who is excluded? For whom does the term present an impossible conflict between racial, ethnic, or religious affiliation and sexual politics? What kinds of policies are enabled by what kinds of usages and which are backgrounded or erased from view?

—Judith Butler, *Bodies that Matter: On the Discursive Limits of "Sex"*

DL offers a new-school remix of the old-school closet, an improvisation on the coming-out narrative that imagines a low-key way of being in the world.

—Jason King, "Remixing the Closet: The Down-Low Way of Knowledge"

As I was inundated with various articles, news stories, and magazines translating this clandestine community of DL men, I became more interested in hearing their voices. Friends had told me of their "sightings of DL brothas" in the club and online, but I had never had conversations with these men with whom they mingled. My intrigue began one single night of being a wallflower on the club wall, as a thirty-something hard-body brushed up against me asking, "How you get down?" And my knee-jerk frown was quickly caught and transitioned into a smirk that welcomed a conversation revealing his articulation of himself as "being on the low" and looking for a "young, nice brother" like me. Our thirty-minute whispering along the wall—as it may have appeared to be a flirtatious exchange—was actually an informal interview, navigated by my intrigue at his refusal to say he was gay, his admission that this was his first time at an "alternative" spot, and the many questions he asked me in hopes of peeling back the mysteries of queer space. Over a year of ethnographic observation, I would interact with over forty

DL men[1] and perform twenty formal interviews with those I had met at the Gate. As I began to sift through the narratives, the saliency of space, music, and the construct of hip-hop masculinity compelled a richer chapter. Thus, while many of the experiences with these men are chronicled through the ethnographic detail, in this [reading] I focus on only two subjects, who speak to the complexity of this space. [...] I must also say that the two experiences distilled here share various representative elements—which speak to the utility of sexual discretion and the architecture, or *architexture*, of black masculinity. DL men—as they are often resistant to dominant narratives and doings of sexuality—write their way out of a largely hegemonic paradigm, entering into spaces and communities that have historically been a part of black male constructions of sexual identity.[2] DL men are new bodies dancing to an old song: the complex rhythms of sexual discretion.

This dance, both literal and metaphorical, is the focus of this [reading]. Here, I am most interested in the ways that DL men negotiate their "private" identity within queer club space. I wish to move from the printed page to the stage, focusing on the black queer club space and DL men's participation within it. As DL presences in predominantly openly gay male spaces may sound contradictory, it unveils the significance of space in expressions of sexual desire. DL men's participation in a queer space, but with a commitment to discretion, questions the popular perception that one is "out" if he is in a gay club. DL presence within the Gate[3] reveals that black masculinity with its diverse textures uniquely enables the possibility for discreet sexual desire. [...] I am interested in understanding how and why certain discreet performances of sexual identity are privileged and what allows for their prevalence within certain spaces. Specifically, what arrangement or structuring of the "black masculine" makes DL presence possible, perhaps comfortable? This particular [reading] explores DL men's travels within a traditionally or predominantly queer club space—where the diverse performances of a certain brand of masculine identity constitute and give credence to a DL positionality. In this club, I discover how "space ... unleashes desire. It presents desire with a transparency which encourages it to surge forth in an attempt to lay claim to an apparently clear field" (Lefebvre 1991, 97).

In my fieldwork, the most "transparent" space has been the Gate, the home of queer black dance on Friday nights, on Chicago's Northwest Side. In this particular club space, DL men perform "straight" masculine identity, while they also engage in homoerotic desires. Following several men in this space, I was able to witness their desires for each other and desires for a cultural space where men could do what I later discuss as "coming in"—finding a style and texture in a space where they fit. Most illuminating and representative were the experiences of twenty-two-year-old "Shawn" and twenty-three-year-old "Tavares."[4] Of all the men I spoke with, Shawn was the first I saw at a gay club. I use his experiences to illuminate, complicate, and outline some of the contradictions and complexities that arise when a DL guy goes "out." Tavares, in contrast to Shawn, is a lifelong friend who had more recently told me of his desire for men. One night, when

I mentioned to him that I was going to the Gate, he asked to join me. I chronicle his first experience in a predominantly male queer setting. Together, their narratives illuminate how what I designate later as the *architexture* of black masculinity can corroborate/collaborate with queer desire. These encounters prompted many questions: How do these men negotiate their commitment to a heteronormative understanding of self, while participating in homonormative social and sexual activities? What is it about DL subjectivity that allows for such possibilities? What is it about the structures and textures of the club space that invites these performers of discreet sexual identity?

BLACK QUEER WORLD-MAKING: GOING INSIDE THE GATE

Growing up in the 1980s and '90s, during a time when white queer politics were in your face and white queer images were dominant, my black queer world consisted of a ravaged imagination with no playground to explore and experiment. This understanding of black gay men as invisible or "quiet" continued with my collegiate experiences, as the predominant gay presence once again were white gay men. The potentiality of a black gay setting where men actually engaged homoerotic desire seemed at best foreign, at worst a fantasy never to be realized. It was not until my senior year in college that I learned that there were many people who had transformed my vivid imagination into a reality. Indeed, across the country and throughout the world, there existed spectacular spaces of black queer expression. In order to understand, experience, and enjoy my black queer self as a part of a living (rather than dormant) tradition, I would have to acknowledge what the critical performance scholar Dwight Conquergood knew well: "That sometimes—you do have to go there to know there."[5]

I first went to the Gate with my best friend, Aaron, after we came home for Christmas break in December 2000. As an undergraduate, I ventured into the white gay club scene under the racist "all black people look alike" mentality that marked the culture of so many white gay establishments, by using the ID of an upperclassman who was two shades darker than I. When I turned twenty-one, however, I was afforded open-door privileges to participate in whatever "adult" activity I desired. My visit to the Gate was my first official "black gay function." I remember asking folks in line, "Is it hot in there?" to which many applied in the affirmative. Many of the clubgoers were also lamenting the closing of the Incinerator, a black gay club that evidently had been the place to be "black and gay, and fabulous" prior to the Gate's arrival, according to one patron.

Interestingly, the Incinerator was a house club, which many argue lost its business to the "rise of hip-hop."[6] What was most significant about the Incinerator was its history as the only black gay club, seven days a week. The Gate, on the other hand, is gay once a week—becoming the Friday-night outlet for a large hip-hop queer mass. While those who attend the Gate have an option of listening to house or hip-hop, all of the club's advertisements and publicity seems to highlight its hip-hop appeal. Together, those who "kicked it" at the Gate partook in what Fiona Buckland, borrowing from Lauren Berlant and Michael Warner, describes as *queer world-making*[7]—"a conscious, active way of fashioning the self and the environment, cognitively and physically, through embodied social practices moving through and clustered in the city" (Buckland 2002, 19). While Buckland does not deny the possibility for a racialized subject to engage this practice, her research does not advance a theoretical application that accounts for racial subjectivity. During that Friday-night party, the Gate's patrons were definitely participating in an act of black queer world-making through their appropriation of a traditionally black heterosexual space and transformation of it into a space of and for queer desire.

Excited to be a part of this black queer world, Aaron and I entered the gates of the Gate. As we approached the cashier, we read a sign announcing, "alternative lifestyle night," which also explained why there was a ten-dollar cover charge. We both looked at each other, astonished at the use of the terms "alternative" and "lifestyle," which clearly marked the space as not only queer, but temporarily non-heterosexual. This framing of our evening of fun suddenly became queer, in the sense of odd, as we had configured this opportunity as not an alternative, but an only option. Second, we were also appalled at what seemed to be an inflated price for clubbing. Both of us, having ventured to predominantly white clubs, had become accustomed to three to five dollars covers for entry. In response to this escalation in price, Aaron referred to the cover as a "rip-off," and I at that time called it a scandal. Later I learned otherwise. Todd, a manager at the Gate, told me that "for black club owners, there is a greater price to pay—for the possibilities of misbehaving and also to make up for the lack of money made through the consumption of alcohol and other club activities." Clearly, the prices for this queer party were the product of something that went beyond scandal and rip-off. It was an example of the way Chicago's system of racism shows its face in every part of black life. However, our sentiments, and those of many others I have talked to, reveal the ways that this customary practice toward black parties informs a (mis)understanding of the economics of queer world-making. As a result, the escalated costs of clubbing at the Gate, when compared to "white" establishments," almost always suggested an unethical and outrageous "lack of appreciation" for black patronage. Due to such high costs, in what seems to always be hard economic times for black people, many choose to stay at home or truly find "alternative" things to do. This, I know, has not only led to disgruntled patrons, but has also contributed to the historical demise of many black gay events in general. Despite the ten-dollar cover, we entered this space of queerdom hoping that what was inside was better than what we had witnessed thus far.

As we entered the Gate, we heard the thump of house music and observed many bodies, mostly men, moving across the dance floor, feeling the groove, standing along the wall; the place was charged with homoerotic energy and rhythmic impulses. Initially, we didn't acknowledge the dynamics of space as much as we were attentive to the music and the "type" of folk in each space. It was not until we entered the second room, the hip-hop room, that we made any real assessment of the differences in clientele on this night: we noticed that it was crowded and filled with a sort of "brute masculinity," as Aaron put it. Immediately, I thought of cavemen when he used this analogy, but I understood the gist of his commentary. Indeed, there was something rough and rugged about the way people moved in this space. In this first episode at the Gate, I only remember us exiting the room quickly, as we began to sweat profusely in the midst of those dancing and moving to DMX's infamous "y'all gon' make me lose my mind up in here."

Feeling that we were literally going to "lose our minds," we returned to the house room, where we felt more comfortable and at home. In retrospect, I am sure that Aaron may have felt out of place in his Kenneth Cole black slacks and fitted white shirt because most of the men in the hip-hop room were not dressed in similar attire. Instead, they were adorned in what had become known as hip-hop gear: loose low-riding jeans, big shirts, and baggy wear. I was wearing a similar ensemble to Aaron, a black shirt (somewhat fitted) and a pair of regular-fitting jeans. I felt a tinge out of place, as well. Nonetheless, our return to the house room made us aware of the great contrast between the two spaces. The house room welcomed us. This was most clear when the vocalist on the DJ's track began to sing, "Divas to the Dance Floor." Quickly, we took to the dance floor as if that were a cattle call to our middle-class, college-going, Kenneth Cole-and DKNY-wearing selves. We thought we were divas—the cream of the crop. But more than this, we felt that we were "free" to express that part of ourselves that we had repressed for so long. This song initiated our move into black gay culture, showing us what we loved most about it: the fabulous music, the fabulous people, the fabulous DRAMA!

Fiona Buckland marks this act of being "fabulous" as a quintessential gay cultural performance sensation. Indeed, it is an essential component of black gay life, as it is in white gay cultural productions. However, the Gate, as a space that contained both house and hip-hop music, seemed to occupy two distinct modes of expression. While the house room and music were "fabulous," it was clear that the hip-hop room and music were deemed "cool." If one simply observed the house room, where one witnesses voguers in high fashion from DKNY to Prada, dancers wearing traditional Kenneth Cole, and the classic tight shirt/tight jeans models, he or she would recognize it as a place where "I'm fabulous and I don't care what you think" is the general sentiment. Whereas the predominant look in the hip-hop room was more uniform—demonstrating people's desire or consciousness of specific fashion trends traditionally associated with hip-hop music and its consumers. This is not to suggest that fabulousness and coolness are determined by fashion. However, clothes are one way that individuals in space can display both their individuality and conformity. Although this binary description may imply otherwise, it is important to note that I am not claiming that hip-hoppers and house-heads, as they are often called, don't share space or blur the lines. Yet, for this project, the distinctions between the two spaces are important as they reflect a larger dominant shift/divide in the black gay cultural experience at this historical moment. Therefore, the dynamics of the hip-hop room as a space that lends access to down-low positionality is of utmost interest. Indeed, this space circulates contradictory messages that supersede traditional boundaries of gender and sexuality, where men negotiate their relationship to and between masculine bravado and black queer culture.

This odd congruence, between hip-hop and queer desire, has "coolness" at its nexus. Here, I wish to discuss coolness as a more general expression, which Marlene Kim Connor in *What Is Cool?: Understanding Black Manhood in America* (2003) understands as a guiding ethic on how to dress, behave, and interact with approval from a largely black and male spectatorship. Coolness is a theory in practice—an embodied rubric that regulates and monitors what is and is not acceptable among black men under and outside of white surveillance. While I argue that coolness is not a uniquely black expression, it is a modern descriptor for a historical tactic. Most importantly, coolness acts as a way of survival, a coping stance/pose that black men utilize, in order to make do with what they do or do not have (Majors and Bill-son 1992, 4–5). Coolness is a performative utterance and action, whereby men define themselves within and against traditional standards. Indeed, like all performances, it changes depending on those involved, dimensions of space/place, and who is reading and interpreting the scene of action.

The Gate's hip-hop room seemed to spill over with coolness. Our quick entrance and exit, a sign of discomfort, was probably a resistance to such odd congruency. Queerness and coolness rarely are coupled in traditional black rhetoric. More pointedly, hip-hop as the impetus or interlocutor for queer desire is foreign to circulating mythologies of sexuality. Indeed, everything we had learned in our experiences about hip-hop and gayness said that "ne'er the twain shall meet." In addition, our tradition of queer experience included white men, techno music, and "fabulous" apparel. Naturally, the Gate's ability to forge a relationship between hip-hop and queerness was fascinating, but also triggered feelings of discomfort. We were queer indeed, but we were not hip-hoppers; we preferred house (more honestly read: techno) music, and we wanted to be fabulous rather than cool.

Indeed, the dynamic duo, hip-hop and queer space (or coolness and queerness), are incongruous at surface level, but a deeper examination can explain this coupling. Historically, hip-hop culture and music have gone against the grain of traditional American music and style—often critiquing dominant structures and modifying other musical forms. Likewise, queerness has also disrupted normative tales of sexuality, restructuring the perceived composition of our society and generally challenging normative socio-sexual rules and regulations. Together, they seem to make a "fabulous" pair. These two world-making apparatuses disrupt norms, interrogate new ground, and encourage exploration outside the domains of normativity. Ultimately, the relationship between hip-hop and black queer expression is a sort of meeting of two queers. Thus, hip-hop music's use as a medium for homoerotic engagements is not odd, but almost anticipatory.

Furthermore, the Gate as a predominantly black establishment would naturally welcome black forms of musical and cultural expression—its patrons are young black men and women who often are consumers of hip-hop in other contexts. And young postmodern black queer subjects are often most inclined to situate sexual identity as only one part of the self, rather than the most privileged point of identification.[8] Whereas white queer subjects may often construct a more peculiar culture, black queer subjects often appropriate traditional black (often heterosexual/sexist) mediums of entertainment for queer use. While this appropriation does, in fact, mark the black queer subject as unique from dominant structures, in these terms black gays can recognize both parts of the self, concomitantly. To follow this line of thought is to understand that black queer participation and enjoyment in hip-hop is congruent with black life—where hip-hop often operates as the nexus between the black and the queer. This reality corroborates the theoretical shift in the academy that understands the black subject as multiple, rather than monolithic. In a world that compartmentalizes different parts of the self (i.e., sexuality from black forms of expression), the black queer male/female subject understands that his/her being in the world is informed by all parts. Therefore, hip-hop is as much a part of queer world-making, as queer world-making is a part of the history of hip-hop.

Indeed, black queer world-making is a way of making history in a society where black experiences of same-sex desire and interaction are too often underrepresented and underappreciated. Hip-hop at the Gate provides a unique experience for black queer subjects to embrace such desires while maintaining an allegiance to macro-cultural forms of expressions. The (un)conscious moving and making of a black queer world constructs a black queer history that is dynamic, though often "down low." The Gate is one place that participates in a black queer world-making in Chicago, where it uniquely creates a conversation between seemingly distant, but clearly familiar, cultural expressions. Black men like Robert, a DL man whom I met five months earlier during an ethnographic observation, illustrates the value of a space like the Gate, where he said he could "feel the body of another man's without feeling ashamed."[9] Nonetheless, he acknowledged the peculiarity of this space while also recognizing the inability for this exchange in other circumstances. Robert marked the key cultural difference between this queer world and the "other" when he told me that in the Gate "there is no need for hiding and hushing." Indeed, the Gate provides such a space where black gay/queer men can express same-sex desire with little or no disgrace. In this sense, black queer world-making is as much about constructing a history as it is building a "home." As Chandan Reddy informs us, home is always a "contradictory location that is open and hybrid" (1997, 367), much like the hip-hop space at the Gate—which blends hip-hop and queer roots on the route to non-normative desire and pleasure.

The Gate, in its rerouting of queer desire and pleasure into social space, constructs a home where a subject can "have his/her cake and eat it too," so to speak. The black queer subject can live in the space of hip-hop, engaging traditional black (read: black heterosexual) musical forms and cultural styles, while also engaging in queer desire. This space, home, "is open and hybrid." As the domestic home has often afforded very little opportunity for black queers to enjoy and celebrate their desire, the Gate offers an opportunity for them to challenge such a limited understanding of home, constructing a temporal "pleasure zone." While the relationship between hip-hop and queerdom presents an enthralling question, of most interest here is how black queer subjects utilize hip-hop in queer space. Particularly, how does hip-hop serve as an interlocutor between discreet performances of sexual identity and explicit engagements of queer desire? How specifically, do DL men utilize queer space, navigating their desire for discretion and the pleasure of homoerotic engagement? How do these men literally dance down low, while simultaneously remixing the closet? To gain any critical understanding of this process, we must go "in da club."

"IN DA CLUB": HOMOEROTIC ACTIVITY IN A HETERONORMATIVE PLAYGROUND

It is about 12:45 a.m. on a cold, below-zero February morning on Chicago's Northwest Side. I stand in front of what once was a site of industrialization—a dark brick building with a one-story front and its raised back—now a structure that contains often contradictory architectures of homo- and heteronormative performances. The Gate is a parade of contrast. The physical appearances and fashion "looks" are definitely diverse and dynamic. As I stand in a line of approximately seventy-five people outside of the club, the "straight" bouncer yells, "Have your IDs ready." I scope the never-ending processional, where there are black men and women of all ages, a few whites and Latinos, a couple of drag queens in pumps, and some folks who appear "to have gotten the night mixed up." After twenty minutes of us taking in the scene, the line begins to move. I am elated because my arms are getting goose bumps, as I am only dressed in a blue polo shirt and loose-fitting blue jeans. Seeing that I don't have much meat on my bones, this "cool" attire was probably a bad choice for this processional in the middle of a Chicago winter. Troubled by the tingling sensation in my fingers and concerned that my elbows will begin to ash, I proceed forward in the line, as a young woman who is adorned in FUBU fashions (that's For Us By Us) passes me and hands the big six-foot-four bouncer her VIP pass. This, to my dismay, allows her to bypass the parade. I hear disgruntled patrons in line expressing their frustration, while my shivering body tells me that I should've been with Miss VIP. Before long, I enter the corridor that leads to the actual club. Plastered on the wall still hangs a sign that announces, "alternative lifestyle night." Near this sign is another that reads: "After 1:00 a.m., the cover is $12.00." "Hell no!" scream some of the folk standing in line as they read the sign. I, of course, pay the cover, unsure about what is so special about the 1:00 a.m. hour, but knowing that there is a rich queer world waiting inside.

Bodies of all ages, sizes, shapes, colors, and fragrances fill the "house" space. I walk past a bar to witness bodies divided across the dance floor by wooden beams in a twenty-by-forty-foot space of sensuality and sexuality. Indeed, this house was divided, clearly quartering off one "type" from the "others." There is a section of men over thirty in one quarter, voguers in another, and the other half contains men and a few women who are under thirty, uninhibited in how they move and groove—who may often be conceived as the liberal or "queeny" types.[10] Both DL men and traditionally "masculine" gay men often read themselves against the latter category. Effeminate men—or the "queens"—are the characters in this dance space who are most often positioned as artificial, fake, or not "real men." Here, the "sissy," "fag," or "punk" is understood as being a pretender or impersonator. These assessments assume that for men, masculinity trumps femininity, denying the possibility for both gendered norms to exist in one body, or more importantly for their development or appearance to be disordered. Not only do such claims allow "masculine" men to deem their performance as natural, but they also reaffirm that gender is a "stylized repetition of acts" (Butler 1999, 270). Interestingly, such claims of inauthenticity could be made for any masculine performance—noting that all gender performances are impersonations.[11] If one accepts RuPaul's oft-cited claim that "we are born and the rest is drag," then all men in queer space are practicing the art of impersonation. Yet this does not situate any one gender as more real or authentic than any other. Still, the prevalence of men in the hip-hop room illustrates which performances are valorized as being most authentic. While the macho bravado or most "thugged-out" images are often deemed as most "real" or "authentic," there are clearly competing versions of what is, or ought to be, the black masculine. However, in the Gate it seems that one particular narrative has won out but has not completely taken over.

While there may be debate over who belongs at the Gate or within which quarter of space, the convening of black queer men for sociosexual engagement is an electric gathering. In the Gate's house room, black men perform gayness and blackness simultaneously. And while there may be shame in the shadows, the rhythms control the character of this space—filling it with pride and celebration. Typically, I join the crowd of men under thirty, where we move to the sound of the urban drumbeat, industrial scratches, gospel riffs, and the rare remixes of rhythm-and-blues songs together. We dance to house music, which seems to release the body from some of its constrictive impulses, exploring its multiple meanings and possibilities. Those who don't wish to dance stand against the wall, smiling, frowning, talking, drinking, and sometimes even singing. These bodies often exchange space, switching between being a dancer and a wallflower. However, many who feel the "groove" remain in their sweat and swing, living on the dance floor. Unfortunately, this house would not be my home today. As I walk past another bar, I follow a crowd into another space, located in the back of this warehouse, the hip-hop room.

The hip-hop space is a strong contrast to the house room. As I push my way through the crowd, I gently brush up against hard muscle, soft and sometimes sweaty flesh, noticing the many costumes of those who inhabit this humid and frenetic space. As I navigate through the crowd, I hear a familiar rhythm and walk up a short flight of stairs onto a passageway above the dance floor, a location where many seem to settle. The new hit by Eminem's protégé 50 Cent—"In Da Club"—is blaring from the speakers:

> You can find me in da club,
> With a bottle full of bub
> But, mama, I got the X [ecstasy]
> If you into taking drugs.
> I'm into having sex,
> I ain't into making love.
> So come give me a hug—if you into getting rubbed.

I become entangled in these lyrics and wonder about their function in this space of desire and dancing. Surveying the action, from what Michel de Certeau has called the "God View,"[12] my critical ethnographic instincts are overactive. Everything is present, alive, right in front of me, above me, and even behind me. The vulnerability I experienced was the result of overstimulation—where the heightened action within the space left me available for unwarranted touching, pushing, and shoving. My body, as it absorbed so much of the vibrant action in the club space, was the receptor of much uninvited, and often unwelcomed, energy. And I wonder, "Why is it here, from this scape, that I typically encounter men on the DL?" Many men I have spoken with have described this point of view as "safe" or the place where they just "chill." This is a unique vantage point as it sets you apart (creating vulnerability), while giving you the scopographic power (providing control with the gaze). As one DL man told me, "I can see all the pickings from here." I would contend that while the God view is a point "which transforms the city's complexity into readability" (de Certeau 1984, 124), it is also a location of power and control. This balcony-like passageway allows the viewer to observe action from afar and potentially locate those whose gestural schemas, and/or "sex appeal," are in line with their ideals. The traveler in this queer world can be a bit more selective about who piques his queer desires. From this spectatorial location, the voyeur has control and is almost unavailable for direct physical interaction. Often when I approach random "strangers" to inquire as to their reason for choosing the hip-hop room or the Gate club, they often cut the conversation short or disregard my attempt to converse.[13] These moments have heightened my awareness as to the navigating powers of the ethnographer—as a trickster-traveler who has to work for access into whatever community with which he/she works.

As I stand at the God view, I am so aware of what is happening in this queer world. This consciousness can be partially attributed to my vantage point, but also to the words of the rap song—the way that the lyrics seem to match the action on and off the dance floor. We were in the club, there were some "bub" (champagne) drinkers, and there was body language that suggested, "I wanna have sex" and not "I wanna make love." Meanwhile, I am doing what I call the sway dance—moving from side to side to the rhythms but not really exerting much energy. I look up and around as the crowd shakes, jiggles, and gets down. This space, though filled with many different bodies and forms of bodily expressions, has a somewhat homogeneous character stamped with a certain "look" or "pose." This aesthetic is discussed in Thomas DeFrantz's "The Black Beat Made Visible," where he suggests that "it is the tightness of the body that speaks most to a hip hop dance. ... These dances are fundamentally concerned with controlling the body, holding it taut, and making it work in a fragmented manner" (2004, 75). While DeFrantz is discussing early hip-hop dance history, the age of break-dancing and pop-locking, similar trends remain in clubs like the Gate. In these dance spaces, the performers limit their movement rather than find multiple ways to flex the muscles and navigate through space. The dancing seems more contained to a specific location, with little mobility, yet much diversity. Though informed by some of the ritualistic expressions of hip-hop in popular culture, each body tells its own story.

As I look above me, below me, and beside me, I observe physical and facial expressions that recall childhood experiences of "mackin'" and "hollerin'" These type of poses and approaches were popular when I was a young boy growing up on Chicago's South Side. Men would often stand, in a neutral position, allowing their eyes to do much of the talking. Then, as they approached the person with whom they had interest, they would quickly perform this "tight" and often "tough guy" posturing. This performance was often accented by a hand on the groin, an expressionless face almost always absent of any hint of a smile, a cool slouch in the shoulders, and the classic concaveness in the chest. A similar aesthetic appreciation is present in the Gate. Interestingly, however, the presence of women in this space is hardly felt. Yet the "mackin'" and "hollerin'" styles of performance are projected on to bodies of the same sex. There is the dancing male/butchfemme binary and its ideological counterpart, heterosexual male/female pairing. Still, it is striking how the style of dress and dance characteristics are consistent, as to suggest that everyone had received a similar cultural memo for the evening. In this space, the dress code is in—and it's called hip-hop fashions (anything produced by fashion gurus like Nelly, P. Diddy, and Russell Simmons). Bodies move slowly and stiffly, with little exaggeration. These are men who through the image of the "thug" or "homey" make the masculine man (or woman) come alive.

> My flow, my show brought me the dough
> That bought me all my fancy things
> My crib, my cars, my pools, my jewels
> Look, nigga, I done came up and I ain't change.

As this bridge plays, I become more excited and decide to come out of my standstill and catch the groove. As I step down from the passageway onto the dance floor, to my surprise I see Shawn. This twenty-two-year-old college student classifies himself as being on the DL and previously vowed that he would never "be caught dead in one of those sissy clubs." It was with even greater surprise that Shawn acknowledges me and proceeds to take my hand and place it on his groin. This was the first time he had ever made such a move, but the time and space encouraged him to lose many of his inhibitions and insecurities. When I later asked Shawn about the incident, particularly the level of comfort he displayed, he insisted that it was due to the alcohol and apologetically said, "I guess I'm becomin' a little bit too comfortable." This statement prompted a longer historical explanation:

> I wasn't always that comfortable. For real. I mean, me and my guy—my best friend—the first time we went to the club in D.C., we practically hid. We wore our hats so far down over our faces; the most you probably could see was my smile and his goatee. We wore real big clothes to conceal our identities. ... Now I don't know who would have known me in D.C., being that I was from the west suburbs of Chicago.

This admission, clearly marking Shawn's evolution from being very discreet to less discreet in his participation in club life, is informative. While it illuminates a certain level of "comfort," it could potentially suggest that Shawn has "come into himself." However, this comfort within the space of the club does not speak to his behavior in company outside of the club. In fact, I observed that Shawn's anxiety over how his fraternity, friends at school, and family would respond to his presence became an almost overwhelming concern. Specifically, he articulated a concern for his reputation among his "brother-hood" as the "pretty-boy ladies' man"—a title that clearly informed Shawn's general performance of masculinity. The most striking image in this narrative is the costume for concealment, the utilization of presumable hip-hop gear to mask identity. Shawn was astutely aware of the value of clothes in the regulation and monitoring of what is properly masculine. In a sense, Shawn and his friends' clothing are the material masks for their queer desire. On the one hand, his cap is a signifier of hip-hop, while, on the other hand, it is also a sign of Shawn's desire to both not see as well as be seen. All at once, hip-hop is the corroborator and the concealer of queer desire.

The more one understands the cultural work of hip-hop, within and outside black queer environments, the less surprising it becomes that DL men patronize the Gate. A couple of weeks prior to the incident with Shawn, a guy standing at the bar had approached me by saying, "I'm here with my girl and her gay friend, but I get down too."[14] After this admission and my mild response, he proceeded to rub my leg. I suppose the wordless realm of physicality was being used to clarify the meaning of potentially ambiguous language.[15] I slowly smiled, grabbed my drink, and continued back to the dance floor.

He attempted to follow. After talking with other gay men who frequented the Gate, I discovered this is not abnormal. Often these spaces allowed for DL men to express desire that would otherwise be neglected and kept dormant. However, as queer space somewhat de-stigmatizes queer sexuality, men could feel less stigmatized by their participation in homoerotic/homosexual behavior.

Likewise, Shawn was able to not only be present at the Gate, but also to activate his sexual desires without the fear of losing his "masculine" card. My astonishment over Shawn's presence at the Gate and his behavior therein was related to his adamant insistence that his identity was "private," a term that connotes a keen sense of discretion. Typically, the men I had encountered previously would not be seen in an announced "gay" or "alternative" night at any club. Since this encounter, I have seen Shawn at one other "gay" club that offered a hip-hop fix. In a later interview, he told me: "I can't stand house music—hip-hop is where it's at!"[16] It became clear that his ability to perform a hip-hop masculinity was part of the impetus for his participation in this particular "alternative" Friday night at the Gate.

50 Cent continues:

> I'm that cat by the bar toasting to the good life
> You that faggot-ass nigga trying to pull me back right?

The last line invokes audience participation. As I deepen the groove of my sway dance, gay men and women shout: "Faggot-ass nigga." Actually, they shout the whole line, but it is this part of the phrase that throws me. It seems contradictory for these queers of color to engage in such a chant. I turn to a friend, giving him a look of shock and disheartenment, and he says, "It's just like the way we use 'nigga' by itself." But why would those who, like myself, have endured being called "faggot, sissy, punk" rearticulate such problematic rhetoric? Why would Shawn, or DL men in general, seemingly draw pleasure from this chant of hate and homophobia? As people threw their hands in the air, almost marching to construct a chorus-like concentric circle of "faggot-ass nigga," something told me that this was "cool."

This performance of heterosexism seemed to work in collaboration with a larger desire to be "cool." The queer subjects who yelled "faggot-ass nigga" could feel a part of a larger black masculine sphere—one that usually excluded them. In this masculine imaginary, the way to often affirm one's normality is through the participation in homophobic or sexist acts. When one takes possession of the "faggot" or the "nigga," it reduces the legitimacy of such ascriptions being made upon the speaker's body. In this way, the utterance of the profane empowers the speaker/chanter, affirming his status as appropriately masculine. This chanting moment was emblematic of the "cooling" of the hip-hop room, while also illuminating the ways in which one type of masculinity seems to pose itself as *the* cool. These so-called performances of heterogender (read: heterosexism) position the hip-hop space as the greater of the two rooms. It is within the hip-hop room that the "real men" reside. Traditional hetero-masculine behavior and codes deemed this space as "hot." This behavior, though highly problematic, suggests, as Robert Farris Thompson does in his aptly titled classic essay "An Aesthetic of the Cool" (1966), that hot is always balanced by cool. Whereas Thompson is speaking to the literal hotness of bodies, I employ "hot" to refer to contemporary black vernacular, where this adjective signifies the best place to be, the spot, and the atmosphere that is most enlivened. Indeed, the men in the hip-hop room understand this room as such, while often the "room of sissies," as one patron referred to the house room, was seen as a place less desired—"really gay," so to speak.

I also read this instance of hip-hop heterosexual rage in queer face to be a moment where gay men can temporarily "de-queer" themselves. I argue that such a chant may work as a way to set these men apart from the "others" in the space. It is a strategy to disavow one brand of masculinity, while embracing another. In this conceptualization, the "others" who are outside of the traditionally masculine—those ascribed titles such as "femmes," "bottoms," "punks"—are marked as inferior, less than those who carry traditional masculine codes and behaviors. Shawn explained the every Fridaynight 50 Cent chorus by saying, "A faggot is a punk—it's not about what he does in the bedroom; it's what he doesn't do." His perspective suggests that the ability to spout this sexual epithet is about condemning the feminine male. In addition, Shawn's comment also ridicules those who perform the non-dominant role during sex.[17] Hence, his comment about "what he does not do" signifies a discomfort not with being the non-dominant sex partner, but those who perform a style of masculinity that signals this sexual preference. Of course, Shawn doesn't consider this style masculine, which begs the question, "Is there a way to masculinize, or even affirm, bottoms in this world of queer world-making?"

For Shawn, I guess not. Shawn's perspective further accentuates the ways in which "femininity is always already devalued in patriarchal societies, those associated with the feminine are also viewed as inferior" (Johnson 2003, 69). There is no room for femininity in the domain of the masculine. A man is considered either masculine/feminine; the different styles of masculinity often remain unaccounted for or unrecognized. Of course, femininity is the less ideal performance of gender, making the distinction between who is properly masculine and who is not. Much of these understandings of gender are residual hegemonic perspectives that almost always uses the effete or feminine to describe the "gay," setting straight men apart from those who are identified as "gay." This act of devaluation of some gay male bodies is modified in the Gate, as some "masculine" gay men can at once feel "straight," while DL men can affirm their allegiance to heterosexuality (read: heteronormativity) through a harsh critique of those who perform queerness and manliness differently. Furthermore, it allows some men to carve a space for the cool, creating a necessary hierarchy of masculine performances within the Gate.

It would be dishonest to ignore the ways in which "faggot-ass nigga" is somewhat of an inside joke. All of those who participate in the "alternative" night at the Gate are aware of their appetite for those of the same sex. Thus, the utterance of the chant also brings with it a reminder that the space is a queer, or "faggot," terrain. In some ways, the mass chant announces, "We are black faggots, but look who's in possession of these words now." In this sense, my friend's comparative analysis between the chanted phrase and the vernacular use of "nigga" is an apt one. Black queer men reappropriate these terms, turn them on their head, and thereby reduce the power of the term in constructing their identities. However, I would suggest this analysis is less applicable for men on the DL, as they often disidentify with traditional identifications of (homo)sexuality in everyday life.

I spend critical time in this [reading] on this moment of hip-hop hetero-sexist and homophobic chanting because it exposes what I believe is the true pleasure of this queer zone, for black gay men and DL men alike. In this space, performances of gender and sexuality are in flux—men are able to be queer, while also acting straight, or even straight while acting queer. Patrons of the Gate are able to realize the treasure of performance that many of us scholars take as given: "Performance is a means by which people reflect on their current conditions, define and/or reinvent themselves and their social world, and either reinforce, resist, or subvert prevailing social orders" (Drewal 1991, 9). The Gate offers an occasion where black queer men can attain pleasure through the stimulation created by the multiple valences within the hip-hop space. In this unique space of queer world-making, these men can "reinforce, resist, [accept], or subvert" dominant modes of gender and sexuality. While black men can identify and perform their queer desire (resist/subvert), they can still participate in the rituals of patriarchy (reinforce/accept). At the Gate, or any queer world-making space for that matter, bodies "produce para-doxical effects which cannot be understood if one tries to force them into a dichotomy of resistance or submission" (Bourdieu 1991, 94). This may be the queerest characteristic of this space—where heterogender, hip-hop, and homoeroticism are married through music and dance.

This queer possibility is what Katrina Hazard-Donald misses when she addresses hip-hop's dance as a form that "encourages a public (and private) male bonding" through the disbursement of male bodies, moving and communicating through space (1996, 229). Her discussion is not only hetero-centric, but it also denies the possibility for queer potential in the spaces where black men gather in the name of hip-hop. Instead, she attempts to frame these "male-bonding" episodes as purely platonic and historically traditional, only significant because of the ability for black men to proclaim a sense of brotherhood. She ignores what Eve Kosofsky Sedgwick has informed us is the homo-erotic potential of all male-bonding circumstances. Sedgwick, when examining what she calls "homosociality," reevaluates the often assumed impossibility for the homo-social to become homoerotic. In *Between Men: English Literature and Male Homosocial Desire*, Sedgwick attempts to demonstrate the "unbrokedness of a continuum between homo-social and homosexual" (1985, 1)—bringing forth a significant discussion of desire's presence in what could be called "male spaces." A discussion about such possibilities has been almost absent in the commentary of those who write about the homosocial domain of hip-hop. My discussion here attempts to expand beyond acknowledging the potential of space in constructing and producing desire, but rather how the Gate, as a unique space, opens doors for a specific desire by a particular group of men. Moreover, this [reading] illuminates the many ways that hip-hop is employed for queer use. In the hip-hop space, all black queer men can participate and feel "normal," almost un-queer, as the culture of the space encourages homoerotic desires for each subject, as he dances in the largely heteronormative playground.

"IN DA HOUSE": BRINGING HIP-HOP HOME

Though my fascination is with the hip-hop space at the Gate, specific performances in the house room are germane to the understanding of masculinity in space. In this section, I map and examine the ways in which hip-hop masculinity travels. Particularly, I look closely at a peculiar moment where a DL man engaged in desire in the house space, though operating under the rubric and rhythm of hip-hop. In short, I am interested in how some men perform "cool" in a space that is often understood as being "fabulous" and filled with "faggotry." Throughout my research, for instance, I have found that some men embrace, appreciate, and even express attraction for the "feminine," while simultaneously subscribing to a hegemonic masculinity themselves.

Indeed, I was surprised when Tavares, my childhood friend of almost sixteen years who was always known as *the* ladies' man," volunteered to join me on a Friday-night venture to the Gate. Tavares was a twenty-two-year-old young man, often in and out of his mother's home in the south suburbs of Chicago. Since the mid-1990s, I observed many black families moving because of gentrification—from the ghettoes of the city into the south suburbs of Chicago—a migration that often had damaging and debilitating effects on minority children, for the sake of middle-upper- and middle-class progress. While this transition was often understood as a mobilizing act by the city for black people, it often facilitated in bringing about greater segregation in the city and schools, while also displacing many poor blacks from their inner-city relatives.[18] I often attributed Tavares's discomfort in his suburban home to his nostalgia for the South Side of Chicago, where most of his friends and family dwell. Unfortunately, on one of his many hiatuses from his mother's home, Tavares began a new hobby of living with, as he said, "big girls who love me" and "serving" marijuana in the neighborhood. Unfortunately, the latter occupation landed Tavares in a Cook County correctional facility, where I would spend much time visiting him and ensuring that he had the support and resources necessary for physical and mental survival. A month after serving time, he came to stay with me for almost two weeks. This visit offered me a fruitful opportunity to not only get reacquainted with my "brother in spirit," but also to listen deeply to his many experiences. Sleeping in my bed, chatting on my computer, rummaging through my videos, and surveying my books, Tavares learned things about me that I had never disclosed to him during our childhood. The first thing he learned was that I love Whitney Houston; the second, that I am gay. The latter bonded us in ways indescribable, while the former simply occasioned weird looks from him.

Tavares's presence in my intimate, so-called private space opened a door to vulnerable, valuable, and very enlightening dialogue. Tavares's entrance into my personal space opened my eyes to what it feels like to be "exposed." Though I was very open with my sexuality, my politics, and my home, it was still awkward to see and experience Tavares making certain evaluations and judgments on my "private" materials—I often felt under investigation. Sometimes he would rummage through my *Advocate* magazines—with queer subtexts in its covers—turning his nose up or simply making an uncomfortable sound. In addition, he would ask questions about the *how* of male-male sex as if he had no clue or was repulsed by the idea. To avoid these conversations, I began to remove these materials during his visit or make them less visible. I quickly realized that my anxieties over his inquisitions were incomparable to the type he felt in terms of his discretions and choices he might make as he attempted to stay "down low." It was these intimate moments that always reminded me that the ethnographic walk is a privileged one—a journey that requires attention to *how* we gather information before being concerned with *what* we gather. On the fragile plain of conversation with Tavares and other men, it has often been difficult to generate more intimate, deeper discussions. Though we were friends of many years, my new role as an ethnographer seemed to create some distance between us. However, our already-established closeness made it possible to turn potential feelings of exposure into moments where the subject could exhale and release many inhibitions.

The potential rewards of such an approach was made most obvious when, on the second night he stayed at my home, Tavares witnessed my "going-out ritual." This included talking on the phone to find out every friend who would be at the Gate, while simultaneously choosing something "hot" to wear. I am sure that this element of preparation made it clear that I was not going to a "straight" club. When I finished on the phone, I ironed my clothes, took a shower, and then I announced that I was leaving. Before I could even ask if he needed anything, Tavares said that he wanted to go with me. I asked him, "Why?" He responded, "What am I going to do, sit here at the computer and listen to Whitney?" I said, "You know where I'm going, right? I'm going to a gay club." He said, unaffected and unflinchingly, "I know."

Tavares's willingness to go to the Gate registered as a queer idea, but not queer in the sexual sense. It was queer because it became an instance when a heterosexual man was doing "straight" differently and defiantly. In this moment, Tavares showed me that his understanding of himself as a man was not contingent upon the disavowal of the effete or homosexual but the ability to not be preoccupied with my sexuality or overdetermine what his participation would signify. His ability to accept my queerness continued when I had to pick up Dedrick, my partner at the time. Together, they shared jokes and bonded—usually through various forms of making fun of me and my idiosyncratic ways. Interestingly, their greatest point of connection was around musical tastes—from Eminem to Do or Die. At the time, I sat silently and took in this moment with great interest. This act of male bonding reaffirmed what I have articulated earlier about the many transgressive possibilities for hip-hop, on and beyond the dance floor. I was most excited to see Tavares and Dedrick in action in the hip-hop room at the Gate. Admittedly, there was a theory being tested—a theory that was proven to be incorrect. In my early trials in the field, I learned quickly not to anticipate outcomes because they almost always turned out differently from what I expected.

When we arrived at the Gate, I paid the whopping thirty-six dollars for all of our admissions, since it was after 1:00 a.m. Moving through the customary procedures, we entered the Gate, and I asked Tavares if he wanted to take his hoodie to the coat check, as it would probably be too hot in the club. He refused. We continued into the Gate, whose energy and tone were pretty standard. It was much more crowded than at visits mentioned earlier. This night the dance floor had no empty spaces, the walls were crowded with people, and there were even lines for the washroom. It was a perfect night to feed the potential anxieties felt by my straight buddy from childhood. In such a crowd, one's body was always touching other bodies; one was constantly being looked up and down. Everyone from drag queens to drunks were attempting to make contact with Tavares. Appropriately, I quickly dashed toward the hip-hop room—an area where I was sure that Tavares would feel most comfortable. Immediately, Dedrick and I hit the dance floor. Tavares stood back against the wall observing the scene, while reggae beats played loud and strong. Quickly, the reggae turned to rap, and Tavares briefly joined us, doing a dance similar to my sway dance—a default move for music with a steady beat and for people who don't want to get too carried away. After a couple of hit songs, Dedrick and I continued dancing, but Tavares went off to the sidelines of the dance floor and simply stood in front of the speaker.

After being engrossed in a moment of dancing with Dedrick, I looked over and realized that in the midst of the large crowd, Tavares had disappeared. I panicked. I assumed that he was looking for me, as Dedrick and I had slightly shifted on the dance floor. I walked up to the "God view," peering out onto the dance floor, but he was not there. I moved to the balcony level, thinking that he might have given himself a personal tour of the hip-hop room. He was nowhere to be found. Maybe he went to the restroom. I walked through the crowd and cut to the front of the line, gazing into the restroom for Tavares. Just as I was about to return to the hip-hop room, Dedrick came and informed me that Tavares was watching the voguers. What? This was the last place I would have expected to find this "ladies' man." Nonetheless, I found Tavares standing, almost entranced, as the voguers waved, flipped, and dropped to the infamous "Ha!"—a musical piece that has historical reverence in the ball culture of black queer life.[19] I asked him, "You like that?" He replied, "It's funny—they crazy—but it's entertaining as hell." His fascination shocked me. Looking at his hooded face, I knew that Tavares's interests had shifted from entertainment to erotic pleasure. He watched the voguers with the same visual pleasure that he had watched all of the "tight females" who used to get off the Third and King Drive bus during our childhood. It was this look of desire that Tavares possessed as he gazed upon the "femme-queens" and the "girls up in pumps." He watched them for the remainder of the evening.

It was not until a later conversation at my home that I understood this erotic impulse that seemed to guide Tavares's desire for femme bodies. Tavares was in my room, at my computer—while I lay in my bed—and he told me that he had "a thing for femme cats." At first, I was preoccupied by the inversion of typical animalistic description of men as "dogs" flipped in this context to "cats." More interesting and informative, however, was how such an appreciation for the feminine disrupted and discounted the assumption that DL men only have interest in the masculine. Here, Tavares gave value and recognition to a desire for something outside of the masculine, showing a moment where his masculinity and heterosexuality were not contingent upon his object choice being a masculine subject. It is for this reason that Tavares's experiences in the house room become most appropriate in this discussion of hip-hop.

I argue that though Tavares prefers a feminine subject of desire, his interests are still in line with a certain heterosexual privileging system. Tavares, as a DL man, maintains his heterosexuality through his pursuit of a surrogate female figure. His relationships with "femme cats"—who are often understood as an androgynous male and/or transgendered female—allow him to still imagine himself inside the dominant matrix of sexuality, as these figures are often referred to and often refer to themselves as women.[20] Like those in the hip-hop space discussed earlier, Tavares attempted to undo his queerness through his participation in what can be understood as un-queer acts. It is no coincidence, then, that when Tavares described the femme cats he had seen and "hollered at" elsewhere, he emphasized the female characteristics as being "so real ... I mean just like a woman's." This thinking reveals the ways in which any feminine/female body acts as a fill-in for the birth-assigned female with which Tavares was most familiar. Still, he cannot deny that he is engaging in queer acts with those who identify themselves in queer ways. This is most apparent when he articulated his same-sex desire in the somewhat ambiguous phrase that he was "feelin' that way toward another dude." Though he may relish the femininity of his sexual object-choice, he is always aware that it is a "dude." It seems, however, that he feels less threatened by his own desires when he imagines and acknowledges those with whom he shares interests as females or femme cats. In this sense, Don Kulick's ethnographic analysis of Brazilian travestis' desire for "straight men" is relevant and instructive for this case study: "Not only is desire meaningful only in relation to difference, it is also what *produces* difference—a male is a man *because* he desires a woman; a travesti can feel like a woman *to the extent that* she desires a man and is desired by him in return" (1998, 126).

The "production of difference" is what triggers Tavares's attraction to-ward "dudes" as being "all good." The difference, rather than sameness, attracts him to feminine subjects; whereas the queer world around him seems to endorse a more homonorma-tive relationship.[21] Consequently, Tavares stands as somewhat of a queer queer, who reconfigures queer desire as heterosexual. As long as the subject of his desire speaks "woman" through performance and pose, he is comfortable and content. This female performance legitimates his desire, marking it as authentically "straight" and "more normal," as he put it. Such desire for normality, normalcy, and normativity seems to be the anchor for expressions of desire in these spaces, where masculinity seems so fragile, contingent, and contained to hetero-patriarchal ideals.

In addition to his ability to establish his heteronormativity through desire choice, Tavares also continued to position himself within hip-hop masculinity by enacting a gendered performance that has its roots in hip-hop culture. He stood rigid, with his hoodie covering and concealing his face, periodically moving to the beat. As he talked with those who passed by who fit his preferred image, he carried himself in a manner that bespoke "coolness" and positioned him as in charge and in control. I even noticed that his voice deepened and hardened in a manner similar to that of young boys courting young girls over the telephone. As he engaged with feminine objects of desire, through his performance of the heterogender, he was able to mark his place in this space of queer desire. Tavares, like many men on the DL, could only come to embrace homoerotic desire through the performance of heterosexuality, or heteronormativity. Together, Tavares and Shawn tell us two different stories about DL desire, disrupting any mainstream, monolithic notion of the performances of discreet sexuality. They serve as examples of the ways in which space "unleashes desire"—forcing them to find ways to compensate for the force-fitting pressure to submit to hegemonic masculinity. Their experiences in the club space accentuate and reiterate the ways in which sexuality is greatly informed by the constant constructs and constraints of a black masculine architecture.

SOMETHING IN THE ARCHITEXTURE: HETEROTOPIA, MASCULINITY, AND HOMOEROTICISM

For this construction of black male identity, we can thank many cultural architects who include Eldridge Cleaver, Amiri Baraka, Louis Farrakhan, Dr. Dre, and 50 Cent.[22] In these constructions of black masculinity, queer desire and performance are suspect, stigmatized, and incompatible with certain notions of blackness. Additionally, we can be grateful to white supremacist capitalist patriarchy, which demands and rewards a certain performance of masculinity for black men in America to gain some access to agency and power.[23] On the one hand, the Gate, in its homage to hip-hop, destabilizes the "queerness" of this space and shapes a heteronormative imaginary with a queer subtext. On the other hand, the Gate uses hip-hop to facilitate, encourage, and even legitimate queer desire. Indeed, something strange occurs in the invocation of hip-hop in queer spaces. This presence of the "strange" reminds me of how my mother would respond to abnormal occurrences within our house by screaming, "I swear there is some-thing in the water!" Likewise, I am professing that there is something in the architexture.

Clearly, I am not the first to connect architecture, as a material form, to ideology within a given culture. In fact, this relationship was discussed as early as 1847 in author-architect's George Wightwick's writings on the body and architecture:

> A building is a body or a "carcass," lettered over with beauty of diction, with poetic illustration, and with the charms of rhetoric. ... [W]hat the skin is to the body, the hair to the head, the eye-brows and lashes to the eyes, and the lips to the mouth—such is the marble casing to the walls, the cornice to the facade, the pediment and the architecture to the windows, and the porch to the door. (1847, 37)

What is most important in Wightwick's discussion of architecture is his focus on the body and space as interdependent. The body is as important as space; each part of the body and space requires the other. In Wightwick's construction, body and space form a dialectic rather than a dichotomy. While Wightwick's discussions seem to get at the dialectic between space and human behavior, I argue that "architecture" as a term does not get us there or sufficiently explain what is happening. In this project, I am as much interested in how certain spaces invite DL men's participation, as I am interested in the interior issues that allow DL men to find liberation, tension, or satisfaction in the Gate. While many would refer to both as "architecture," I want to employ a more appropriate term: *architexture*. While "architecture" alone accounts for physical space, the addition of "texture" tells us more about the "feeling" of space—the expansive cultural fabric that dwells in specific sites of queer production. "Architexture" is a term that describes the dialectic between the interior and exterior manifestations of masculinity. In Maurice Wallace's *Constructing the Black Masculine* (2002), he argues that in order to understand the construction of the black masculine, we must consider the architectural structures in which it resides and also those structural foundations around which it is built. To this end, I utilize the term "architexture" to describe the contours of black masculinity with regards to spatial characteristics and cultural dimensions.

Architexture, as a material structure and a meaning-making apparatus, is a produc-tive point of entry for my discussion of DL men in the hip-hop room of the Gate. At the Gate, there seems to be a constant thread of masculinity that impacts the music and the men. As a performer-witness at the Gate, I have experienced the impact of certain commitments to masculinity, while also participating in its construction and reinforcement. Between my first visit to the Gate and my subsequent journeys, I have learned that there are many codes, characteristics, and necessities in order to gain greater access into men's lives. The Gate's physical space assists in the masculine characteristic of the club. The industrial and working-class motif in addition to the separation of house and hip-hop into separate rooms signify the value and visible difference between two worlds. The industrial features are in alignment with the black masculine subjects in the space, and their character concurs with the cultural fabric of the Gate's patrons. "Architexture" seems most applicable, then, as a term that best accounts for this strong relationship between the physical space that helps shape what is possible and the internal presence that helps dancing subjects to make sense of what is possible.

It was only through a concerted effort to understand *how* men *do* the DL—a rehearsal of sorts—that I was able to refine and often reproduce the style of masculinity being produced in and outside the club space. At the Gate, either you follow the rules of hip-hop, or you are deemed outside the realm of normality. The Gate houses a brand of masculinity that reifies, reproduces, and rewards Shawn's and Tavares's heteronormative ideals, making it a space more open for DL presence and participation. Todd Boyd has called this gendered performance "the desire to be hard," which is much like "cool" in its somewhat visual posturing often associated with gangsta culture that is most often conveyed through style and image (2004, 70). The Gate, through its patrons' dress and gestural style—and its architectural design's sterility and staleness—promotes and projects a sense of the "hard." As the music fills the space with a hard sound in order to narrate a hard ideal, it prompts "hard, tight dancing," to which those who find queer performance difficult can engage in with less anxiety.

It is DL men's physical presence in the queer club [...] that much of media has latched on to, as they stake claim to an "out" DL subject. In actuality, most men at the Gate are not "coming out" but participating in a sort of "comin' in." They have arrived in a queer space that welcomes them but does not require them to become an official member. The Gate is a black home they can come into, where the relatives understand the fullness of diversity, liberalness, and transgressiveness, and are most honest about different forms of desire. The discursive demand that one must be "out" to participate in gay activities ignores that all gay activity does not take place in public, and that participation does not always guarantee membership.

Indeed, DL men are out in the club in the sense that they are a part of a queer world-making moment. However, outside of this club space, they live very discreet lives, void of public displays of pleasure and desire for those of the same sex. Shawn referred to his life outside the club as "being out in the real world." When men would mark this difference in this way, I would often reply, "Is the club space not the 'real world'?" During our conversations, I was often aware of how Shawn and others dichotomized the queer world and his everyday heteronormative performance of identity. These admissions clearly gesture toward the ways in which the Gate allows DL men to imagine themselves in a sort of utopia (but not quite). This pleasure, attained through a queer world-making experience, may be the answer to the problematic question "Why are they in a gay club if they are not gay?"

This "utopia, but not quite" pleasure is what Foucault has referred to as a state of *heterotopia*. Heterotopias, unlike utopias, are real places. In his public lecture "Of Other Spaces," Foucault uses the mirror as an example:

> The mirror functions as a heterotopia in this respect: it makes this place that I occupy at the moment when I look at myself in the glass at once absolutely real, connected with all the space that surrounds it, and absolutely unreal, since in order to be perceived it has to pass through this virtual point which is over there. (1987, 24)

Here, I find the difference between the real and the unreal, heterotopia and utopia, to be contingent upon time. As Foucault makes clear, "The heterotopia begins to function at full capacity when men arrive at a sort of absolute break with their traditional time" (26). While the subject appears to be in the mirror, everything that he experiences is real; but once he exits the mirror, he is no longer in the mirror, and his image and its surroundings have a different meaning. The image that he acquired in the mirror is gone, and he is left with the everyday imagining of himself rather than the situational, specific look of the mirror.

For Foucault, then, heterotopias are spaces where people temporally reside. These spaces allow individuals to lose sense of time and to picture themselves and their world in ways that mark time as inconsequential. For DL men, the club is one of many potential heterotopias. Queer spaces that allow DL men to live queerly—though constrained by time—allows them to explore often unavailable, or inconvenient, possibilities. Unlike a heterotopia, a utopia is without material grounding, potentially timeless, and available only to the imagination. While Foucault uses an abstract space to speak to the possibilities of heterotopias, his material examples provide clearer understanding: "theatre, cinema, garden, cemetery, prison." Each of these spaces serves a specific purpose, allowing its residents to go to a different world for a specific period of time. The Gate's hip-hop room is a hetero-topic space. Though Foucault omitted the club in his original theorization, its characteristics definitely fit within his paradigm. As DL men travel to spaces like the black queer club, they enact desires that are often foreign to heteronormative understandings of manhood. As they participate in queer world-making, they are engaging with heterotopic sites.

As heterotopias break with the ordinary, everyday life, they serve as monitors of our social conditions. For example, the necessity for the creation of queer dance spaces in general alerts us to the lack of queer social sites, places where queer men and women can act erotically without scrutiny. Because most clubs embrace a heteronormative understanding of what is acceptable, queer men and women must develop their own spaces. In essence, queer world-making is a way of creating a heterotopia. The Gate's hip-hop room offers those who are sexually marginalized but who have specific cultural roots to "have their cake and eat it too." Particularly, it offers black queer men an opportunity to take traces of the everyday and mix them with the extraordinary to create a scene where they can make their erotic imaginings real. The Gate, in its use of hip-hop and its preference for a certain texture of masculinity, is a unique place—where contradiction seems to fuel its energy and erotic possibilities. Here, black men can imagine themselves within and outside of societal ideals—mapping their own reality, making real what only seemed imaginable.

Heterotopias are sites structured in privilege. The Gate allows men the privilege to engage in, enjoy, or perform same-sex desire. Hence, they are similar to "safe spaces." Like heterotopias, the Gate "always presuppose[s] a system of opening and closing that both isolates and makes them penetrable" (Foucault 1986, 26). Thus, for DL men, the Gate has as many real risks as rewards. However, because of its "curious exclusions" (26), the risks are limited and its rewards multiple.[24] Indeed, Judith Butler's rhetorical questions at the outset of this [reading] are apropos as racialized queers often cannot afford or desire to be "out." Thus, the closet as a threshold apparatus does not fully illustrate the ways in which the patrons of the Gate work through their sexuality. Black queer people have always done queer differently. Symbolically, the Gate, unlike the closet, is not a place of residence but a place for possibilities to be explored. The Gate is a heterotopic playground whose architexture allows its patrons to explore and enjoy temporal pleasure—through its conjoining of oft-thought disparate traditions. In a sense, rather than being a container for sexuality, the DL act as a frame (or fence)—through which men can better imagine and articulate sexuality on their own terms, privileging sexual discretion anchored in a traditionally masculine framework.

In this [reading], I have attempted to highlight one complicated space that exhibits black queers "making do" within a heteronormative society and cultural tradition. As media and other intellectual endeavors pursue this topic, it is important that they listen deeply and "down low," and be attentive to sociohistorical circumstances of black men and the histories connected to the spaces in which these men put their bodies on the line. As Aaron Betsky informs us, "Queer space is not one place: it is an act of appropriating the modern world for the continual act of self-construction ... Queer space queers reality to produce a space to live" (1997, 193). Whether it is on a phone chat line or on the Internet [...] or in the hip-hop section of a black gay club, DL men and many black gay men search for spaces where they can imagine a world that allows them to "just be." In this sense, "to be" is engaged in a politics of "becoming"—a black queer world-making—where one's positionality can shift without scrutiny but with understanding.

A few years ago, the Gate's Friday-night party came to a sudden end.[25] As I sit at my desk, reimagining the space of the Gate and the many possibilities within, I am drawn back to the underground dance scenes in Isaac Julien's film *Looking for Langston* (1988). I return to a masterful moment when he flashes back to a historic scene in which black men are gathered in a discreet space to party and partake in homoerotic desires. Some stand with drinks, some chat, and some dance with each other—all feeling the pulse of the erotic and the pleasure of this rare opportunity. Dressed in period suits and clothes, drinking and tasting the finest things, these men engage in desire on their own terms, in their own way, somewhere "down low" and outside the radar of heteronormative gazes. This moment in film mirrors so much of what I saw at the Gate. Black men and black queer men engaging in desire and using space, style, and music to guide their performances. The Gate is no contemporary coincidence; it is a space that resurrects an older, rich tradition. It is a retelling of black queer men, cautiously and creatively, dancing desire. It is an illustration of black queer performance happening outside the closet, but inside the Gate.

NOTES

1   Often men would give me a brief moment of their time, stating their disinterest in a longer interview but a willingness to simply chat with me for a minute or two. These moments often gave me what I call soft data; not a lot to extrapolate a fortune of meaning, but yet illuminating of the threaded presences within the Dl experience of club space and even everyday life handlings of desire.

2   The late Charles Clifton, as he explored historical presences of homoeroticism, illuminated the importance of recognizing the role and service that discreet sexual identity has played in the lives of black men. See Clifton 2000, 342.

3   The name of this club has been modified, to secure confidentiality for the men with whom I speak, as well as the club and its other patrons.

4   Like the name of the club, I have used pseudonyms to protect subjects' anonymity.

5   As a student of Dwight Conquergood, this was one of his common sayings.

6   For more information on the transition from house to hip-hop and its effects on the club space and its business, see Kai Fikentscher's *"You Better Work!": Underground Dance Music in New York City* (2000).

7   See Berlant and Warner 1998, 558.

8   Here, I contest William Hawkeswood's discussion in *One of the Children: Gay Black Men in Harlem*, where he mislabels the population of men with whom he speaks as "gay black men," when they clearly prioritized blackness before gayness (1996, 11–12). "Black gay men" seems to better articulate the way in which many understand themselves and often (even in Hawkeswood's study) show strongest allegiance. Such recognition further explains the black gay affinity for hip-hop, as it assists in an authenticated blackness.

9   Though Robert speaks generally about the Gate as a club, I would suspect that his sentiments are his interpretation of his experiences in the hip-hop section of the space.

10   Note how the uninhibited, self-expressive, and energetic gets read as being feminine or over the top.

11   See Mark Simpson's *Male Impersonators: Males Performing Masculinity* (1993) for a broader discussion on the art of gender impersonation.

12   In Michel de Certeau's *Practice of Everyday Life* (1984), he refers to this viewpoint as a (dis) advantage point above the city, away from the masses. While this perspective provides a place to feel the energy and activity in the space, it also positions me outside the participatory realm, in a place of power and privilege that I often find too titillating or, at times, troubling.

13   Usually, those who elicit initial eye contact or conversation are not interested in my research questions. Most often, they are interested in me as an object of attraction. For this reason, there are many more dead-ends than there are live wires. However, I can sometimes turn their attraction into a fruitful conversation with minimized flirtation.

14   This term is an indirect admission that one has sexual relations with men. Typically, "to get down" suggests a temporal queer experience; whereas the person who "gets down" only does this periodically, or when it is convenient for them.

15   Often when faced with issues of sexuality, nonverbal expression can provide greater clarity; while language often creates greater tensions and even over-articulates what the subject desires. In this case, erotic physical performance clarifies homoerotic desire.

16   Here, Houston Baker's discussion of disco music has great resonance when he states, "There are gender-coded reasons for the refusal of disco. Disco's club DJs were often gay, and the culture of Eurodisco was populously gay" (1995, 198). This may also explain the consistent disdain for "house" music as it often queers spaces and carries a queer aesthetic.

17   Interestingly, Shawn has admitted to me several times that he often performs both roles, as active and passive participant in sex. This contradiction is consistent within all initial conversations with men on the DL, but often operates the same way in traditional black gay discourses.

18   For more on gentrification and its effects on black people, see Mary Pattillo's *Black Picket Fences* (1999), as well as her recent book, *Black on the Block* (2007).

19   For more information on this dance form and the musical significance of the "Ha!," see Marlon Bailey's *Butch Queen Up in Pumps* (2013).

20   It is important to note that this relationship with "femmes" or transgendered individuals is not peculiar to DL men. For example, many gay men prefer relationships with "femme" men or transgendered women. However, since I have been doing this research, the investment in these relationships are often predicated on something very different from those of many gay men. It seems that many DL men engage in a gender attraction, whereby they are captivated by certain ideals that are grounded in hetero-patriarchal ideals. It is also important to note that my use of the term "relationship" is by no means to suggest that Tavares has ever sustained relationships with those with whom he shares interests. "Relationship" is used to describe the connection or association between Tavares and those he desires.

21 While one could argue that male-transgender relationships are a part of homonormativity—the lack of acceptance of this relationship within black queer "communities" counters this supposition. More specifically, for Tavares the only way he can even fathom a relationship with a "man" is if he appears to be a "woman" or "womanly."

22 Philip Brian Harper (1999) highlights the ways in which certain leaders within the black community have continued to create heterosexual anxiety over queer presences.

23 bell hooks (2003) illustrates the detrimental effects of this structure on black male understandings of self and also locates white supremacist patriarchal culture as the hidden culprit in perpetuating and legitimating both sexism and homophobia. It is important to recognize how these forms of domination reward black men for acting out in sexist and homophobic ways, reiterating its use value and almost necessity within black male life.

24 One of the cited reasons for attendance by many DL men, in spite of the possibilities of being "found out," is that the Gate typically attracts the same "type" of people. In other words, the likelihood of incidentally encountering a spouse, family member, or friend is unlikely. In addition, many have said that their anxiety is lessened because those who would frequent the Gate are probably more likely to "be cool" with what men do at the Gate.

25 There are multiple rumors circulating as to what caused the party's demise. Some attribute the Gate's party closure to mismanagement of funds by party promoters and organizers. Others have concluded that the Gate's owner began to demand more money to utilize the space and the party was not generating enough revenue to be profitable. Many have speculated that the party become too much of an eighteen-and-up club, which meant less revenue to be generated—as the demographic shift produced a more unpredictable presence and profit. And many have told me that they believed the owner saw more profit in "straight parties" than "gay parties." Whatever the truth here, what is for certain is that this brand of black queer world-making in this underground industrial space has not been matched in the Chicagoland area.

REFERENCES

Bailey, Marlon. 2013. *Butch Queens Up in Pumps: Gender, Performance, and Ballroom Culture in Detroit.* Ann Arbor: University of Michigan Press.

Baker, Houston A., Jr. 1995. *Black Studies, Rap, and the Academy.* Chicago: University of Chicago Press.

Berlant, Lauren, and Michael Warner. 1998. "Sex in Public." *Critical Inquiry* 24, no. 2 (Winter): 547–66.

Clifton, Charles. 2000. "Rereading Voices from the Past: Images of Homo-Eroticism in the Slave Narrative." In *The Greatest Taboo: Homosexuality in Black Communities,* edited by Delroy Constantine-Simms. New York: Alyson, 2000.

de Certeau, Michel. 1984. *The Practice of Everyday Life,* translated by Steven Rendall. Berkeley: University of California Press.

Fikentscher, Kai. 2000. *"You Better Work!": Underground Dance Music in New York City.* Hanover, NJ: Wesleyan University Press.

Harper, Philip Brian. 1999. *Private Affairs: Critical Ventures in the Culture of Social Relations.* New York: New York University Press.

Hawkeswood, William. 1996. *One of the Children: Gay Black Men in Harlem.* Berkeley: University of California Press.

hooks, bell. 2003. *We Real Cool: Black Men and Masculinity.* New York: Routledge.

Pattillo, Mary. 2007. *Black on the Block: The Politics of Race and Class in the City.* Chicago: University of Chicago Press.

_____. 1999. *Black Picket Fences: Privilege and Peril among the Black Middle Class.* Chicago: University of Chicago Press.

Simpson, Mark. 1993. *Male Impersonators: Males Performing Masculinity.* London: Cassell.

DISCUSSION QUESTIONS

1. How does a feminist consciousness rooted in hip hop (hip hop feminism) allow artists, performers, activists, and fans to resist oppression and inequality?

2. How does hip hop provide those with marginalized identities a way to express or perform their identities?

3. Do the authors in this section discuss hip hop as resisting or perpetuating inequality? How?

4 Hip Hop as Resistance

By Kierra Toney

H ip hop gave sound to the resistance movements of the 1970s and 1980s as Black and Latinx communities responded to the pressure of heightened systemic racism. Artists became the voice of their communities by fighting for the acknowledgment of their grievances and justice to be delivered. Hip hop was unlike many other musical genres of the period because it reflected the Black community's culture while simultaneously carrying on the spirit of rebellion from its musical and literal ancestors (i.e., jazz, blues, and funk). Hip hop is an art that reflects the experiences and dreams of those who create it. The artists' use of hip hop to resist institutions and bring attention to oppression has varied forms ranging from the militant political commentary of Public Enemy's "Fight the Power," to the womanist anthem of Queen Latifah's "U.N.I.T.Y.," to Ice Cube's "It Was a Good Day," which covertly narrates the daily tribulations faced in urban Black and Latinx communities. The diversity of approaches to resistance in hip hop is necessary to communicate multifaceted obstacles and stories of those who experience them. Each generation of hip-hop artists and fans connect with this liberating element of the art. Although the music may sound different and the oppressive systems being addressed may have changed forms, hip hop artists continue to use their platform to carry on the legacy of inspiring their audiences to fight the powers that be.

As an adolescent, hip hop was as familiar to me as my own heartbeat. The sounds of hip hop were heard in my parents' cars, my room, family cookouts, and even on the school bus. I listened to a variety of artists from N.W.A. and 2Pac to Lil Wayne and Outkast. I never questioned hip hop's place in my life nor I in it. I wish I could say the same for my undergraduate journey. During the 2015–2016 academic year, I was a junior at a flagship university in the South. Being a Black, female, first-generation college student at a large predominately white institution (PWI) made me very aware of all of the labels that defined my existence. Walking to class would sometimes be overwhelming when all the faces racing around me like cars in city traffic did not look like mine. It was in those moments where I felt especially intimidated. My defense was putting on my headphones, listening to my favorite hip hop album—at the time Kendrick Lamar's *To Pimp a Butterfly*—and becoming empowered by the music and feeling like nothing could hold me back.

I was very involved on campus and spent the bulk of my time with organizations focused on diversity and social justice. At the start of the 2015–2016 school year, it seemed the university was making strides toward becoming a more welcoming campus with the establishment of the Office of Diversity and Inclusion and a newly hired vice chancellor (VC) for diversity and inclusion. The VC was a soft-spoken and well-dressed Black man who seemed eager to make the university a welcoming environment for all. Unfortunately, he wasn't in office long enough to see the bulk of his plans come to fruition.

The local news had caught wind of a student-authored op-ed on the office website, which gave an overview of nonbinary pronouns one might prefer. This was somehow spun into a controversial local news headline suggesting university administrators completely banned staff and students from using *he* and *she* pronouns. State legislators were outraged and directly targeted the LGBTQ Pride Center and Office for Diversity and Inclusion for defunding. I became involved in numerous campus protests and demonstrations involving a coalition of students, faculty, and staff from the LGBTQ community, racial and ethnic minority groups, religious minorities, and allies. It was a tremendously empowering and eye-opening time in my life. Unfortunately, we were not successful in our efforts to retain the diversity resources the school had recently established. Stakeholders and concerned parents of students used the VC as a scapegoat and he was fired. Eventually the Office of Diversity and Inclusion and the Pride Center were defunded.

In April 2016, after two long semesters of protest, news of the firing and defunding reached a group-chat comprised of members of the diversity ally coalition. As a coalition, the combined efforts and relationships we built across groups felt cosmically unstoppable. Yet, here we were. Stopped. Our spirits were low, and I could feel everyone's mix of anxiety and anger through my phone screen as we all responded to the news. I typed a simple message in response to the heavy hearts of the chat. "We Gon' Be Alright—K Dot." The group message lit up with pictures, GIFs, and words of encouragement. After that, more demonstrations on behalf of the coalition were planned for the end of the semester and throughout the summer, all with the tag line and chant "We Gon' Be Alright!" The message of Kendrick Lamar's (K-Dot) "Alright" inspired and motivated the group to remember why we started. We started this journey not because of a single injustice but rather because the spirit of resistance was passed on to us by those who fought for equality on our behalf generations earlier. We knew that while we had lost this single battle, we had not lost the war. In fact, we had gained something greater than what we lost: our united voice. While hip hop may look different today than it did in the 1970s and 1980s, the power of anthems like "Alright" carry on the legacy of calling out oppressive systems while simultaneously giving hope to people burdened by the same.

The articles selected for this section examine the historical and contemporary presence of resistance in hip hop. The purpose of this section is to bring attention to the social commentary present in hip hop, which often goes unacknowledged or underestimated. Each article covers historical and/or theoretical context for resistance in hip hop using songs and personal experiences of artists as examples. Examining hip hop as a form of resistance is integral to interpreting the art form and understanding the worldview of those who participate in its culture, as creators and consumers.

In "'Fight the Power' by Public Enemy," David Stovall contextualizes the importance and impact of one of Public Enemy's most popular songs. The author is reflective of his own journey as an educator and encourages his colleagues to be justice-oriented in their approach to interacting with youth. Stovall makes the case that "Fight the Power" is as relevant to the youth of today as it was in the 1990s. Corporate influence on mainstream hip hop often steers artists toward shallow desires and away from being social justice–oriented. However, as Stovall points out, it is the job of old-school hip hop lovers not to shame the youth for their music but rather to educate and inspire them to remember and connect with their roots. This article reminds us of the power and revolutionary sounds of the 1980s and calls us to remember that the fight is not over yet.

In "Criminal-Justice Minded: Retribution, Punishment, and Authority," Erin I. Kelly uses retributivist and consequentialist philosophies of punishment to analyze the lyrics of gangsta artists who rap about taking justice into their own hands. Her primary claim is that the lyrics are their attempt to expose the fallacies of the legal justice system. Gangsta rappers are often demonized and/or excluded from academic conversations because of the materialism, misogyny, homophobia, and violence that are often found in their music. According to Kelly, when we neglect this style of rap, we miss the ways that many gangsta rappers are using their personal experiences with the legal system, inner city life, and vengeance to interrogate forms of racial inequality and social control. Kelly challenges us to view gangsta rappers' use of vengeful lyricism as a "provocatively aggressive" strategy to insight awareness and protest against unfair systems of oppression.

In "'Hip Hop Is Dead' by Nas," Michael Benitez Jr. explores the evolution, definition, and boundaries of hip hop culture particularly as it relates to the historical and sociopolitical context in which it is situated. Many purists compare the current state of hip hop to its past and believe it has lost its edge and strayed from its roots. Hence the common phrase, "Hip hop is dead." Nas is a hip hop artist who regularly tackles social problems facing his community. In his song "Hip Hop Is Dead," he addresses the hip hop community and calls out corporate commodification, free speech infringement, lack of knowledge representation, and disregard for the origins of art, which many people point to as the reason, if you agree with his position, hip hop is dying. The song and Benitez's analysis nuance the narrative of hip hop dying and allow space for change and constructive critique of the genre. Benitez encourages educators to continue to incorporate the hip hop of today into their pedagogy as it is the voice of the younger generation's social movements. Because of the critical and controversial nature of hip hop, the author is certain that it will continue to be the music of young activism.

Collectively, these articles demonstrate how and why resistance has been and continues to be a central theme—if not *the* central theme—in the art. Without resistance, hip hop is merely benign spoken-word poetry accompanied by rhythmically appeasing sounds.

READING 4.1

"Fight the Power" by Public Enemy

By David Stovall

TO BANG, BLAST, AND STRUGGLE FOR FREEDOM

When I was first approached by the editors to contribute the following [reading], I was a bit conflicted. Public Enemy (PE) is one of my favorite groups of all time, but "Fight the Power" (Shocklee, Sadler, & Ridenhour, 1989) is not my favorite song (Black Steel in the Hour of Chaos is still the *ultimate* PE banger!). Despite the fact that it is considered one of their most, if not *the* most, important contributions (and one of the more important songs in Hip Hop, for that matter), I felt that it became the opus that unfortunately overshadowed the breadth and depth of their body of work. Nevertheless, despite its timelessness and current relevance, "Fight the Power" should be contextualized to the conditions and events of the late 1980s and the reality of how the song is a reflection of the lives of Black and Latino/a urban youth in that historical moment. Bridging the 1980s to the current moment, songs like "Fight the Power" have a critical connection that should be explored in relevance to the lives of the same group of young people. Wrongly interpreted by mainstream media as "rage-filled" or "hateful" music, the songs and lyrics of PE deserve to be understood as reflective of the counter-stories of oppressed peoples.

For the reasons listed above, the following [reading] is a call to action more than a tribute. Because 22 years is a lifetime in the world of youth culture, PE and "Fight the Power" may appear ancient to some. However, as a college professor and volunteer high school social studies teacher, the song (and those like it) continually present a challenge to all adults who work with young people: *in our attempts to demonstrate solidarity with youth, we must be keenly aware and remain willing to engage the things we do not know.* Waxing poetic serves little purpose to young people who are dealing with the realities of high-stakes testing, homelessness, sexual exploitation, poverty, the prison industrial complex, the military industrial complex, racism, police brutality, gentrification, and disenfranchisement. We need to understand the current situation of young people in urban space as intense. For these reasons we must use this context to create thoughtful, clear, justice-oriented curriculum that work to develop the skills of our students to navigate and change the current reality—not as a lofty vision, but in the practical spaces that constitute the victories and defeats that we experience in the fight for educational justice.

Simultaneously, the following [reading] is not a manifesto. Instead, it should be considered reflections on my own struggle to engage students with relevant, thoughtful, action-provoking curriculum in a moment when many of them have been deemed disposable by the State. Because many communities that have historically had the least are getting even less in terms of access to state, local, and federal resources, "Fight the Power" is both relevant and somewhat prophetic. In the rebellious and protest tradition of jazz, blues, folk, punk, and rock (i.e., Last Poets, Watts Prophets, Black Jazz Ensemble, Oscar Brown Jr., Abbey Lincoln, Max Roach, Odetta, Joan Baez, Bob Dylan, Woodie Guthrie, Pete Seger, The Clash, The Ramones, New York Dolls, etc.) "Fight the Power" provides social commentary accepted by few but understood by many.

Returning to the practical matters of the document, the [reading] is divided into three sections. The first section engages the political, economic, and social context of the late 1980s for urban youth. Part two engages the song sonically and visually. Providing context for PE, the lyrics and visuals of "Fight the Power" provide an overlooked critique and call to action. As the visual advent of music video enhanced (or numbed) our connection to a particular song, "Fight the Power" is deeply connected to a particular socio-political revival. The concluding section connects the song to the present-day, placing it in the context of urban classrooms and the tangible connections to the current moment. Included is a discussion of how the neoliberal turn in education and society at large has intensified the struggle for justice. Highlighted in a set of examples of student, family, teacher and community resistance, the hope is for readers to understand the struggle and possibilities for equity and justice.

WELCOME TO THE TERRORDOME: THE WRATH OF THE 1980S, PROTEST AND THE POLITICS OF DISPOSABILITY

The decade predating the 1990 release of PE's album *Fear of a Black Planet* has particular significance in understanding the prominent underpinnings of a song like "Fight the Power." The devastation of the crack epidemic, along with government disinvestment in programming centered in social welfare (K–12 education, higher education, employment development programs, etc.) wreaked havoc on Black and Latino/a communities throughout the mid-1970s and 1980s. Continuing the legacy of de-industrialization in the 1970s, the subsequent War on Drugs heightened under the Reagan Administration utilized legislative tools like mandatory minimums and extended sentences (e.g., Rockefeller

Laws in the state of New York) to imprison a generation of young African-American and Latino/a males. Excellently documented in the accounts of Alexander (2012), Wacquant (2009), and Brown (1999), the advent of the prison industrial complex (PIC) remains as one of the most totalizing forces that continues to deem a generation of young people as disposable. Due to its reciprocal effects through felony disenfranchisement (the process whereby convicted felons cannot vote or hold certain occupations depending on the laws of the state), underground economies are in some cases understood as the most viable means for sustenance.

Despite images of the flashy, opulent, over-indulgent drug-dealer/pimp archetype glamorized in 1970s Blaxploitation films like *Superfly or The Candy Tangerine Man*, this was not the case for the vast multitude of persons participating in the illicit drug-trade. Where many aspired to live the lives of Bumpy Johnson, Frank Lucas, and Nicky Barnes and their reincarnations in the form of Azie (AZ) Faison, Alberto (Alpo) Martinez, and Rich Porter in Harlem, "Freeway" Ricky Ross in Los Angeles, Flukey Stokes in Chicago, or the original 50-Cent in Queens, their opulence remained pipe dreams for most. Nevertheless an unusual relationship developed in many communities in urban America: for some, the drug kingpin became the anti-hero of sorts—despised by the larger world, they operated as the one group of people who were willing to support those who were down-and-out when few others would. Through their material support of the block, many understood the wrongdoings of the drug-dealer, but they were the few people who were willing to support the downtrodden. We knew their enterprise was problematic, but these men and women were often the people we grew up with who took "different paths" from the mainstream and began an engagement with a world with seismic risks for the prospect of considerable gains.

Conversely, there were also members of the same group of young people in urban spaces who began to educate themselves on the realities of racism not as solely a contemporary phenomenon, but as part of a larger historical continuum. College campuses across the country had thousands of students participating in campaigns against the Apartheid state in South Africa, nuclear proliferation, Israeli settlements, and police brutality at the local and national level. Popularized in the Artists Against Apartheid song "Sun City," numbers of mainstream artists were willing to lend their efforts to popularize the efforts of activists both locally and internationally.

In the later part of the decade, much of the divestment work loaned itself to a renaissance of the sentiment displayed in the Black Power movement of the late 1960s and early 1970s. Dubbed in many circles as Afro centricity or Afrocentrism, the international interest in the plight of People of Color internationally lent itself to return to a study of Black and Brown people in the United States. Books like Carter G. Woodson's *Miseducation of the Negro*, Harold Cruise's *The Crisis of the Negro Intellectual* and bell hooks' *Ain't I a Woman* were showing up in reading circles, challenging those who engaged to return to the idea that our communities were valuable and deserving of change. For a brief moment a burgeoning of African-American studies departments were beginning to expand to provide graduate degrees. K–12 educators began to re-incorporate ethnic studies into their social studies and history curricula. College students who transitioned the anti-Apartheid/divestment work onto local student and community struggles returned home to work for community organizations instead of Fortune 500 companies. National media coverage on the 1989 Virginia Beach Greekfest riots and the Tawana Brawley rape accusation had African-American students (and other students of color) question their position in the larger society. Police brutality, discrimination, and the perpetual regulation of Black bodies became rallying cries for scores of youth disillusioned with the ideal of the "American dream." Instead of looking outward for people to assist us in changing our conditions, the Afrocentric renaissance returned many to Ella Baker's notion that we are the ones we've been waiting for. For many, her sentiments held considerable weight in communities ravaged by policies of the Reagan administration coupled with local and state disinvestment.

Because the movement was not without its contradictions (our continued inability to critically engage sexism, homophobia, ageism, ableism, and anti-Semitism), it was one that resonated with young people in that it challenged common notions of an elite class that would provide the saving grace for the masses of poor, working class urban youth. In addition to PE, groups like X-Clan and their community partners the Blackwatch Movement were seemingly committed to the uplifting of historically disenfranchised communities. Paired with these sentiments, in many cities there was a sense of what was needed to reclaim our communities. The work of Sonny Carson in Brooklyn, New York was of particular importance as the video for "Fight the Power" was shot in conjunction with the Brooklyn March to End Violence.

For myself, this was my coming of age moment in that I was immersed in a space where people involved in the cultural, political, and nationalist movements were reaching back to the younger generation to pose alternatives for our current condition. As students at my high school became more versed with PE through albums like *Yo! Bum Rush the Show,* a growing militancy began to emerge in our consciousness. In addition to hearing songs like "Public Enemy #1" and "You're Gonna Get Yours," we also began to read the teachings of Malcolm X and H. Rap Brown. Earlier civil rights struggles became viewed as docile and accommodating. For a young person in the late 1980s, I was affirmed by the suggestion of taking power instead of asking for it.

As a Chicagoan, I was familiar with the Nation of Islam (NOI) and the teachings of Elijah Muhammad. By way of some relative independence granted by my parents (the ability to drive and take public transportation), I was able to venture out to other parts of the city. In the fall of 1988, one of my classmates (who was a member of the NOI) got a group of friends together in study hall and asked us to go to attend a service at Mosque Maryam (NOI national headquarters). Out of curiosity and my initial knowledge of PE, I thought it was definitely something to check out. The security detail of the NOI, commonly known as the Fruit of Islam (FOI) used to perform a precise military marching drill that was duplicated by members of PE known as the S1Ws (short for Security of the First World). Because some S1Ws were FOI members, the use of military drill was an exciting element to PE shows. All of my classmates were fascinated with this imagery and wanted to know more.

While I was truly impressed with the Minister Louis Farrakhan's oratory skills, I was equally astounded by the centrality of self-reliance and community development in his sermon. Some of my classmates were so impressed that two of them joined the NOI directly after the service. Despite the speech I remained a skeptic, as I wasn't as comfortable with their ideas around gender. Nevertheless, I respected Farrakhan's unwavering commitment to his beliefs. I wasn't used to hearing sentiment like his. The brash militancy and call to action was something that stuck with me. PE's songs were a way for me to localize many of the national struggles against racism and marginalization. As a young person I knew something was wrong in our communities, but I had no clue as to how to address it. In this moment "Fight the Power" became the anthem by which to direct my energies.

INTO THE VISUAL: IMAGERY, REFLECTION AND "FIGHT THE POWER" AS FORMATIVE CONSCIOUSNESS RAISING

In the earlier years of music video production and television shows solely dedicated to the viewing of music videos, viewers were often treated to long-form or "full-length" videos. My preparation to write this [reading] had me view the full-length version of "Fight the Power." In my own recollection, I hadn't watched the full-length video in at least 15 years. Totally forgotten was the footage from the 1963 March on Washington by Universal International Newsreel. The announcer states that the march was an attempt to end forever the blight of racial inequity. Directly following the footage the video transitions to a march in Brooklyn led by PE. Chuck D (lead emcee), is holding a megaphone and states:

> We rollin' this way—that march in 1963, that was a bit of nonsense. We ain't rolling like that no more—(as a) matter of fact, in young Black America we rollin' up with seminars, press conferences, and straight up rallies. Am I right? (crowd roars back—Yeah!) We gonna get what we got to get coming to us. Word up—we ain't going out like that '63 nonsense. (D'Ambrosio, 2005)

I had forgotten that the video had been positioned as a critique of the 1963 march through the use of similar imagery. Long placards that had the names of cities, states, and New York City boroughs were identical to the ones used in the March on Washington. What was different, however, was the addition of posters with seminal figures in African-American

History (Harriet Tubman, Medgar Evers, Sojourner Truth, Malcolm X, Martin Luther King, Marcus Garvey, Angela Davis, etc.). Because our images of the March on Washington are passive in the sense of people holding hands and singing spirituals, imagery from the video for "Fight the Power" were visceral. Young people were orderly and at the same time excited, jumping up and down, holding up two fingers for peace, sitting on each other's shoulders and carrying banners that stretched across the street. The song was the rallying cry for the march, with young people yelling to "fight the power." The visuals were powerful in that they created another dimension for the song through the connection of song lyrics to celluloid imagery. For me, as a seventeen-year-old in 1989, the coupling was magical. Rarely did we see images of ourselves as young people claiming space and pushing to change our condition. Strengthening this concept was the fact that Spike Lee used "Fight the Power" as the unofficial theme song for his 1989 seminal film *Do the Right Thing*. The popularity of this film with my friends in high school made the video even more enticing.

Contributing to my personal excitement was the affirmation of my personal feelings about the music industry at large. Upon learning about the ingrained structural racism of the music business, Chuck D's verse was affirmation of the way I felt about Elvis as the "king" of rock and roll: "Elvis was a hero to most, But he never meant shit to me, Straight up racist that sucka was simple and plain, Motherfuck him and John Wayne!" (Shocklee, Sadler, & Ridenhour, 1989). The next few lines, "'Cause I'm Black and I'm proud, I'm ready and hyped plus I'm amped, Most of my heroes don't appear on no stamps" (Shocklee et al., 1989) were the ultimate voicing of truth to power at the time. Between N.W.A. and PE, the fact that someone was willing to tell the truth in an uncompromising way served as my inspiration to engage. It inspired me to learn more about Muddy Waters, Big Mama Thornton, Sister Rosetta Tharpe, Howlin Wolf, Dizzy Gillespie, Otis Dixon, Koko Taylor, Chuck Berry, Little Richard, and the countless R&B, jazz, blues, and soul artists that were never given their proper due. The veil of whiteness had been lifted to expose fallacy while encouraging others to right the wrongs of the current historical record. Hip Hop was at its punk moment when a bevy of artists began to name the unseen and overlooked.

WE ROCK ON AND ON AND ON AND ON: "FIGHT THE POWER" AS LEGACY AND PRAXIS

Instead of reminiscing about Hip Hop's "golden age," it's much more important to recognize the changing landscape of Hip Hop. The advent of corporate media influences along with the demise of the record company in its traditional sense has taken Hip Hop in an entirely different direction than its genesis in the South Bronx in the late seventies. The world of PE, Eric B. and Rakim, MC Lyte, Queen Latifah, Lakim Shabazz, Digable

Planets, De La Soul, KRS-ONE, Gang Starr, EPMD, and X-Clan is not the world of 2 Chainz, Lil Wayne, LFMAO, Tyga, Nikki Minaj, Drake, Rick Ross, Meek Mill, and Wacka Flocka Flame. Where the end of the modern record company should provided more visibility to do-it-yourself artists, the corporate influence has morphed to use the same outlets to steer tastes and desire.

For these reasons and countless others, PE and "Fight the Power" deserve to be contextualized in the current milieu in the fight against disparities with regard to race, class, employment, housing, gender, sexuality, and ability. The same forces that Chuck D addressed in 1989 remain salient. Some of the faces may have changed, but the work remains the same. We are *still* the ones we've been waiting for.

REFERENCES

Alexander, M. (2012). *The new Jim Crow: Mass incarceration in the age of colorblindness.* New York, NY: New Press.

Brown, M. (1999). *Race, money and the American welfare state.* Ithaca, NY: Cornell University Press.

D'Ambrosio, A. (2005). Interview: Chuck D. *The Progressive.* Retrieved August 22, 2013, from www.progressive.org/mag_chuckd

Shocklee, H., Sadler, E., & Ridenhour, C. (1989). Fight the power [Recorded by Public Enemy]. On *Fight the power* [Cassette, single]. New York, NY: Motown Records.

Wacquant, L. (2009a). *Prisons of poverty.* Minneapolis, MN: University of Minnesota Press.

Criminal-Justice Minded

Retribution, Punishment, and Authority

By Erin I. Kelly

The payback attitude heard in gangsta rap sounds like a call for retribution. As 50 cent puts it, "Nigga you play around, I lay you down / That's how it's goin' down."[1] Justice as retribution echoes the feeling that vengeance is sweet, redeeming those who've suffered the humiliation of being wronged. This appeals to many people. It fact, it seems to express the attitude many law-abiding citizens would direct at gangstas themselves. Yet the desire for retribution that some rappers express isn't proposed as a legitimate basis for a system of punishment. To begin with, the situations they portray are sometimes way outside of the law, as Nas depicts in "Every Ghetto": "Circle the block where the beef's at / And park in front of my enemy's eyes / They see that it's war we life-stealers, hollow-tip lead busters."[2]

Behind rappers' desire to settle the score often lies a firm belief that the law does not, and doesn't aim to, protect them. If the law doesn't protect you and won't deliver justice, you may have to protect your own honor and reputation by seeking vengeance against your enemies. In Dr. Dre's words, "And if motherfuckers come at me wrong / I straight put my.44 Desert Eagle to his motherfuckin' dome / and show him why they call me the notorious one."[3]

Many rappers are skeptical about justice in America and alarmed by our system of punishment. They suggest that racial bias in our criminal justice institutions—police, courts, and prisons—undermines the notion that criminals are getting their "just deserts." Rappers also call into question whether the massive effort to incarcerate black men serves the purpose of public safety. The rhetoric of both retribution and the public good seem to them to be a front for unjust forms of social control that help to maintain

---

1 50 Cent, "Rotten Apple," *Guess Who's Back* (Full Clip, 2002).

2 Nas, "Every Ghetto," *Stillmatic* (Sony, 2001).

3 Dr. Dre, "Nigga Witta Gun," *The Chronic* (Priority, 1992).

a system of racial privilege for whites. I will discuss "retributivist" and "consequentialist" philosophies of punishment and how rap music aims to snatch the disguise from the ugly face of the system.

PUNISHMENT AS RETRIBUTION

Retribution as a justification for the state-sanctioned, legal practice of punishment has become popular. Punishment as retribution is based on the idea that criminal wrong-doing calls for punishment—quite apart from the consequences of punishment, such as incapacitating or deterring offenders. The demand for retribution would be considered justified even at substantial economic and social cost. The point is that justice is done only when wrongdoers suffer. This punishment is imposed through the formal proce-dures of the law, where punishment takes place well after the crime and for reasons other than self-defense.

In lawless circumstances, by contrast, the line between retribution and self-defense gets blurred. Retaliation and even preemptive action might seem necessary to defend person and property. "Ready to rhyme / Standin' my ground / Never back down," says OutKast, "Willin' to rob, steal, and kill any thang that threatens mine."[4] But advocates of retribution (a.k.a. retributivists) are not interested in retaliation as a means to personal safety or as a reaction to a threat. They advocate retaliation for wrongdoing as a matter of justice. This has led famous retributivists, the philosophers Immanuel Kant (1724–1804) and, in our time, Robert Nozick (1938–2002), to stress differences between vengeance and retribution. Vengeance is emotional, personal, reckless, and often disproportion-ate to the wrong. Retribution is impartially applied by a dispassionate and legitimate authority, and carefully calculated to fit the crime. In a civilized society, these philosophers claim, retribution should replace vengeance. This does not mean that retribution will be less violent or brutal. The death penalty and maximum-security prisons are hardly gentler alternatives to vigilante vengeance—as the French philosopher Michel Foucault (1926–1984) emphasizes in *Discipline and Punish: The Birth of the Prison* (1975).

Yet the ideal of retribution carries with it more than a trace of vengeance. Indeed, some recent books, such as Peter French's *The Virtues of Vengeance* and Jeffrie Murphy's *Getting Even*, urge us to embrace the emotional, personal, and expressive value of punishment as retribution. These philosophers accept continuity between vengeance and the justification of punishment. French offers four conditions that vengeance must meet if it's to count as justice:

1. *Communication*. The penalty must effectively communicate that what the offender did was wrong.

---

4   OutKast, "Return of the 'G,'" *Aquemini* (La Face, 1998).

2. *Desert*. The penalty must be deserved.
3. *Proportionality*. The penalty must fit the crime.
4. *Authority*. Someone with legitimate authority must administer the penalty.

When these conditions are met, vengeance guides us to justice, or so it is claimed.

DOUBTS ABOUT THE JUSTICE OF RETRIBUTION

Rappers tell a cautionary tale—the retributivist's conditions for justice aren't met. Here is Public Enemy's angle on political authority:

> I got a letter from the government
> The other day
> I opened and read it
> It said they were suckers
> They wanted me for their army or whatever
> Picture me givin' a damn—I said never
> Here is a land that never gave a damn
> About a brother like me and myself
> Because they never did
> I wasn't wit' it, but just that very minute ...
> It occurred to me
> The suckers had authority.[5]

PE's Chuck D implies that the authority of a government that doesn't care about some of its people can't be legitimate. A legitimate government serves the interests of all of its people, including minority groups. A government that fails to do this exercises only power, not legitimate authority—might, not right.

The most basic rights associated with our criminal justice system, guaranteed by the U.S. Constitution, are these: people should not be subjected to unreasonable searches and seizures (Fourth Amendment); people are innocent until proven guilty through due process of the law (Fifth Amendment); people should not be subjected to cruel or unusual punishment (Eighth Amendment); people should be equally protected by the law (Fourteenth Amendment). Many rap artists point to violations of these basic constitutional rights—police and prosecutorial misconduct, lack of access to legal counsel, unfair sentencing policy, and inhumane prison conditions. These are well-documented problems that disproportionately affect African Americans and Latinos.

---

5 Public Enemy, "Black Steel in the Hour of Chaos," *It Takes a Nation of Millions to Hold Us Back* (Def Jam, 1988).

Consider, for example, racial profiling. As Mos Def describes it, "The po-po stop him and show no respect / 'Is there a problem officer?' / Damn straight, it's called race."[6] Racial profiling is a policing strategy that is strongly correlated with the excessive use of force and with disproportionate incarceration of minorities.[7] Problems such as these threaten not only U.S. Constitutional rights but also internationally recognized human rights. They give us reason to doubt whether many punishments have been justly imposed.

But grounds for doubt about punishment as retribution may extend beyond worries about racial bias in its application. How could we know whether the desert condition or the proportionality condition for justice as retribution has been satisfied? Consider this discussion about fitting the punishment to the crime:

> Tailoring the fit appears to depend on the moral sensitivity or intuitions of the punisher(s). When is the fit 'just right'? When does a suit of clothes fit? When it feels right? Yes, but also when it looks right to the wearer and to others. ... Morality is an art, not a science.[8]

Statements such as this should worry if not alarm us. The lack of a cohesive moral community and a shared basis for moral judgment in multicultural, multiethnic, multire-ligious America dooms this justification of punishment. We simply don't agree about who deserves what. The haphazard nature of desert judgments cannot justify the high-stakes social policy of criminal punishment. Our system of punishment costs us almost 60 billion dollars per year;[9] it disrupts families and communities; and it deprives offenders of their most basic liberty, sometimes for a very long time. Metaphorical and biblical references to cosmic balance, the scales of justice, "an eye for an eye," or the art of morality are inadequate as rational and public justifications for a system of punishment. We must look elsewhere for a more plausible rationale.

PUNISHMENT AS SOCIAL CONTROL

The main alternative rationale for punishment is about social control, not desert. Many rappers know this all too well through personal experience. The standard philosophical theories of punishment as social control come from a tradition influenced by the work

---

6   Mos Def, "Mr. Nigga," *Black on Both Sides* (Rawkus, 1999).

7   See Amnesty International's report, *Threat and Humiliation: Racial Profiling, Domestic Security, and Human Rights in the United States* (New York: Amnesty International USA, 2004).

8   Peter French, *The Virtues of Vengeance* (Lawrence: University Press of Kansas, 2001), p. 227.

9   Unless otherwise specified, the statistics in this essay come from the Bureau of Justice Statistics, United States Government.

of Jeremy Bentham (1748–1832). Bentham and other "consequentialist" philosophers have argued that punishment can only be justified when it has good consequences for society. In particular, punishment can be justified by considerations of deterrence, rehabilitation, or incapacitation.

Deterrence is achieved when, by punishing offenders, criminals or potential criminals are effectively discouraged from committing crimes. Rehabilitation is achieved when an offender's desire to re-offend is extinguished and replaced by respect for the law. Incapacitation is achieved when the guilty are rendered incapable of re-offending because they're locked up. Rappers express skepticism about whether anything but incapacitation is achieved by punishment.

We have seen that the moral authority of the criminal justice system is precarious when the rights of members of minority groups are not protected. This makes it hard to secure respect for the law, which dims the prospects for rehabilitating criminals. A deterrence rationale is also on unsteady ground, since deterrence is ineffective when the conditions outside prison are like the "jungle" that Melle Mel describes in "The Message":

> Broken glass everywhere
> People pissin' on the stairs
> You know they just don't care
> I can't take the smell, can't take the noise
> Got no money to move out, I guess I got no choice
> Rats in the front room, roaches in the back
> Junkies in the alley with a baseball bat
> I tried to get away but I couldn't get far
> 'Cause a man with a tow truck repossessed my car.[10]

When people are poor, unemployed, without hope, and subject to street violence and police abuse, prison may seem a lot less like something to fear, as Dead Prez makes clear in "Behind Enemy Lines":

> You ain't gotta be locked up to be in prison
> Look how we livin'
> 30,000 niggas a day, up in the bing, standin' routine
> They put us in a box, just like our life on the block.[11]

Of course, prison is in many ways worse than "life on the block." The point is that people in difficult social circumstances are more willing to take risks, especially when they're

---

10 Grandmaster Flash and the Furious Five, "The Message," *The Message* (Sugarhill, 1982).

11 Dead Prez, "Behind Enemy Lines," *Let's Get Free* (Loud, 2000).

angry or desperate. This fact, which might be called "the ghetto factor," substantially weakens the effectiveness of punishment as a deterrent.

We're left with incapacitation, and herein lies a deeper story. It begins with an agonizing recognition of the prospects facing many people who get caught up in the system: "They're scared of us, rather beware than dare to trust / Always in jail, million dollar bail, left there to rust."[12] Incapacitation could be a legitimate rationale for punishment only if the aim is public safety. But rappers charge that the long sentences that many African Americans face often serve interests that reach beyond the safety of the public.

For instance, federal sentences for cocaine possession and distribution are much harsher for the drug in crack form as compared to powder form. Possession of five grams of crack triggers a five-year mandatory minimum sentence, whereas it takes five hundred grams of powder cocaine to trigger the same sentence. Although evidence indicates there are far more white crack users and dealers than black ones, 84 percent of crack defendants are African American.[13] By contrast, only 31 percent of powder cocaine defendants are African American. The racial disparity may be explained by a concentration of drug law enforcement in urban, minority communities in which crack, the cheaper form of cocaine, is more prevalent than powder cocaine. The media also hyped the "evils" of crack as the government launched its "war on drugs" in the 1980s. The result is what Human Rights Watch has described as "an indefensible sentencing differential [that] becomes unconscionable in light of its racial impact."[14]

The idea that our criminal justice system punishes not only crime but also race comes up time and again in rap tracks. In the words of Ice Cube: "I think back to when I was robbin' my own kind / The police didn't pay it no mind / But when I start robbin' the white folks / Now I'm in the pen wit' the soap-ona-rope."[15]

PRISON/GHETTO

Let's further probe the relationship between prison and ghetto. Here's Goodie Mob's "Cell Therapy": "Loc up folks they in the hood, got an eye on every move / I make open your face to info you ain't know / 'Cause it's kept low how the new world plan / Reeks the planet without the black man."[16] The ambiguity of the line, "Loc up folks they in the hood, got an eye on every move," implies that both prison and ghetto serve to control and to segregate African Americans, especially young men.

---

12 Big Punisher, "Capital Punishment," *Capital Punishment* (Loud, 1998).

13 U.S. Sentencing Commission, 2000 Sourcebook of Federal Sentencing Statistics.

14 Human Rights Watch Presentation to the United States Sentencing Commission (25th February, 2002).

15 Ice Cube, "AmeriKKKa's Most Wanted," *AmeriKKKa's Most Wanted* (Priority, 1990).

16 Goodie Mob, "Cell Therapy," *Soul Food* (La Face, 1995).

Similarities between prison and ghetto have caught the attention of sociologists. The ghetto is a physical space that segregates, stigmatizes, coerces, and makes people vulnerable to economic exploitation.[17] Ghettos have worked this way, in apartheid South Africa, the Jim Crow American South, Chicago, and New York City. The racial profile of the U.S. prison population—65 percent of the prison population is non-white—suggests that prison too contributes to racial segregation. No doubt it also stigmatizes. And further, private companies are making big money marketing products and services. Telephone companies, for instance, are reaping hundreds of millions of dollars on unregulated phone rates for calls from prisons, some as high as $2.20 per minute.[18]

Greater racial integration in American society achieved by the civil rights movement of the 1960s has been followed by a massive increase in the incarceration rate. The total U.S. prison population has shot up, incredibly, from less than 200,000 to almost 1.4 million today—about seven times. In addition, close to 700,000 people are held in local jails. This brings us to a grand total of 2.1 million people behind bars in America today. At the current rate, about 1 in 3 black men will do time at some point in their lives. Sociologist Loïc Wacquant remarks on the post-civil rights era: "As the walls of the ghetto shook and threatened to crumble, the walls of the prison were correspondingly extended, enlarged and fortified, and 'confinement of differentiation,' aimed at keeping a group apart ... gained primacy over 'confinement of safety'."[19] Wacquant draws a contrast here between incarceration as a way to make society safer and incarceration as a way to stigmatize and ostracize a despised group. His point is that our prison system has increasingly functioned to stigmatize and to ostracize African Americans; the advancement of public safety cannot plausibly be characterized as its primary aim. Some rappers, like Nas, seem to be making the same point:

> My country shitted on me (My country)
> She wants to get rid of me (Naw, never)
> 'Cause the things I seen (We know too much)
> 'Cause the things I seen (We seen too much).[20]

Rappers challenge us to be more aware and critical of the systematic abuse, exclusion, and marginalization of the black urban poor. They protest the endless cycling of black men between ghetto and prison. Their strategy is aggressively provocative—by being provocatively aggressive. Ice-T's "Cop Killer" is an early example that prompted

---

17   See Loïc Wacquant, "From Slavery to Mass Incarceration," *New Left Review* 13 (2002), pp. 49–54.

18   Kim Curtis and Bob Porterfield, "California Inmates' Calls Home Prove Costly to Families, Friends." *The Boston Globe* (6th September, 2004).

19   Wacquant, "From Slavery to Mass Incarceration," p. 52.

20   Nas, "My Country," *Stillmatic* (Sony, 2001).

a censorship debate in the 1990s. The lines I quoted from OutKast are more subtle. We don't know whether "standin' my ground, never back down" is a matter of rhyming or something more threatening. We often find rappers playing on words, or signifying, in order to drive home a deeper message. Think of KRS-One's play on the similarity between the words "officer" and "overseer" to draw a parallel between the control and violence that people in each role have exercised over the lives of African Americans.[21] An aim in the music here, as elsewhere, is to destabilize our perceptions of state legitimacy and criminal justice.

Criminal "justice" in an unjust society is suspect. The burden on those who shoulder it is heavy. Despite the materialistic, consumerist values frequently found in rap tracks, sometimes a simpler, deeper, and more soulful plea can be heard, as in Dead Prez's cry for freedom:

> Yo, this world is oh so cold, I think about my ancestors
> Being sold, and it make me wanna break the mold ...
>
> I don't wanna be no movie star
> I don't wanna drive no fancy car
> I just wanna be free, to live my life, to live my own life.[22]

BEATS & RHYMES!

A SELECTED DISCOGRAPHY

Big Punisher. *Capital Punishment* (Loud, 1998).
Dead Prez. *Let's Get Free* (Loud, 2000).
Dr. Dre. *The Chronic* (Interscope, 1992).
50 Cent. *Guess Who's Back* (Full Clip, 2002).
Goodie Mob. *Soul Food* (La Face, 1995).
Grandmaster Flash. *Message from Beat Street: Best of Grandmaster Flash* (Rhino, 1994).
Ice Cube. *AmeriKKKa's Most Wanted* (Priority, 1990).
KRS-One. *Return of the Boom Bap* (Jive, 1993).
Mos Def. *Black on Both Sides* (Rawkus, 1999).
Nas. *Stillmatic* (Sony, 2001).
OutKast. *Aquemini* (La Face, 1998).
Public Enemy. *It Takes a Nation of Millions to Hold Us Back* (Def Jam, 1988).

---

21 See KRS-One, "Sound of Da Police," *Return of the Boom Bap* (Jive, 1993).

22 Dead Prez, "We Want Freedom," *Let's Get Free* (Loud, 2000).

"Hip Hop is Dead" by Nas

By Michael Benitez Jr.

INTRODUCTION

Many artists, critics, scholars, and fans alike have, throughout the past decade, engaged in a prolonged dialogue over the state of Hip Hop and the extent to which Hip Hop is either dead or dying. Ever since the bricks and rods were laid out and the foundation paved, Hip Hop has become a worldwide phenomenon that serves as a vehicle of agency through which many oppressed people's voices are heard and their stories told. Conversely, Hip Hop in its cultural expressive form has also become a genre of preference for many who do not directly identify with the experiences and struggles faced by the very same youth who pioneered the movement. In the late 1980s and into the 1990s, Hip Hop was soon met with corporate intrusion and money vultures seeking profit by commoditizing Hip Hop culture and capitalizing on its gained popularity, eventually leading to what is now a constant debate putting to question the extent to which Hip Hop remains credible and whether or not what is being produced is Hip Hop or, as Dyson (2004) alludes to, pop rap. I like to refer to this fusion of pop and rap as *pap*.

While many Hip Hop artists have come and gone, some have been able to adapt and transcend time, switching up their game over the years in order to remain relevant while staying true to the social issues that continue to plague inner cities and urban communities. One of these Hip Hop artists is Queens-bred Nasir Jones, mainly known and recognized in the rap game as Nasty Nas or Nas. Nas's debut album *Illmatic* was released in 1994 and quickly became an instant classic with hits like *The Genesis*, *N. Y. State of Mind*, *One Love*, among others. Since then, Nas has released a flurry of mix tapes and albums, including *Hip Hop is Dead* in 2006. While all the other albums Nas dropped did not quite enjoy the same classic status as his *Illmatic*, Nas has always been able to stay on top of his game in order to remain fresh, relevant, and a top emcee in the Hip Hop music industry. No doubt he will go down as one of the nicest—if not *the* nicest—of his time, with fresh beats by the illest producers, dope rhymes, and sick punch-lines. His last two albums have also stirred up quite the controversy with *Hip Hop is Dead* and thereafter in 2008, *Untitled*—which he originally was going to title *Nigger*, triggering a stir of sentiments and responses about the use of the racially charged term (Nas drops "Nigger" album title, 2008). Hence, bringing me to my intention with this [reading].

So what exactly is the difference between Hip Hop yesterday and Hip Hop today? Is there a difference? Who gets to define what does or does not constitute Hip Hop? Is it the people, the clothes, the dialect, the aesthetic? Is it urban America, an industry, a culture? Is it a way of being, acting, thinking, living? And why is it critical for today's educators to afford Hip Hop the same respect afforded to other generations defined by their historical and sociopolitical context and conditions? In this [reading] I aim to answer these questions using Nas's song as an important discourse in the use of Hip Hop as social movement. Thus, I provide a cultural lens into, and analysis of, Nas's song, *Hip Hop is Dead* (Jones, 2006a) from his 2006 album in the space of Hip Hop. In doing so, I provide a brief understanding of Hip Hop culture and the sociopolitical context it is situated in, further elucidate the message of Nas's message from a cultural perspective, and end by speaking to the value inherent in Hip Hop as a tool for transforming consciousness in education.

THE CULTURE THAT MADE NAS

> I got so many rhymes I don't think I'm too sane
> Life is parallel to Hell but I must maintain
> And be prosperous, though we live dangerous
> Cops could just arrest me, blamin us, we're held like hostages
> It's only right that I was born to use mics
> And the stuff that I write, is even tougher than dykes. (Jones, 1994)

The quote above from Nas's first album, *Illmatic,* provides a bit of insight into the lived experiences of Black urban youth and many Hip Hop artists' preference to relay their story and message utilizing poetic artistry in the form of rap music, while also doing it a manner that is aesthetically playful and, simultaneously, raw. Close to half a decade has passed since the marking of what many today refer to and have come to know as Hip Hop—a cultural movement, enduring phenomenon, and adaptive form of self-being and expression that presently speaks to the psyche of many but is rooted in the historic struggle of oppressed people forgotten by a system that ignored conditions of racism and hardships of urban poverty. One can trace Hip Hop culture, primarily recognized as rap, to ancient African oral traditions that have influenced contemporary African American cultural practice (Dyson, 2004), including the radical genius and entrepreneurial prowess of legends such as the late Gil Scott-Heron, Last Poets, DJ Kool Herc, African Bambatta, and Mele Mel, among others, from the gritty streets of New York City. It won't be long before the likes of Nas, Jay-Z, and 2-Pac also become legends, though they are already legends in the context of respective cohort generation. Such legends are what can be described as Hip Hop geniuses. Sam Seidel (2011) describes Hip Hop genius as the creative resourcefulness in the face of limited resources or flipping something out of nothing. Thus, Hip Hop does not reflect an inability of inner city youth who do not make it in mainstream or popular culture. Rather, Hip Hop is a representation of subjects and voices stemming from Black youth culture that has since the conception of slavery been discriminated against, marginalized, and/or denied equitable opportunities at attaining mobility in a society. Hip Hop critiques a society that unfortunately continues to devalue Black culture and/or non-white culture. Rooted in the 1970s and early 1980s as a form of resistance to oppressive conditions and as an alternative to mainstream media that did not reflect the experiences of inner city communities, Hip Hop has over the past four decades shaped and informed the values and ideas of many who have grown up listening and relating to Hip Hop, grown with it, and helped shape it. This includes many of today's Hip Hop artists as well as middle-aged professionals from urban communities across different economic and political sectors of society (i.e., health, law, education, government). However, it is important to note that Hip Hop as a culture may have influenced many, but it will always remain at the helm of youth cultural expression. This is critical to understand as Hip Hop relies on the youth to continuously redefine and refresh what Hip Hop looks like based on the needs and issues faced of the time and context. Thus, it is a culture primarily cultivated by youth who continue to face societal, economic, and political challenges and hardships pressed onto those who reside in inner cities of the United States, and eventually expanded to include struggles beyond inner cities and outside U.S. borders.

THE ELEMENT OF RAP (MCEEING)

Though Hip Hop's elements transcend the musical modules of the movement beyond "Mceeing" and "DJing" to include Graffiti (Hip Hop in form of artistry and breakdancing, Hip Hop in the form of dance), it is through its musical elements, largely, that most people experiencing similar conditions of poverty, hardship, and strife across the globe have been introduced to it and the sociopolitical realities that inform it. It is also from this elemental tradition of rap in Hip Hop that this [reading] will be addressed. Rap is a form of lyrical and oratory flow that Trica Rose (1994) describes as "a black cultural expression that prioritizes lack voices from the margins of Urban America" (p. 2). Hence, Hip Hop culture provides a space where Black youth (African-American,

Afro-Caribbean) primarily, and to some extent other racially minoritized groups from New York City, could be creative, innovative, and are encouraged to engage their entrepreneurial spirits in order to rise above the pit of poverty and racism as described by Mumia Abu-Jamal:

> ... the music arises from a generation that feels with some justice that they have been betrayed by those who came before them. That they are at best tolerated in schools, feared on the streets, and almost inevitably destined for the hell-holes of prison. They grew up hungry, hated and unloved. And this is the psychic fuel that generates the anger that seems endemic in much of the music and poetry. One senses very little hope above the personal goals of wealth to climb above the pit of poverty. (Immortal Technique, 2003)

Hip Hop culture has become a vanguard of social commentary that aesthetically aims to challenge the conditions in which Hip Hop culture has fermented. The flipside is that while much rap has positive and uplifting conscious messages, there is also much rap that reinforces practices of internalized oppression and display Black and non-white youth cultures in a negative light. This includes, but is not limited to, romanticized ghettoism (i.e., drugs, poverty, etc.), misogynistic representations and disrespect of women, overemphasis on materialism, and reinforcement of violence within these very same communities. And though much of this cultural insight into Hip Hop culture is very real, there are those rappers who shed light on these issues differently. Tricia Rose (1994) goes on to describe this paradox:

> Rap music brings together a tangle of some of the most complex social, cultural, and political issues in contemporary American society. Rap's contradictory articulations are not signs of absent intellectual clarity; they are a common feature of community and popular cultural dialogues that always offer more than one cultural, social, or political viewpoint. (p. 2)

On one hand you have rappers who make an effort to raise awareness about the lived experiences of young Black and Brown youth—sort of like a verbal museum of how the broader system impacts their lives. On the other hand, you have rappers who rap about these same issues in a commoditized manner, where dominant and monetary value is assigned to oppressive representations of minoritized people. Unfortunately, this latter approach benefits the profit-driven mission of media corporations at the expense of Hip Hop culture and humanity. Hence, the Hip Hop aesthetics (a way of expression without rules and boundaries that encourages liberation creativity, learning, speaking without fear, peer reinforcement, and a need to be heard) often utilized to pass on the message that guides much of Hip Hop lyricism has been partly high jacked by corporate entertainment giants. It is here at this production of knowledge threshold between authentic and commoditized representations of Hip Hop culture that Nas's song "Hip Hop is Dead" is situated.

NAS'S HIP HOP IS DEAD

In the 2006 release of his studio album *Hip Hop is Dead*, Nas titled one of his tracks after the album. His album is a challenge to the Hip Hop world about the state of Hip Hop; in particular, the rap game. In his song "Hip Hop is Dead," featuring will.i.am of the Black Eyed Peas, Nas takes on the topic head on, which lead to others shining in and responding to Nas's cultural and political message on the state of Hip Hop. In the chorus itself he goes on to rap, "if Hip Hop should die before I wake/ I'll put and extended clip and body 'em all day/ roll to every station wreck the DJ/ roll to every station, wreck the DJ" (Jones, 2006a). Culturally speaking, Nas engages in a satiric and raw conversation with his listeners, proposing to go after the disc jockeys (DJs) who no longer have the independence to play to the taste and call of its cultural base. Instead, DJs are under an obligation to play a repeated play list of co-opted "pap" provided by the corporations who own the air waves as a result of the Telecom Act of 1996 that deregulated ownership restrictions on media outlets. This led to fewer companies owning the radio stations and having control over public consumption of music. The result: pop rap with very little social commentary, if any; pop rap often focuses on making dollars, spreading misogynistic messages, materialism, and individual mobility (not to be confused for individual style—very much a symbol of Hip Hop) without the collective community that makes Hip Hop what it is. I recall prior to 1996 being able to listen to Hip Hop vibes from different cultural locations that represented local tastes and diverse forms of Hip Hop. Today, it doesn't matter where you go because chances are radio stations are playing the same shortened playlists. Thus, his challenge that Hip Hop is dying may be partly directed to the DJs, but behind the lyrics he targets the corporations who make the decisions and the artists who buy into businesses' demoralized money making philosophy. Even at the beginning of the video production for the song, the screen reads:

> A new law has been passed today by the U.S. government. Hip Hop has been abolished and is no longer to be heard. All claiming the title MC will be arrested and given the worst penalty under the law. (Terrero, 2006)

In the track, he also goes on to rap, "everybody sound the same/ commercialize the game/ reminiscing' when it wasn't all business/ it forgot where it started/ so we all gather here for the dearly departed" (Jones, 2006a). His message has more to do more with a corporeal intrusion and commercialization, free speech infringement, and a departure from the roots of Hip Hop, as opposed to the death of Hip Hop. He illustrates this in the following lyrics: "Went from turntables to MP3s/ From 'Beat Street' to commercials on Mickey D's/ From gold cables to Jacobs/ From plain facials to Botox and face lifts" (Jones, 2006a).

In the track "Hip Hop is Dead," Nas also hints at other underlying issues that often go unnoticed without a critical ear to the lyrical verbiage he spits, such as knowledge representation and neocolonial dependence. The issue of knowledge representation deals with the production of knowledge through Hip Hop and should bring to light questions such as: Who is producing the music being consumed and under what conditions? Who is making decisions about the content of the music? Whose message is it? What Hip Hop music exists that is not receiving any air time and why? Who is listening to, and consuming public controlled radio? These questions are all important to consider given the deep history of corporate culture and social movements (i.e., abolition of slavery, civil rights movements; musical genres such as jazz, blues, and funk, etc.). One of his better tracks that gets at these issues of knowledge representation, I believe, is his collaboration with Damian Marley on their collaborative album *Distant Relatives* (Jones & Marley, 2010). In it they rhyme: "Discovering the world before this world. A World buried in time/ uncover with rhymes. It gets no realer." Both Nas and Damian Marley provide provocative, insightful, and critical verses about knowledge in their song "Patience." First Damian Marley shines in with:

> On the TV the picture is/Savages in villages/And the scientist still can't explain the pyramids, huh/Evangelists making a living on the videos of ribs of the little kids/Stereotyping the image of the images And this is what the image is. (Nas & Marley, 2010)

Nas chimes in with challenging epistemological questions, "Who made up words? who made up numbers? And what kind of spell is mankind under?" He goes on to question our consciousness of neocolonialism when he rhymes:

> Anything along the land we consuming/Eatin', deletin', ruin/Trying to get paper/ Gotta have land, gotta have acres/So I can sit back like Jack Nicholson/ Watch niggas play the game like the Lakers. (Nas & Marley, 2010)

Both Nas's and Damian's indictment of knowledge representation is quite evident in the lyrics; however, neocolonialism is another issue exposed indirectly, yet rather swiftly. Therefore, it is important to also illuminate the role of neocolonialism on Hip Hop culture, which refers to the dependence by the people on the structure to live and survive, thus having to adhere to some extent to the cultural practices of the dominant and ruling group.

In the track, "Hip Hop is Dead," Nas goes on to rap, "Any ghetto will tell ya', Nas helped grow us up/ my face once graced promotional Sony trucks/ hundred million and billin', I helped blow 'em up" (Jones, 2006a). His lyrics towards the end of his first verse suggest a dependence on each other by both the artist (the people) and the structure (the corporation). Nas's sales produced massive profit for the record companies he partnered with. In turn, Nas also implicates himself by admitting to: 1) helping the entertainment corporations get bigger and 2) benefiting financially from his partnership with the record label. As such, it is important to also illuminate how Nas himself has engaged in the poetic process that on one hand tells an important story, and on the other hand has worked to perpetuate the very same stereotypes about women, violence, and materialism through his lyrical candidness. Still, Nas makes it a point to remind us that he hasn't bought into the glamour of creating Hip Hop with no substance at the expense of the values and ethics that inform Hip Hop, as illustrated in the lyrics of "Let there be Light" (also on the album *Hip Hop is Dead*):

> No gang banging in New York tonight
> Just murals of Biggie Smalls, bigger than life
> Turn up the kid mic cuz ya'll ain't listening right
> What's all this talk that Nas got bought?
> I'd rather outline my body in white chalk. (Jones, 2006c)

Conversely, Nas uses his lyrics to continuously also remind us about the harsh cultural lived experiences and realities behind Hip Hop and the dangers associated with consuming ghettoized ideologies without addressing the conditions that have over time made Hip Hop a powerful and attractive avenue for urban youth identity development (Dyson & Daulatzai, 2010). Other tracks on the album *Hip Hop is Dead* reiterate the influences of Hip Hop culture, such as in the lyrics of "Black Republican":

> Could it be the forces of darkness
> Against hood angels of good that forms street politics
> Makes a sweet honest kid turn illegal for commerce
> To get his feet out of them Converse (Jones, 2006b)

As Nas explained in an interview with MTV:

> When I say "hip-hop is dead," basically America is dead. There is no political voice. Music is dead … Our way of thinking is dead, our commerce is dead. … what I mean by "hip-hop is dead" is we're at a vulnerable state. If we don't change, we gonna disappear like Rome. Hip-hop is Rome for the 'hood. I think hip-hop could help rebuild America, once hip-hoppers own hip-hop. … We are our own politicians, our own government, we have something to say. We're warriors. (Reid, 2006)

Thus Nas's lyrics, as well as much of Hip Hop lyricism in general, could be a powerful tool no different than the books already utilized for teaching about social ills that continue to plague the lives of youth and the youth movements that continue to challenge the conditions created by those in positions of power and privilege. This includes educators associated with, and implicated in, education. In many ways, Hip Hop culture has recently, more than before, managed to permeate and exert its way into the soul of academia and helped cultivate a collective of students and educators alike to conceptualize Hip Hop as a means for teaching, learning, and raising consciousness. Given the rise in interest and use of Hip Hop in education and the academy, it is important to consider how Hip Hop can be effectively utilized as an educational pedagogy both in form and in content to examine the use of Hip Hop as a way to learn about cultural spaces. Hip Hop as pedagogy offers direct insight into lived experiences and realities of minoritized racial and ethnic people who have faced and continue to encounter oppression and marginalization. Nas's critical insight and controversial position on Hip Hop illuminates a need to reclaim the role of Hip Hop for generations to come. If more than anything, what his "Hip Hop is Dead" track suggests is that Hip Hop culture will always be around as long as there are: 1) social ills such as poverty and racism plaguing different communities and 2) new generations springing up that will use Hip Hop to tell their story their way. Ultimately, as long as there is a youth base faced with these issues, there will always be Hip Hop.

REFERENCES

Dyson, M. E. (2004). The culture of hip hop. In M. Forman & M. A. Neal, *That's the joint: The hip hop studies reader* (pp. 61–68). New York, NY: Routledge.

Dyson, M. E., & Daulatzai, S. (Eds.). (2010). *Born to use mics: Reading Nas's Illmatic*. New York, NY: Basic Civitas Books.

Immortal Technique. (2003). Homeland security and hip hop [featuring Mumia Abu-Jamal]. On *Revolutionary volume 2* [CD]. New York, NY: Viper Records.

Jones, N. (1994). New York state of mind [Recorded by Nas]. On *Illmatic* [CD]. New York, NY: Columbia.

Jones, N. (2006a). Hip hop is dead [Recorded by Nas]. On *Hip Hop is Dead* [CD]. New York, NY: Def Jam.

Jones, N. (2006b). Black Republican [Recorded by Nas]. On *Hip Hop is Dead* [CD]. New York, NY: Def Jam.

Jones, N. (2006c). Let there be light [Recorded by Nas]. On *Hip Hop is Dead* [CD]. New York, NY: Def Jam.

Jones, N., & Marley, D. (2010). Patience [Recorded by Nas]. On *Distant Relatives* [CD]. Los Angeles, CA: Universal Republic and Def Jam.

Nas drops "Nigger" album title: Controversial release will now be untitled. (2008, May 20). *First for Music News*. Retrieved August 22, 2013 from http://www. nme.com/news/nas/36731

Reid, S. (2006, October 10). MTV News Exclusive: Nas Previews *Hip-Hop Is Dead ... the N. MTV News*. Retrieved on August 28, 2013 from http://www.mtv.com/news/articles/1542740/mtv-news-exclusive-nas-previews-new-lp.jhtml

Rose, T. (1994). *Black noise: Rap music and black culture in contemporary America*. Hanover, NH. Wesleyan University Press.

Seidel, S. (2011). *Hip hop genius: Remixing high school education*. New York, NY: Rowman and Littlefield.

Terrero, U. (Director). (2006). Hip hop is dead [Music video]. New York, NY: Def Jam.

DISCUSSION QUESTIONS

1. Referring to the Kelly article, how might the use of materialism, violence, and misogyny in gangsta rappers' lyrics help them achieve their goal of bringing awareness to corrupt legal justice systems? How might this strategy be harmful?

2. How are Public Enemy's "Fight the Power" and Nas's "Hip Hop Is Dead" similar and different based on the systems they are protesting?

3. The Stovall and Benitez articles both touch on generational shifts in the art form since the golden age of hip hop. What are the reasons for these changes based on their arguments?

CPSIA information can be obtained
at www.ICGtesting.com
Printed in the USA
LVHW060206310721
694167LV00005B/63

9 781516 587322